Modern German p

MANCHESTER
UNIVERSITY PRESS

Modern German pronunciation
An introduction for speakers of English

Christopher Hall

Manchester University Press
Manchester and New York

Distributed exclusively in the USA by Palgrave

The right of Christopher Hall to be identified as the author of this work has been asserted by him in accordance with the Copyright, Designs and Patents Act 1988

Published by Manchester University Press, Oxford Road, Manchester M13 9NR, UK
and Room 400, 175 Fifth Avenue, New York, NY 10010, USA

www.manchesteruniversitypress.co.uk

Distributed exclusively in the USA by
Palgrave, 175 Fifth Avenue, New York, NY 10010, USA

Distributed exclusively in Canada by
UBC Press, University of British Columbia, 2029 West Mall,
Vancouver, BC, Canada V6T 1Z2

British Library Cataloguing-in-Publication Data
A catalogue record for this book is available from the British Library

Library of Congress Cataloging-in-Publication data
Hall, Christopher
    Modern German pronunciation: an introduction for speakers
of English / Christopher Hall
    p.   cm.
    Includes bibliographical references and index.
    ISBN 0-7190-3580-5 (hardback). —ISBN 0-7190-3581-3 (pbk.)
    1. German language—Pronunciation.   2. German language—Textbooks for foreign
speakers—English.   I.   Title.
PF3137.H27   1992
438.3'421—dcZU   91-38793

ISBN 0 7190 3581 3 *paperback*

First published 1992

Typeset in Hong Kong
by Best-set Typesetter Ltd

First digital, on-demand edition published by Anthony Rowe, 2001

Contents

List of illustrations

Preface

This book is designed to help English-speaking learners acquire a better pronunciation of German. Together with the accompanying cassette, it can be used either as part of a course for those studying at university or college, or by those studying on their own at home. Chapters 1 and 2 are of an introductory nature and have deliberately been kept as short as possible. Chapters 3 and 4 provide detailed descriptions of the individual consonant and vowel sounds of German. Examples of each of the sounds are provided on the accompanying cassette, and are indicated by the use of the symbol ⊡ in the margin. These chapters should be worked through carefully before going on to chapters 5 and 6 on stress and intonation and words in connected speech.

In addition to the examples of each individual sound, a number of exercises on those sounds which English-speaking learners tend to find difficult in German are provided in chapter 7 and on the tape. These exercises are divided into nineteen units, which should be worked through in conjunction with the relevant descriptive material of the earlier chapters. Instructions for the use of the exercises are provided at the beginning of chapter 7.

The choice of vocabulary in the examples and exercises reflects the intended readership: learners at an intermediate or advanced level. Beginners will probably find the exercises too difficult because they do not know the vocabulary, but a certain amount of pronunciation practice is extremely valuable at the early stages of language learning, so teachers working with beginners might like to construct exercises similar to the ones contained in this book using vocabulary with which their students are familiar.

Acknowledgements

This book has grown out of numerous pronunciation courses I have taught at the University of Leicester since 1986 and before that at the University of Tampere. I am endebted to a number of friends and colleagues from other universities who have read and commented on earlier drafts, in particular to Prof Martin Durrell (Manchester), Dr Eckart Weiher (Bonn) and Dr Jon West (Newcastle), whose encouragement has sustained me and whose perceptive criticisms have helped me clarify my views and avoid many pitfalls. Thanks are also due to Prof Antti Iivonen (Helsinki), Prof Werner König (Augsburg) and Martin Barry (Manchester), who gave generously of their time to discuss specific points with me. Needless to say, we do not agree on every issue, and the final responsibility for what is in the book is mine. I hope the colleagues mentioned do not feel too let down by what I have made of their advice.

I also owe a debt to a number of published works, which is acknowledged in the relevant sections of the *Sources and Further Reading* at the end of the book.

For the accompanying recording I am endebted to Gabriele Esser-Hall and Thorsten Afflerbach, who undertook the task cheerfully and competently in conditions which were far from ideal. The recording was supported by a grant from the University of Leicester, which is gratefully acknowledged.

Finally I would like to express my gratitude to the Head of the German Department at the University of Leicester, Miss Patricia Boswell, for her support throughout the period when this book was being written.

List of phonetic symbols

A. The sounds of German

Consonants

p	as in	*Paß*
b		*Baum*
t		*Tag*
d		*Dach*
k		*Kind*
g		*gut*
f		*Fuß*
v		*Wein*
s		*weiß*
z		*See*
ʃ		*Schnee*
ʒ		*Genie*
x		*Buch*
ç		*ich*
j		*jung*
h		*Haus*
m		*Mann*
n		*Nuß*
ŋ		*lang*
l		*Luft*
r		*rot* – voiced apico-alveolar roll
ʀ		*rot* – voiced uvular roll
ʁ		*rot* – voiced uvular fricative
ɰ		*Ware* – voiced uvular or velar approximant
ɾ		*Ware* – voiced alveolar flap
β		*aber* (quick pronunciation) – voiced bilabial fricative

ɣ   ma*ch*' ich (quick pronunciation) – voiced velar fricative
ʔ   *eins* [ʔaɪns] – glottal stop

Vowels

iː	as in	Sp*ie*l
ɪ		st*i*ll
eː		T*ee*
ɛ		F*e*ld
ɛː		sp*ä*t
aː		S*aa*l
a		*a*lt
oː		S*oh*n
ɔ		G*o*ld
uː		H*u*t
ʊ		M*u*nd
yː		fr*üð*h
ʏ		Gl*ü*ck
øː		*Ö*l
œ		zw*ö*lf
ə		Seit*e*
ɐ		bess*er*
aɪ		M*ai*
aʊ		H*au*s
ɔʏ		d*eu*tsch

B. Some English sounds

θ	as in	English (Southern British Standard) *th*ink
ð		SBS *th*at
r		SBS *r*ed
w		SBS *w*ine
ɫ		SBS ho*l*e ('dark l')
æ		SBS m*a*n
ɑː		SBS f*a*ther
ʌ		SBS b*u*t
ɒ		SBS g*o*t
ɜː		SBS b*ir*d
eɪ		SBS w*ai*t
əʊ		SBS b*oa*t

C. Other symbols

ˈ primary stress on the following syllable, e.g. ˈbesser

ˌ secondary stress on the following syllable, e.g. ˈKrankenˌhaus

̥ voiceless sound, e.g. German *Platz* [pl̥ats], English *place* [pl̥eɪs]

ˌ syllabic consonant, e.g. German *hatten* [ˈhatn̩], English *button* [ˈbʌtn̩]

̯ non-syllabic vowel, e.g. German *Nation* [naˈtsi̯oːn]

ʰ aspiration of plosive, e.g. German *Paß* [pʰas], English *pie* [pʰaɪ]

‾ unaspirated release of plosive, e.g. German *spät* [ʃp̄ɛːtʰ], English *spin* [sp̄ɪn]

˺ no audible release of plosive, e.g. German *Haupt* [haʊp˺tʰ], English *apt* [æp˺tʰ]

˜ nasalisation, e.g. French *bon* [bɔ̃]

/ / phonemic transcription

[ ] phonetic (allophonic) transcription

D. Intonation marks

Nuclear tones

ˋ Fall

ˊ Rise

ˉ Level

ˆ Rise–fall

ˇ Fall–rise

Non-nuclear stresses

ˈ High-stressed syllable

ˌ Low-stressed syllable

1

Introduction

1.1 **Why pronunciation?**

In the days when foreign languages were principally used, and taught, for reading foreign literature and writing business letters to associates abroad, it was understandable that pronunciation played little or no role in the teaching or learning processes. If learners were never going to have the opportunity to speak the language anyway, it was unimportant what kind of accent they had. Those days are long past, however, and nowadays foreign languages are spoken and heard just as often as they are written and read. People travel abroad in their millions every year, many of them to the German-speaking countries, and they have more opportunities of meeting people and making friends there than ever before. In this situation, the ability to communicate in the spoken language has rightly come to be emphasised more and more in schools and universities, and improvements in the speaking ability of language learners at all levels have undoubtedly been made. It is the aim of this book to help make further improvements in the area of pronunciation.

It is a common misconception that a good pronunciation in a foreign language is very difficult to achieve. In fact, the effort involved in acquiring a passable pronunciation in German is not very great, provided the task is approached systematically and at the right time. Teachers can do a lot to help: if a small amount of pronunciation is taught in the early stages of foreign language learning, before bad habits become established, there is no reason why most pupils should not achieve a reasonable standard.

On the other hand, a good pronunciation in a foreign language is not acquired simply by listening, as is the case with a child learning its mother tongue. In the normal foreign language learning situation, with schoolchildren or adults, the pronunciation habits of the mother tongue are well established and are automatically transferred to the foreign language unless countermeasures are taken. Even a prolonged stay abroad is no guarantee of success, as is shown by the number of foreigners who have spent many years in an English-speaking country and yet still speak English with a strong foreign accent. It is a simple fact that a certain amount of systematic tuition in both listening and pronouncing is needed by the great majority of learners.

It is worth putting some effort into acquiring a good pronunciation in a foreign language for a number of reasons. Foreign learners with poor pronunciation in German run the risk of being misunderstood, or perhaps not understood at all, in communication with Germans. It can also be tiresome to talk to someone who is difficult to understand, so a poor pronunciation may have a detrimental effect on the learner's social contacts. More subtly, the command of a language is an important part of the impression made by foreigners on native speakers with whom they come into contact. Pronunciation is one of the most obvious indicators of competence in a language, simply because it affects every single word that is spoken by the foreigner. We have a certain amount of choice as to which words and grammatical structures we use when speaking a foreign language and can avoid expressions and constructions of which we are unsure. Indeed, this is one of the skills beginners have to acquire in a foreign language – expressing themselves within the limits of their knowledge. Pronunciation, however, can never be avoided when speaking the language and it therefore has a strong influence on native speakers' judgements of a foreigner's command of the language.

Learning a new pronunciation should be regarded as a natural part of learning a new language. Just as in grammar and vocabulary we must learn that German is not just English with different words, we must also learn that German cannot simply be spoken using English sounds, but has a pronunciation system of its own which has to be learnt if we wish to acquire an acceptable level of competence in the language.

1.2 Regional variation and standard pronunciation

In any language there is not just one form of pronunciation, as all native speakers of English know for their own language. The question therefore arises as to which form of German pronunciation the learner should aim to acquire. The most obvious differences in pronunciation are those which reflect the regional background of the speaker and which enable us to recognise that a speaker comes from Bavaria, Switzerland, the Rhineland, Hamburg, etc. Regional variation occurs in pronunciation, in which case we speak of *regional accents*, and also in grammar and vocabulary, in which case we speak of *dialects*. Regional accents are considerably more widespread than dialects, since a person speaking dialect will always use a regional accent, whereas the reverse does not apply: there are many people who speak Standard German as far as grammar and vocabulary are concerned and yet have some degree of regional accent in their speech.

Regional forms of German differ from one another so sharply that local accents and dialects from the south of the German-speaking area are not readily understood by North Germans and vice versa. The variation in the German language is certainly encouraged by the fact that it is spoken in a number of different countries. Norms which are in certain respects distinct from those in use in Germany have been established in Austria and Switzerland, a situation which has prompted scholars to speak of German as a 'pluricentric' language, i.e. a language with more than one centre and more than one standard.

But even in Germany, by far the largest, economically most powerful and most influential of these countries, there is great variation, particularly between north and south. Politically speaking, of course, Germany was a 'pluricentric' country until the formation of the German Empire in 1871. The regional variation in the German language is to some extent a reflection of this historical political fragmentation.

However, if a language which is spoken over a large area is to fulfil its communicative function successfully, some form of standardisation is obviously necessary. Moves towards standardisation started towards the end of the Middle Ages, and as a result of a process lasting several centuries the written German language (G. *die Schriftsprache*) is now highly standardised. This standardisation is somewhat variable (most complete in spelling, least so in vocabulary), but overall the written German language varies very little between the German-speaking countries or between the different regions of Germany.

The spoken German language is much less standardised than the written form. There are a number of reasons for this, e.g. the standardising influence of the school is felt much less strongly in spoken language (which is largely learnt at home and in the community) than in the written language (which is largely learnt at school). And in times before the introduction of modern means of transport and the invention of the electronic media, communication between regions (which was where the need for standardisation was felt) was predominantly written communication, whereas spoken communication was predominantly within the local community.

These are general, if not universal, factors, of course, and so it is generally true that written language is more standardised than spoken language. But whereas in politically more united countries like England and France pronunciation standards such as **Southern British Standard** (or **Received Pronunciation**) and Parisian French emerged, the situation in the politically more fragmented Germany was less favourable towards the emergence of a spoken standard.

However, the need for a spoken standard in German was felt in some areas, particularly in the theatre for productions of classical drama. In response to this need, Theodor Siebs (Professor of German at the University of Greifswald) produced, in consultation with representatives of the universities and the theatre, a set of guidelines for a standard pronunciation of German for the stage, published in 1898 as *Deutsche Bühnenaussprache*. Siebs's standard did not represent the actual speech of any region of Germany, but was a compromise between a number of regional forms, although it leaned strongly towards North German pronunciation, which was regarded in some circles as the 'purest' form of the spoken language. It was in fact the closest to the written language, owing to the fact that North Germans, originally speakers of Low German, had had to learn High German from books at school. Their 'pure' pronunciation was thus a spelling pronunciation of the High German written forms. Although Siebs's standard was criticised in the south, and was never accepted in Austria and Switzerland, it gained acceptance in the theatre as an ideal norm for actors to aim at. It was later even suggested that it should be used for more general purposes, e.g. in schools, to which end some modifications were made and the title of the book changed to *Deutsche Hochlautung*. But Siebs's pronunciation was too far removed from the way people actually spoke in real life for its use of spread, so it remained largely restricted to the theatre, for which it had originally been developed.

In the 1950s projects were started to describe a pronunciation closer to actual usage. These resulted in the publication of two pronouncing dictionaries, the West German *Duden-Aussprachewörterbuch* (1966; 3rd edition, 1990) and the East German *Wörterbuch der deutschen Aussprache* (1969; new edition, *Großes Wörterbuch der deutschen Aussprache*, 1982). Although these dictionaries describe a pronunciation much closer to the way German is actually spoken, one feature of Siebs is retained, namely that the pronunciation is a compromise between the various regional forms of German speech in which the North German influence dominates.

This form of German pronunciation is usually referred to as *Hochlautung* or *Standardlautung*, sometimes also as *Hochdeutsch* (although this term more usually refers to the standard dialect, i.e. the standard forms of grammar and vocabulary). It can be regarded as the 'standard' in the sense that it is the codified form, the one used for descriptions of German and in teaching German pronunciation to foreigners. Secondly, it enjoys high prestige and is widely regarded (even by many German-speakers who do not use it themselves) as the 'best' pronunciation, and finally it is tolerably close to the usage of many educated Germans. However, it must be remembered that German pronunciation is not uniform, and that most speakers have some regional features in their speech, ranging from the almost imperceptible to the strong regional form.

The 'standard' pronunciation described in this book is the obvious one for foreign learners to adopt, but they will also need a basic passive command of the most important regionalisms in German pronunciation, first in order to understand genuine samples of spoken German and secondly in order to be able to judge whether to imitate pronunciations they hear from German-speakers. For these reasons, some information on regional variation in the pronunciation of German is included in the description offered here, but only the standard forms are intended for use as a model.

1.3 Stylistic variation

Even standard pronunciations are not monolithic, and a certain amount of variation does take place within the standard, most importantly variation according to the situation or **stylistic variation.** In formal situations speakers tend to speak more carefully, more slowly and with greater tension of the articulatory muscles than in informal situations, in which more rapid and relaxed speech leads to characteristic reductions or simplifications in pronunciation. This variation in pronunciation is affected by personal factors, but the general tendencies are sufficiently clear to distinguish a number of pronunciation styles, following Meinhold (1973). The most important of these are formal pronunciation and conversational pronunciation, each of which can be further subdivided:

1 **Formal pronunciation** (G. *gehobene Formstufe*): this style is restricted to the reading of texts in formal situations. It is possible to differentiate between
   (a) **recitation style** (G. *hoher Stil*), reserved for the recitation of poetic and literary texts, and the somewhat more relaxed
   (b) **moderate formal style** (G. *gemäßigte Formstufe*), used for instance by newsreaders on radio and television and often in reading formal lectures before large audiences.
2 **Conversational pronunciation** (G. *Gesprächsstufe*) is associated with the genuine, spontaneous use of language in conversational situations. Again it is possible to differentiate between

(a) **careful conversational style** (G. *gehobene Gesprächsstufe*), used
     for instance in talking to small audiences, in discussions and
     more formal dialogue, and
(b) **relaxed conversational style** (G. *lässige Gesprächsstufe*), which is
     the style most typically used between good friends and in the
     family.

These styles all belong to standard pronunciation. They form a scale
ranging from 1(a), which is more precise and closer to the written language, to 2(b), which contains more reduced or simplified forms and is
further removed from the written language. Notice that all the types of
standard pronunciation contain come reductions or simplifications. The
differences between them are thus differences of degree rather than
absolute differences.

A distinction can be made between these forms of standard pronunciation and non-standard pronunciation types. Recitation style can be
distinguished from **full pronunciation** (G. *Höchstlautung* or *Überlautung*),
a very clearly articulated pronunciation closely following the spelling of
words, which would sound unnatural and overarticulated in normal
speech, but which can be used when communication is difficult, e.g. in a
noisy room, when there is a bad line on the telephone, when speaking to
someone who is hard of hearing, or when shouting over long distances.
Most importantly, it is the form of pronunciation used for classical singing
in German.

At the other end of the scale, it is not always easy to draw a distinction
between relaxed conversational style and **regional accent** (G. *Regional-
lautung* or *regionaler Akzent*), as many speakers use a regional form of
pronunciation in informal situations. However, the types of reduction,
assimilation, etc., which characterise the relaxed conversational style of
standard pronunciation are not tied to any regional accents, but occur
throughout the German-speaking area, and are thus also to be found in
the speech of people whose pronunciation has few, if any, regional
characteristics.

All the types of pronunciation mentioned above are legitimate, and it is
the context that determines which is used. Thus it would sound unnatural
to use formal pronunciation (especially recitation style) in everyday
situations with one's family or friends, and it would sound very odd to
use relaxed conversational style when acting in a classical drama on the
stage. The great majority of speakers of Standard German quite naturally
use more than one of these different types of pronunciation, choosing
(consciously or unconsciously) the style which is best suited to the
situation.

It is important for the learner of German to distinguish between various types of pronunciation and recognise the situations in which the different types are appropriate. All learners should aim at a good knowledge of formal and conversational pronunciation. The other forms, full pronunciation and regional accent, will not normally be required by the learner; in fact they are best avoided. This applies particularly to regional accents, which learners who have spent some time in one or other of the regions of Germany are often tempted to use. This is not usually a good idea for foreign learners, unless they are also thoroughly conversant with the formal and conversational pronunciations, and unless their command of the language is very good indeed, since few things in foreign language learning sound more ridiculous than people with an inadequate command of the language trying to copy regional dialects and pronunciations. Another reason for avoiding regional accents is that the situations in which they can legitimately be used outside Germany, or indeed outside their regions of origin, are extremely limited, and they are also definitely best avoided when teaching the language in schools.

Thus the pronunciation described in this book is the **formal** (more precisely the **moderate formal**) and **conversational pronunciation** of Modern Standard German, and it is, in fact, simpler to describe the formal pronunciation first and then to describe the particular features of conversational pronunciation on the basis of this. A second reason for describing the moderate formal pronunciation first is that it is natural for the beginner to start with a careful, precise pronunciation. Conversational pronunciation requires a certain amount of fluency and familiarity with the language, and therefore comes into its own at a later stage.

1.4 Social and individual variation

In addition to the regional and stylistic differences already mentioned, there are also social and individual variations in language. **Social** varieties reflect differences in the social position of speakers. Although there are some areas in which linguistic variation correlates directly with social factors, e.g. the jargon of certain professional, social and other groups, this is actually not the most common kind of social variation. In most areas of language, and certainly in pronunciation, the correlation between social factors and linguistic forms is indirect, in that speakers at the top of the social scale tend to have less regional forms in their speech than those lower down the social scale. There is thus a close connection between regional and social variation, and, although the latter is an interesting field of study in its own right,[1] it is not necessary to treat it separately in a book of this nature.

[1] See 'Sources and further reading' for literature.

Individual variation is that caused by the preferences, habits and peculiarities of the individual. In pronunciation these are the features which enable us to recognise a voice when we cannot see the speaker, e.g. on the telephone. By definition individual variation is impossible to describe systematically for a large number of speakers and it has been ignored here.

1.5 Learning the sounds of language

Learning pronunciation is a very individual thing: some people have an ear for sounds and learn very quickly, while others have to work hard to achieve a good pronunciation in a foreign language. But we are, after all, doing something which comes perfectly naturally to all human beings as small children, for, unless they suffer from a handicap such as deafness or from a speech defect, everyone learns the pronunciation of their own language perfectly. However, the small child's sharpness of hearing starts to deteriorate after the age of about five, and after puberty learning a foreign pronunciation becomes a lot more laborious. But acquiring an acceptable pronunciation in a foreign language is not an impossible task, and *everyone* can improve with practice.

In spite of individual differences, however, there is one essential element that is the same for everybody: the only way to acquire a good pronunciation in a foreign language is by *listening* to the way it is spoken and *trying out* the sounds oneself. That is the purpose of the exercises included at the end of this book and of the accompanying cassette. It is not possible to learn pronunciation just from a book, but for older schoolchildren and for adults, who are used to approaching learning in a systematic way, a more cognitive approach, in which the articulation of sounds is explained in detail, has been found to be very useful.

In learning pronunciation, as in all other learning, we should start from what the learner already knows. In this case, the learner already has a knowledge of English pronunciation, which can be put to good use when starting with German, since many German sounds are the same as, or very close to, the corresponding sound in English. A contrastive approach has therefore been adopted for the description of German sounds in chapters 3 and 4: German sounds are contrasted with those of English, sounds which are the same in both languages are treated rather briefly, and attention is focused on the sounds which are either different from the corresponding sounds of English or completely absent from English. This contrastive approach cannot be carried too far, however, for a number of reasons:

1   It has to be remembered that the English pronunciation of learners will differ, and that the problems they have in learning German differ accordingly. The form of English used for the comparison with German is **Southern British Standard** or RP (typified by traditional newsreaders on BBC radio and television), but some common regional features of English pronunciation are also taken into account.[2]

2   A precise phonetic description of familiar sounds is the best way of familiarising learners with phonetic terminology.

3   Sometimes difficult sounds in German can be described by reference to ones familiar to the learner from English, e.g. the consonant in German *ich* (phonetic symbol [ç]) has the same tongue position as the first sound of English *yes* (phonetic symbol [j]).

Our aims in teaching and learning pronunciation should be ambitious but achievable. The aim of most learners will not be to sound exactly like a native speaker of German, but to acquire a 'near-native' pronunciation, which is easily understood by Germans, which does not draw attention to itself, and in which all the important German sounds are clearly articulated and the most disturbing elements of an 'English accent' are missing. This course aims to help learners achieve such a 'near-native' German pronunciation, but, as in all language learning, it is not only in the language laboratory or the classroom that learning takes place: once you have become aware of the details of German pronunciation you will be able to observe and learn whenever listening to Germans speaking.

[2] The term 'Southern British Standard', used in Wells & Colson (1971), is preferred here to the older, better-known label 'Received Pronunciation' (or RP), as it indicates the geographical area in which this accent is accepted as a standard: southern Britain, i.e. England and to a certain extent Wales, but not Scotland.

2

The production and description of speech sounds

2.1 Articulatory, acoustic and auditory phonetics

Phonetics is the study of the sounds of natural language. The use of sounds in speech involves three distinct phases: (1) the production of sounds by the speaker, (2) the transmission of sounds between the speaker and the hearer, and (3) the reception of the sounds by the hearer. Each of these phases, especially (1) and (3), which clearly involve the human brain, is an extremely complicated process, each needs to be understood if we wish to have a full understanding of the workings of human speech, and each requires its own methods of study. The science of phonetics thus consists of three main branches, each devoted to the study of one of the phases of speech.

Articulatory phonetics is the study of the way in which speech sounds are produced or 'articulated' by the speaker. It includes a description of the organs of speech, such as the vocal cords, the tongue and the palate, and how they are used to produce sounds. The description of speech in articulatory terms has a long history, going back to ancient times, and is still considered the most useful type of description for language teaching purposes. **Acoustic phonetics** is the study of the transmission of speech sounds through the air in the form of air waves. Precise studies of the transmission stage of speech rely heavily on electronic equipment which has only been available since the 1930s and 1940s, but in the relatively short space of time since then great strides have been made in our understanding of the transmission of speech sounds. Acoustic phonetics is not as important in pronunciation teaching as articulatory phonetics, but it can be of valuable assistance in certain areas such as the description of vowel sounds or intonation, which are not easily described in articulatory terms. **Auditory phonetics**, finally, studies the processes in the ear, auditory nerve and brain which lead to the perception of sounds by the hearer. The results of auditory phonetics do not have a direct application in language teaching, and we will not go into this subject further here.

The description of German pronunciation in this book will be pre-dominantly in articulatory terms, with occasional references to acoustic descriptions where they are found to be useful.

2.2 The organs of speech

Speech is a relatively late development in the history of the human species, and it utilises organs whose primary function is connected with the basic physical functions of the human body, such as breathing and eating. Thus in making the sounds of speech we utilise the air coming from the lungs (breathing), which we modify by using the larynx (which also acts as a valve at the top of the windpipe), the tongue, the teeth and the lips (all needed for eating). There is no organ which is only used in speech, as is witnessed by the fact that similar organs are present in animals, which do not have the power of speech. However, the precise configuration of speech organs which enable us to produce the variety of sounds required for language is unique to the human race.

Figure 1 is a simplified diagram of the **organs of speech** (G. *die Artikulationsorgane* or *die Sprechwerkzeuge*) in the **vocal tract** (G. *das*

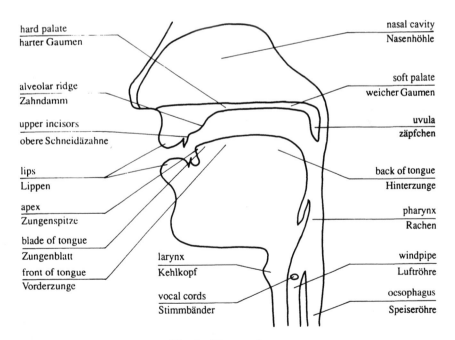

Fig. 1: The vocal tract

Ansatzrohr), seen from the side, in which the phonetically important terms are given in English and German.

In describing the sounds of speech, it is best to start with the stream of air leaving the lungs when we breathe out, which is known as the **pulmonic egressive** airstream, the term 'pulmonic' referring to the fact that it originates in the lungs. This airstream is utilised in all languages, whereas an **ingressive** airstream (breathing in) is very rarely used in speech.[1] Other, non-pulmonic sources of air are also used in some languages for making speech sounds, the best-known examples being the clicks of the Khoisan languages of southern Africa (e.g. Hottentot), but since these are of no relevance to the description of either German or English they will be ignored here.[2] As the airstream passes from the lungs through the throat and mouth and past the lips, it is modified in a number of ways, giving us the distinctive sounds of speech. We will describe these modifications in the order in which they occur, starting with the larynx and finishing with the lips.

The **larynx** (G. *der Kehlkopf*) is a box-like structure consisting of cartilages, easily visible in men as the 'Adam's apple'. This contains the **glottis** (G. *die Glottis, die Stimmritze*), an opening through which the airstream can pass, on either side of which are bands of tissue known as the **vocal cords** or **vocal folds** (G. *die Stimmbänder* or *Stimmlippen*). There are three main position for the vocal cords, as shown in figure 2.

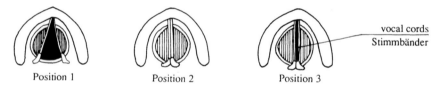

| | vocal cords |
| | Stimmbänder |

Position 1   Position 2   Position 3

Fig. 2: The vocal cords

1 When they are open, air can pass freely in and out of the lungs through the **windpipe** or **trachea** (G. *die Luftröhre*). This is the position for normal relaxed breathing.

2 The vocal cords can also be pressed tightly together closing the glottis altogether, so that no air can pass through into, or out of, the lungs. In this position the vocal cords block off the passage to the lungs, thus

---

[1] A pulmonic ingressive airstream (a sharp intake of breath) is, however, used as non-linguistic gesture of surprise or apprehension.

[2] Non-pulmonic, ingressive sounds are also used for non-linguistic purposes by English (and German) speakers, e.g. for showing disapproval ('tutting', generally represented in writing as *tut-tut*), for geeing on a horse, and for 'blowing kisses'.

preventing the entry of food, liquid or other foreign bodies. A good way to demonstrate to yourself what it feels like to close the glottis is to imagine you are lifting a heavy load, as it is usual to close the vocal cords in that situation. The action of coughing is closing the vocal cords and then releasing them suddenly, allowing the air which has been dammed behind them to rush out with an audible noise.

3   In their third position the vocal cords are placed gently together, so that the airstream is not stopped, as in position 2, but can force the vocal cords aside and escape into the mouth. As the pressure builds up behind the vocal cords, they are forced aside to allow the air to escape, but when the air escapes the pressure is reduced and the vocal cords fall back together again. In this position, the vocal cords vibrate, i.e. open and close very rapidly, giving the characteristic sound known as **voice** (G. *die Stimmhaftigkeit*). One good way of demonstrating this to yourself is to close your lips and pronounce a long-drawn-out m-sound. The sound you can hear is the vibrating of the vocal cords, and you can feel the vibrations if you place the tips of your forefinger and thumb on your larynx or if you put your fingers in your ears. The vocal cords vibrate at different speeds depending on the size of the larynx; typical ranges are 80–200 vibrations a second (or hertz = Hz) for adult males, 150–300 Hz for adult females and 200–500 Hz for children.[3] Within these limits the speed of the vibrations can be varied at will, thus changing the pitch of the voice, as happens for instance in intonation (see chapter 5) and of course in singing.

There are other positions which the vocal cords can take up, for whispering and so-called 'creaky voice', but as these are of no importance for the pronunciation of Standard German they will be ignored here.

The sounds of speech can be produced with vibrations of the vocal cords, in which case they are called **voiced** sounds (G. *stimmhafte Laute*), or without vibrations, in which case they are **voiceless** (G. *stimmlos*).

The area above the vocal cords, the **pharynx** (G. *der Rachen* or *die Rachenhöhle*), leads to the **mouth** or **oral cavity** (G. *die Mundhöhle*), which is divided off from the **nasal cavity** (G. *die Nasenhöhle*) by the roof of the mouth or **palate** (G. *der Gaumen*). The palate plays a very important part in the production of many consonant sounds. It divides naturally into a number of different parts: the front part, from just behind the teeth to the roof of the mouth proper, has the form of a steep ridge, known as the teeth ridge or, more technically, the **alveolar ridge** (G. *der Zahndamm* or *die Alveolen*). This is a hard, bony structure, as is the part of the palate immediately behind the alveolar ridge, extending back just

---

[3] Figures from Clark & Yallop (1990: 215).

about as far as most people can reach back with the tip of their tongue, which is known as the **hard palate** (G. *der harte Gaumen*). The bone comes to an end about in the middle of the palate, and the back part consists of muscular tissue which, because it is not restricted by any bone, can be moved quite freely. This is known as the **soft palate** or **velum** (G. *der weiche Gaumen* or *das Gaumensegel*): most people cannot feel it with their tongue, but it is easy to feel the difference between the hard and soft palates by pressing gently with your fingertips. The soft palate ends in the **uvula** (G. *das Zäpfchen* or *die Uvula*), which is a fleshy appendage hanging down into the pharynx, visible in a mirror when the mouth is wide open.

There are two positions that the soft palate can take up. For relaxed breathing it is **lowered** (G. *gesenkt*), away from the back wall of the pharynx, so that air can pass freely into the nasal cavity. This is the position it occupies for most of the time. It can, however, also be **raised** (G. *gehoben*) and pressed against the back of the pharynx, thus preventing any air escaping through the nasal cavity. This raised position is required for most sounds of language, in fact for all but one group of sounds of English and German.

Below the palate we have the **tongue** (G. *die Zunge*), which is by far the most important active organ of speech. The most important attribute of the tongue is its flexibility, which is fully utilised in speech as well as in its primary functions (e.g. eating). The tip of the tongue can be moved to reach any part of the front of the mouth, and as far back as the end of the hard palate. It can also touch the sides of the mouth and take up an endless number of positions in the mouth. Unlike the palate, the tongue does not consist of any easily discernible separate parts, so it is usual to divide the tongue into parts according to which part of the palate lies directly above when the tongue is in a relaxed position. The **back of the tongue** (G. *die Hinterzunge*) lies directly below the soft palate, the **front of the tongue** (G. *die Vorderzunge*) lies below the hard palate, and the **blade** or **lamina** of the tongue (G. *das Zungenblatt*) is the part below the alveolar ridge. In addition to these three, we distinguish the **tip of the tongue** or **apex** (G. *die Zungenspitze*), which is the part at the very end. In view of the lack of natural divisions in the tongue, it is perhaps not surprising that there are variations in the terminology used to describe its various parts. Many German phoneticians, for instance, do not make a distinction between the tip and the blade of the tongue, so the term *Zungenspitze* is often used for both, and another division of the tongue into five rather than four parts is also sometimes used.

The flexibility of the tongue is not restricted to backwards and sideways movements; the body of the tongue can also adopt various shapes; in particular, it can be either **grooved** (G. *gerillt*) or **flat** (G. *flach*). You can test this for yourself by putting your tongue in the position for the first sound of the English word *so* and breathing in sharply. You will feel a rush of cold air in the middle of the tongue, which forms the bottom of the groove, and much less at the sides of the tongue, which are close to the palate. Contrast this with the first sound of the word *show*: if you breathe in sharply with the tongue in this position you will feel the cold air over the whole breadth of the tongue, which is in the flat position for this consonant.

The **teeth** (G. *die Zähne*) are used for a number of sounds, particularly the **upper front teeth** or **incisors** (G. *die oberen Schneidezähne*) in conjunction with the tip of the tongue or the bottom lip.

Finally, the **lips** (G. *die Lippen*), like the tongue, are very flexible and can take up a large number of different positions. As was mentioned above, the bottom lip can be used in conjunction with the top front teeth, and the lips can be used together, either in contact with one another or to adjust the size and shape of the oral cavity.

2.3 Letters, sounds and phonemes

Even among language students there is sometimes confusion between the concepts 'letters' and 'sounds', yet the distinction between the two is perfectly clear, and should always be made: letters belong to writing, and sounds belong to speech. All natural languages originated in their spoken forms, some (but by no means all) have later been written down, so that it is clear that the spoken form is the primary one and that the written form is a representation of speech in another medium. In alphabetic writing systems, the letters are, or at least were originally, meant to represent the sounds of language directly, but this representation of sounds in writing is not always very precise, one of the most irregular examples, of course, being English. Even in relatively precise or 'phonetic' writing systems, such as those of Finnish or Serbo-Croat, there are some irregularities in which pronunciation is not accurately represented by the spelling.

In this respect, German is somewhere in the middle of a scale between very regular spelling systems such as Finnish, and very irregular ones such as English. Some examples of irregularity in German spelling are:

1   The same sound is represented by different letters (or combinations of letters):
    Vater – Fahne – Phantasie
    König – ich
    Haus – müssen – muß

> *kam – Saal – nahm*
> *mein – Hain – Bayern*
> *Not – Boot – Kohle – Niveau*

2 Different sounds are represented by the same letter(s):
> *Vater – Vase*
> *lachen – lächeln – sechs*
> *so – das – Stein*

3 Two sounds are represented by one letter:
> *Zoo* (t + s)
> *Hexe* (k + s)

4 One sound is represented by two or more letters:
> *Chor, Lack*
> *Bach*
> *frisch*

The lack of a one-to-one correspondence between sounds and letters in spelling does not prevent a writing system from functioning perfectly well, but it obviously causes great problems for the description of pronunciation, in answer to which various phonetic alphabets have been created, based on the principle that *each symbol represents one and only one sound*. The alphabet in general use is that of the **International Phonetic Association (IPA)**, which has a large repertoire of symbols and diacritics that can be used to represent the pronunciation of any language. A complete list of the symbols needed for the representation of the sounds of German is given on pp. xiii–xiv. As will be seen, the list is not long, and the majority of the symbols are taken from the Latin alphabet so they will be familiar to the reader. Some additional symbols have been taken from other alphabets or have been created by altering or combining existing symbols. For any student with a serious interest in pronunciation it is essential to learn these phonetic symbols and the pronunciation associated with them, since otherwise it is not possible to use pronouncing dictionaries and other aids to pronunciation.

The small number of symbols required for phonetic transcription does not, of course, mean that speakers of German use only a small number of sounds when speaking. For one thing, the human ear and the organs of speech are not accurate enough to produce exactly the same sound consistently over and over again. Even in the same speaker there are minute differences between various instances of what is meant to be the 'same' sound, differences which may go unnoticed in everyday situations, but which can be easily picked up by modern electronic equipment. And the variations are obviously much greater between different speakers. There is, however, only a relatively small number of **distinctive** sounds in any language, that is sounds that can distinguish words from one another. The clearest evidence for the distinctive function of sounds comes from so-called **minimal pairs**, which are pairs of words in a language which are differentiated from one another by one sound only, for instance:

Segen	['ze:gən]	:	*Regen*	['re:gən]
so	[zo:]	:	*roh*	[ro:]
sein	[zaɪn]	:	*rein*	[raɪn]

These words differ only in their initial sounds, which can thus be shown to have distinctive function in German. These distinctive sounds are known as **phonemes**, and they are indicated in transcription by the use of slash brackets, e.g. /s/, /r/. On the basis of further minimal pairs we can distinguish other phonemes of German, e.g.:

	Minimal pairs				*Phonemes*		
reisen	/'raɪzn̩/	:	*reißen*	/'raɪsn̩/	/s/	:	/z/
fand	/fant/	:	*Wand*	/vant/	/f/	:	/v/
Miete	/'mi:tə/	:	*Mitte*	/'mɪtə/	/i:/	:	/ɪ/
tun	/tu:n/	:	*Ton*	/to:n/	/u:/	:	/o:/

Not all the sounds of a language which are discernibly different have this distinctive function, though. The front [r] of German (apical roll) is clearly different from the back [ʀ] (uvular roll), yet they do not serve to distinguish words, e.g. both the pronunciations [re:gən] and [ʀe:gən] are understood by Germans as the same word: *Regen*. Sounds which are different but not distinctive in this way are said to be **allophones** or variants of a single phoneme; in our example, the different r-sounds [r] and [ʀ] are allophones of the single phoneme /r/. In transcription allophones are enclosed in square brackets. A phoneme, then, is an abstract unit consisting of a number of different, though related, sounds (allophones) which function as though they were a single sound, in other words which are perceived by the speakers of a language as being 'the same sound'.

The allophones of /r/ that we have discussed so far are known as **free variants**, as speakers are free to use whichever they prefer in any context. The choice of one or other of the variants of /r/ usually depends on the region of Germany which the speaker comes from. This form of allophonic variation is not uncommon, but there is another type which is even more widespread: **contextual variants**, so called because the variations are determined by the context, in other words by the position in the word and by the neighbouring sounds. The reason for this type of variation is that the sounds of speech are not produced in isolation, but together with other sounds in a continuum, and neighbouring sounds influence each other to a greater or lesser degree. A good illustration of this phenomenon is /h/ in both German and English, which is produced by a strong puff of breath (or aspiration), causing friction in the glottis. The position of the other organs of speech (tongue, lips, etc.) is unimportant in the production of /h/, so they tend to take up the position of the following vowel. To demonstrate this to yourself, try starting to say the following words, but stop after the first sound, before you get to the vowel: *Hand, hielt, Hut, Hüte*. In each case you should hear a clearly different h-sound, and in fact there are as many h-sounds in a language as there are vowels, because the position of the tongue and the lips is different for each [h] depending on which vowel follows. All the same, we do not need nineteen different symbols for /h/ in German, because it is entirely predictable which type of [h] will be used before each vowel. One single symbol is therefore perfectly adequate, as long as we make allowances for the influence of neighbouring sounds on the production of h-sounds.

Another example of variation in the pronunciation of German consonants is /p/, which is pronounced with strong aspiration, or a puff of air, when it occurs at the beginning of a word. You can demonstrate this to yourself by holding a piece of paper directly in front of your lips and saying the word *Paar*. You should see the paper moving as you pronounce the /p/. This aspirated /p/ is sometimes indicated in phonetic transcription by means of a raised h: [pʰaːɐ]. /p/ is not always aspirated in this way; in particular there is no aspiration when it follows /ʃ/, as you can demonstrate by putting the piece of paper in front of your mouth again and saying the word *Spar* [ʃpaːɐ]. This time you should find that the paper does not move.

Allophonic variation in speech has a parallel in writing with which we are all familiar: in writing, too, we have abstract, distinctive units, known as **graphemes**, such as ⟨r⟩, ⟨g⟩, etc. (angled brackets ⟨ ⟩ are used to represent graphemes). Each of these graphemes may have several variants, known as **allographs**. For example, ⟨r⟩ can be written in various ways, e.g. ꭇ or ɼ: it does not matter which of these a writer uses; the important thing is that whatever symbol is used is recognisable as an ⟨r⟩ and is always kept distinct from any other letter.

A full list of the phonemes, or distinctive sounds, of German contains thirty-nine units:

The German consonants			*The German vowels*		
1	/p/	as in	**P**aß	1	/iː/	as in	Sp**ie**l
2	/b/		**B**aum	2	/ɪ/		st**i**ll

3	/t/	*T*ag		3	/e:/	T*ee*
4	/d/	*D*ach		4	/ɛ/	F*e*ld
5	/k/	*K*ind		5	/ɛ:/	sp*ä*t
6	/g/	*g*ut		6	/a:/	S*aa*l
7	/f/	*F*uß		7	/a/	*a*lt
8	/v/	*W*ein		8	/o:/	S*oh*n
9	/s/	wei*ß*		9	/ɔ/	G*o*ld
10	/z/	*S*ee		10	/u:/	H*u*t
11	/ʃ/	*Sch*nee		11	/ʊ/	M*u*nd
12	/ʒ/	*G*enie		12	/y:/	fr*üh*
13	/x/	Bu*ch*		13	/ʏ/	Gl*ü*ck
14	/j/	*j*ung		14	/ø:/	*Ö*l
15	/h/	*H*aus		15	/œ/	zw*ö*lf
16	/m/	*M*ann		16	/ə/	Seit*e*
17	/n/	*N*uß		17	/aɪ/	M*ai*
18	/ŋ/	la*ng*		18	/aʊ/	bl*au*
19	/l/	*L*uft		19	/ɔʏ/	d*eu*tsch
20	/r/	*r*ot				

Each of these phonemes may have a number of different allophones, some of which, like the allophones of /h/, pose no problems at all for the learner, as it is quite natural to put the tongue and lips into the correct position for the following vowel while an h-sound is being articulated. On the other hand, some allophones, like those of /r/, cannot be predicted and must therefore be practised by the learner. Our approach in the following chapters on the German consonants and vowels will be to describe only those allophones of each phoneme which the learner is likely to have trouble with and which will probably need practice, at least by some learners.

The following table shows the thirty-nine phonemes of German with their most important allophones:

	Consonants		*Vowels*
/p/	[p, pʰ]	/iː/	[iː, i, i̯]
/b/	[b, b̥]	/ɪ/	[ɪ]
/t/	[t, tʰ]	/eː/	[eː, e]
/d/	[d, d̥]	/ɛ/	[ɛ]
/k/	[k, k̥ʰ]	/ɛː/	[ɛː]
/g/	[g, g̊]	/aː/	[aː]
/f/	[f]	/a/	[a]
/v/	[v, v̥]	/oː/	[oː, o, o̯]
/s/	[s]	/ɔ/	[ɔ]
/z/	[z, z̥]	/uː/	[uː, u, u̯]

	Consonants		*Vowels*
/ʃ/	[ʃ]	/ʊ/	[ʊ]
/ʒ/	[ʒ, ʒ̊]	/y:/	[y:, y]
/x/	[x, ç]	/ʏ/	[ʏ]
/j/	[j]	/ø:/	[ø:, ø]
/h/	[h]	/œ/	[œ]
/m/	[m]	/ə/	[ə]
/n/	[n]	/aɪ/	[aɪ]
/ŋ/	[ŋ]	/aʊ/	[aʊ]
/l/	[l]	/ɔʏ/	[ɔʏ]
/r/	[r, ʀ, ʁ, ʁ̥, ɾ, ɐ]		

It is possible to transcribe the sounds of language using various de-grees of detail. A transcription may show only the distinctive units or phonemes, in which case it is referred to as **phonemic**, or it may contain details of the allophonic variants, in which case it is known as **allophonic** or **phonetic**. Allophonic transcriptions may also vary in the amount of detail given, from a **broad** transcription with little detail to a **narrow** or precise transcription. In this book, we are dealing with an articulatory description of German sounds, and we shall be giving only the inform-ation necessary for learners of German (rather than all the information it would be possible to give), so we shall be using a **broad allophonic** transcription.

2.4 Coarticulation and assimilation

In discussing the various allophones of /h/ above, it was indicated that the pronunciation of sounds is affected by the context in which they occur. The reason for this is **coarticulation** (G. *die Koartikulation*), the fact that sounds are not isolated, discrete units like (printed) letters, but are articulated in chains during which the organs of speech (articulators) are in constant movement. Not every articulator is actively involved in every sound; thus for /h/ the tongue is free to take up the position of the following sound.

A result of coarticulation is **assimilation** (G. *die Assimilation*), which can be defined as the process by which the articulation of a sound is modified to make it more similar to a neighbouring sound, as in the pronunciation of English *newspaper* as ['nju:speɪpə] with a voiceless /s/ because of the following voiceless consonant /p/, or in the conversational pronunciation of German *haben* ['ha:bm̩] – the final /n/ has become /m/, which as a bilabial sound is more similar to the preceding bilabial /b/.

Assimilation has to do with the economy of speech, i.e. minimising the effort and movement of the muscles that we have to make in order to pronounce words. Thus it is clear that it is most evident in rapid, relaxed speech, which may contain a large number of assimilations, and least evident in slow, careful speech, and we will obviously need to pay closer attention to this phenomenon in the discussion of conversational style in chapter 6. In chapters 3 and 4 on the consonant and vowel sounds of German the treatment of assimilation will be restricted to those phenomena which occur in individual words in formal pronunciation.

2.5 Basis of articulation

In the following chapters, the individual consonant and vowel sounds of German will be described in detail. Before we look at individual sounds, however, it is as well to consider some general differences that exist between German and English pronunciation. These are generally described under the heading of **basis of articulation** or **articulatory settings** (G. *die Artikulationsbasis*). This term refers to the typical positions adopted and the types of movement made by the various articulators in the pronunciation of different languages. Languages can differ not only in individual sounds, but also in more general ways which affect large numbers of sounds. Differences in the basis of articulation are largely responsible for residual foreign accents in speakers who have a fair degree of accuracy in the pronunciation of the individual sounds of a language. Such differences between English and German are:

1 **Articulatory tension**: German is pronounced with greater articulatory tension (G. *die Artikulationsspannung*) than English, i.e. the muscles in the various articulators are more tense, or in non-technical terms: the pronunciation of German is more forceful than that of English.

2 **Lip movement** is more pronounced in German than in English. This applies particularly to vowels such as [u:] and [y:], which are articulated with strongly rounded and protruding lips (G. *stark gerundete und vorgestülpte Lippen*) in German. Lip-spreading (G. *Spreizung der Lippen*) is also pronounced for sounds like [i:]. In English, on the other hand, lip movements are much less vigorous and strong lip-rounding is avoided.

3 **Tongue position**: German has more extreme tongue positions as a result of the greater articulatory tension (point 1), leading to different vowel qualities from those of English. For example, the tongue is more raised and more fronted for the [i:] sound in German than in English.

4 **Position of the glottis**: closure of the glottis, i.e. a glottal stop [ʔ], before initial vowels is a typical feature of German pronunciation which differs markedly from English. The glottal stop is possible before any initial vowel in German, e.g. [ʔɪç], [ˈʔaʊto], [ˈʔyːbən], which means that

in German words beginning with a vowel are cut off from the preceding word, whereas in English there is a strong tendency to link words beginning with a vowel to the end of the previous word to form a smooth chain, cf. the following German and English examples:

G. [ʔ]*Ich* [ʔ]*esse* ([ʔ])*ein* [ʔ]*Eis.*
E. *I'm eating an ice-cream.*
G. [ʔ]*An* ([ʔ])*einem* [ʔ]*Abend* ([ʔ])*in* [ʔ]*Irland* . . .
E. *On an evening in Ireland* . . .

The glottal stop is usually omitted in German before unstressed vowels within an utterance – this has been indicated in the above examples by the use of round brackets. In English the use of a glottal stop before initial vowels is also possible, but here it is limited to cases in which the word is given particular emphasis, e.g.:

I'm [ʔ]absolutely *certain.*
It's been [ʔ]ages *since I saw him.*

5 **Position of the soft palate**: in contrast to French with its large number of nasal vowels, English and German both have a raised soft palate for all sounds except the nasal consonants. The only difference between English and German on this point is that nasal vowels are retained in varieties of educated German pronunciation of French loan words to a far greater extent than in English, e.g. German *Engagement* [ãgaʒə'mãː], *Terrain* [tɛ'rɛ̃]. This only applies to more recent or more unusual loan words, however, as there is a strong tendency to replace the nasal vowel by a native German approximation in common loan words, e.g. *Beton* [be'tɔŋ] or [be'toːn] instead of [be'tɔ̃], *Balkon* [bal'kɔŋ] or [bal'koːn] instead of [bal'kɔ̃], etc.

As these features apply to a large number of sounds in German, it is clear that it is not possible to acquire a good German pronunciation without paying close attention to them. Reference will be made to them in the following chapters wherever the pronunciation of individual consonants or vowels is affected by them.

3

The German consonants

There are good reasons for starting our description of the sounds of German with the consonants (G. *der Konsonant*). For one thing, consonants are simpler to describe than vowels, because the organs of speech are brought into contact or close proximity with one another and it is relatively simple to feel their position and to describe it in articulatory terms. For learners, the tactile feedback provided by contact between the organs of speech means that it is generally not too difficult to understand articulatory descriptions of consonants and to reproduce the positions for themselves.

Consonants are also more important in German, first because they are more frequent than vowels, making up about 61 per cent of the sounds in German utterances, with vowels making up about 39 per cent.[1] Secondly, consonants are more important to the understanding of German than vowels. We can demonstrate this using a children's song, 'Drei Chinesen mit dem Kontrabaß, saßen auf der Straße und erzählten sich was . . .', which is sung through several times using only one vowel sound throughout each time, e.g.

[iː]: [driː çiːniːziːn miːt diːm kiːntriːbiːs . . .]
[eː]: [dreː çeːneːseːn meːt deːm keːntreːbeːs . . .], etc.

Even when the vowels are all the same, it is fairly easy to recognise the words, whereas if all the consonants were the same this would be completely impossible. This is not part of the children's song, but for the purposes of illustration we can demonstrate what it would sound like if all the consonants were replaced by [t]:

[ttaɪ titeːtət tɪt teːt tɔttatat . . .]

[1] Figures from König (1985: 115); see also Meinhold & Stock (1982: 100).

We can achieve a similar effect in writing: if we just have the vowels of a German utterance, it is mostly impossible to understand it, as in the following example:

_i__e_ _e_ __u_ _ie__ ei_ __ei_e_ _ü____e_ __ä____e_.

But if we only have the consonants we can generally make out the meaning without too much difficulty:

H_nt_r d_m Fl_ß l__gt __n kl__n_s h_bsch_s St_dtch_n.

Because they play such an important role in the recognition of words, a good command of the consonants is absolutely essential for successful communication in German. Problems with the pronunciation of the vowels are less likely to cause misunderstandings when speaking with Germans. However, if we wish to acquire a good German pronunciation, we must also devote some time and effort to practising the vowels, as they include many of the obvious marks of an English accent in German.

3.1 The description of consonants

Consonants can be defined in two ways, either in terms of their articulation or in terms of their position:

1 **Articulatory definition:** a consonant is formed by obstructing the airstream in the vocal tract by means of a complete closure or a narrowing of the organs of speech. For vowels, on the other hand, the air is allowed to escape without hindrance.
2 **Positional definition:** consonants occur at the edge of the syllable, whereas vowels occupy the position at the centre of the syllable.

We will see that there are situations where these two definitions clash, and that consonants can sometimes occur in the centre and vowels at the edge of the syllable, but these are exceptional cases rather than the rule.

For a description of the way consonants are produced, we need to know a number of things, the most important of which are:

1 **how** the sound is formed, i.e. what type of closure or narrowing is involved (this is known as the **manner of articulation**, G. *die Artikulationsart*);
2 **where** the sound is formed, i.e. at what position in the vocal tract the closure or narrowing takes place (this is known as the **place of articulation**, G. *der Artikulationsort*);

3 whether the sound is **voiced** or **voiceless**, i.e. whether it involves
   any vibrations of the vocal cords or not (this is known as **voice** or
   phonation).

We will look at these three areas in greater detail in the following
sections.

3.1.1 **Manner of articulation**

For German consonants, the obstruction in the vocal tract is one of the
following seven types:

1 **Plosives** or **stop consonants** (G. *der Verschlußlaut*) are formed with a
   total closure in the vocal tract, e.g. [p], [d].
2 **Fricatives** (G. *der Reibelaut* or *der Frikativ*) are formed by bringing
   the organs of speech close together, so that the air escaping from the
   month causes friction, e.g. [f], [z].
3 **Nasals** (G. *der Nasenlaut* or *der Nasal*) have a total oral closure, but as
   the soft palate is lowered air can escape through the nose, e.g. [n],
   [m].
4 **Laterals** (G. *der Seitenlaut* or *der Lateral*) involve a partial closure in
   the centre of the mouth, but air can escape along the sides of tongue,
   e.g. [l].
5 **Approximants** or **frictionless continuants** (G. *der Approximant* or *der
   friktionslose Dauerlaut*) are formed by bringing the organs of speech
   close together, as for fricatives, but they are articulated with less
   force, so there is no audible friction, e.g. [j] [ʁ].
6 **Rolls** or **trills** (G. *der Schwinglaut* or *der Vibrant*) are formed by the
   tip of the tongue vibrating rapidly and striking the alveolar ridge or by
   the uvula striking the back of the tongue, e.g. [r], [ʀ].
7 **Affricates** (G. *die Affrikate*) are plosives in which the closure is
   released slowly, resulting in friction as the air escapes, e.g. [ts], [pf].

The term **obstruent** (G. *der Obstruent*) is used to refer to the classes of
the plosives, fricatives and affricates, which are phonetically related (i.e.
formed in a similar manner) and which it is frequently useful to be able to
group together.

3.1.2 **Place of articulation**

In order to pronounce a consonant we have to obstruct the airstream at
some point in the vocal tract. This involves either contact between two of
the organs of speech, or a movement of one towards another. The place
at which this obstruction occurs can be described by naming the active
articulator, i.e. the organ that moves, and the passive articulator, i.e. the

organ which the active articulator touches or towards which it moves. For instance, in the case of [t] or [d] the passive articulator is the alveolar ridge, against which the active articulator, the blade (or, for some people, the tip) of the tongue, presses to form a closure. For [f] and [v] the active articulator is the lower lip, which is moved very close to the passive articulator, the upper incisors. [t] and [d] can thus be described as lamino-alveolar or apico-alveolar, and [f] and [v] as labio-dental consonants. In practice, when the tongue is the active articulator, it is usually sufficient to specify the passive articulator, as the active articulator is almost always the part of the tongue which lies directly below this. Thus the place of articulation for [t] and [d] is normally simply described as alveolar, and it is understood that the part of the tongue nearest to the alveolar ridge, the blade, is the active articulator. For consonants involving the lips, both articulators must be specified, as there are two potential articulations, one involving the lower lips and the upper teeth (labio-dental), as for [f] and [v], and one involving both upper and lower lips (bilabial), as for [p] and [b].

The example of bilabial consonants like [p] shows that it is not always correct to speak of an active and a passive articulator, for there are cases in which both articulators are active. You can easily demonstrate this to yourself by pronouncing a [p] in front of a mirror, and you will see that both lips clearly move. For the majority of articulations, however, it makes sense to speak of an active and a passive articulator, so these terms have been retained where appropriate.

The following table gives the main places of articulation for the German consonants:

Place of articulation	Passive articulator	Active articulator
bilabial		upper and lower lips
labio-dental	upper incisors	lower lip
alveolar	alveolar ridge	blade of the tongue
palato-alveolar	back of alveolar ridge/ front of hard palate	blade of the tongue
palatal	hard palate	front of the tongue
velar	soft palate	back of the tongue
uvular		back of the tongue/uvula
glottal		vocal cords

3.1.3 Voice

Voiced consonants are produced with vibrations of the vocal cords, whereas for unvoiced consonants there are no vibrations. You can test this for yourself by pronouncing [s] and [z] with your thumb and fore-finger on your larynx or with your fingers in your ears (it is best to pronounce them alternately [szszszszsz]): you will find that you feel the vibrations only for the [z].

However, this distinction is often lost in standard German pronunciation because of variations in the degree of voicing in voiced obstruents. The basic rule is that voiceless obstruents are always voiceless, but voiced obstruents are not always voiced. In fact, they are only fully voiced when they occur between voiced sounds, e.g. in intervocalic position; in other positions they are either partially or fully **devoiced** (G. *entstimmt*). This devoicing can be attributed to the influence of the neighbouring voiceless segment, which can be either a voiceless sound or – in the case of initial and final obstruents – a pause, during which, of course, the vocal cords are not vibrating. Devoicing is indicated in phonetic notation by [̥] placed under the symbol in question: [b̥] (or on top if the symbol descends beneath the line, e.g. [g̊]).

Devoicing is illustrated in the following diagrams, in which [〜] indicates vibrations of the vocal cords and [—] indicates the absence of vibrations.

Voiced obstruents, fully voiced intervocalically:

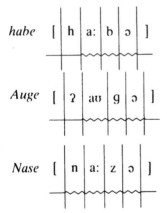

Voiced obstruents, partially or fully devoiced initially:

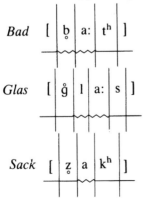

Devoicing also affects the consonants /l/ and /r/ following voiceless plosives (see section 3.2).

When using the term 'voiced', then, we must be aware that these sounds are often not fully voiced. They are, however, potentially voiced, that is they may be pronounced with at least partial voicing, even if this is not always the most common German pronunciation.

3.1.4 Lenis and fortis

Even when they are fully devoiced, there is a difference between voiced obstruents and their voiceless counterparts, i.e. [b̥] is not the same as [p], [z̥] is not the same as [s], etc. The reason for this is that in German (and English, but not in many other languages, e.g. French) voiceless obstruents are pronounced with greater force and muscular effort than voiced ones. The voiceless obstruents are said to be **fortis** or strong, and voiced obstruents correspondingly to be **lenis** or weak. Because of the frequent devoicing of German obstruents, in many situations it is the distinction between fortis and lenis articulation which actually distinguishes pairs of consonants like [s] and [z̥], [p] and [b̥], etc., and it seems that for obstruents this distinction is more important than that between voiced and voiceless.

3.1.5 Auslautverhärtung

One general difference between English obstruents and their German counterparts concerns their distribution. In German, lenis (voiced) obstruents cannot occur (a) in word-final position, or (b) in syllable-final position before a morpheme boundary (a morpheme is the smallest unit of grammar, including stems like *Hand* and *brav* and affixes like *-lich* and *-heit*). In these positions the lenis obstruents are replaced by their fortis counterparts, a process which is known in German as *Auslautverhärtung*. Thus words which have [b], [d], [g], [v], [z], and [ʒ] in the non-final position, for instance before endings, have [p], [t], [k], [f], [s] and [ʃ] when the obstruent is in the final position:

Non-final		Word-final	Syllable-final
Liebe [ˈliːbə]	but	*lieb* [liːp]	*lieblich* [ˈliːplɪç]
Hände [ˈhɛndə]		*Hand* [hant]	*handlich* [ˈhantlɪç]
Wege [ˈveːgə]		*Weg* [veːk]	*Wegrand* [ˈveːkrant]
brave [ˈbraːvə]		*brav* [braːf]	*Bravheit* [ˈbraːfhaɪt]
Felsen [ˈfɛlzn̩]		*Fels* [fɛls]	*Felsblock* [ˈfɛlsblɔk]
beiges [ˈbeːʒəs]		*beige* [beːʃ]	*beigefarben* [ˈbeːʃfarbən]

The same phenomenon occurs before a fortis consonant in the same syllable:

gebe [ˈgeːbə] but *gibst* [giːpst]
lade [ˈlaːdə]   *lädst* [lɛːtst]
lege [ˈleːgə]   *legst* [leːkst]

3.1.6 Three-term labels

In addition to the information we have described so far, an exhaustive description of consonants would include other information, such as the source and direction of the airstream. However, in German (as in English), all sounds are made with **pulmonic egressive** airstream, so this need not be mentioned for individual consonant sounds. A concise description consisting of information on voice, place of articulation and manner of articulation (in that order), known as a **three-term label,** is perfectly adequate to distinguish all the consonant phonemes of German, e.g. voiced bilabial nasal (/m/). For the obstruents, the three-term label contains information on the distinction between fortis and lenis rather than on voice, as these consonants are frequently devoiced, e.g. lenis alveolar plosive (/d/), or fortis labio-dental fricative (/f/). A description in the form of a three-term label is given for each of the German consonants in the sections below.

3.1.7 The description of individual German consonants

In the remainder of this chapter, all the German consonants will be described in detail in groups according to the manner of articulation. There will be four sections on each consonant:

(a) a description and diagram showing the exact manner and place of articulation;
(b) its distribution, or occurrence, in German words, together with examples;
(c) a discussion of the most common problems which English-speaking learners have with each sound, together with advice on how to overcome them;
(d) the major regional variants within the German-speaking countries.

For some of the groups of consonants, sections (c) and (d) have been placed together at the end, so that features common to all the consonants in the group can be discussed in one place.

3.2 **Plosives**

(1) *Formation of plosives*

The plosives or stop consonants involve a total closure of the air passage. The soft palate is raised, so that no air can escape through the nose, and in addition to this the stream of air coming from the lungs is stopped for a fraction of a second by a closure at some point in the mouth (thus the alternative term 'stop consonant'). There are three distinct phases in the formation of a plosive:

(a) **closing stage** (G. *die Schließungsphase*): the articulators are brought together to form the closure;

(b) **hold** or **compression stage** (G. *die Verschlußphase*): while the articulators are together, the air coming from the lungs cannot escape and so pressure builds up behind the closure;

(c) **release stage** (G. *die Öffnungsphase*): when the closure is released the air that has been trapped escapes with a slight puff or explosion (thus the term 'plosive').

(2) *The German plosive phonemes*

In German, as in English, there are six plosive phonemes, which form three groups of two according to the place of articulation. They are: /p/ and /b/, /t/ and /d/, /k/ and /g/. The first-mentioned members of these pairs are voiceless and fortis, the others are (potentially) voiced and lenis.

(3) *Aspiration of plosives*

In some environments, fortis plosives are **aspirated** (G. *behaucht*), whereas lenis plosives never are. Aspiration is a strong release of an oral closure with an audible puff of air. The presence of aspiration in fortis plosives can be tested (as described in chapter 2) by holding a piece of paper directly in front of your mouth and pronouncing pairs of words such as *Paar* and *Bar*, *Torf* and *Dorf*, *Kuß* and *Guß*. You will see a clear movement of the paper caused by the puff of air as the fortis consonants /p/, /t/ and /k/ are released, whereas there will be very little, if any, movement when the lenis consonants are released. (In this experiment the movement of the paper is most obvious in the case of bilabial /p/, as it is released right at the front of the mouth, very close to the paper. /t/ and /k/ are released further back in the mouth, giving the air time to dissipate somewhat before it reaches the paper.) As this puff of air is similar to the consonant /h/, it is often represented by an [h] or a raised [ʰ] in a narrow transcription.

There are variations in the degree of aspiration:

(a) Fortis plosives are most strongly aspirated (= [ph, th, kh]) in the initial position before stressed vowels: *Paß* [phas], *Tal* [thaːl], *komm* [khɔm].

(b) The aspiration is weaker, but still present (= [pʰ, tʰ, kʰ]), before unstressed vowels and at the end of words: *Lippe* [ˈlɪpʰə], *populär* [pʰopʰuˈlɛːɐ̯], *Hand* [hantʰ].

(c) Aspiration is very weak or completely absent (= [p⁻, t⁻, k⁻]) following initial /ʃ/ or /s/: *still* [ʃt⁻ɪl], *Skandal* [sk⁻anˈdaːl]. The non-aspirated fortis plosives in German can be compared to the non-aspiration of the same sounds in English following /s/, as can be demonstrated by saying the following words with a piece of paper held in front of the mouth:

	Aspirated	*Unaspirated*
English:	*pin, till, car*	*spin, still, scar*
German:	*Paar, Teil, kann*	*spar, steil, Skandal*

In each case, a movement of the paper will be observed for the initial plosives, but not for those following /s/ or /ʃ/.

Following an initial fortis plosive the consonants /l/ and /r/ are devoiced: *Kreis* [kr̥ais], *Klasse* [ˈkl̥asɔ], *träge* [ˈtr̥ɛːgə], *Plan* [pl̥aːn]. You can hear the devoiced pronunciation of these consonants if you say the words very slowly and deliberately.

(4) Devoicing of lenis plosives

The German lenis plosives /b, d, g/ are subject to devoicing (see section 3.1.3 above). Even when they are fully devoiced, the lenis plosives are still distinguished from the corresponding fortis consonants by the difference in aspiration: e.g.:

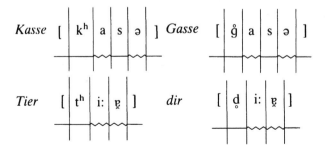

(5)   *Clusters of plosives*

When two plosives occur together, either within words or at word
boundaries, the first of them is usually pronounced with no audible release.
This means that the closing and hold stages of the first plosive are formed
in the normal way, but before it is released the closure for the following
plosive is in place, thus preventing the air from escaping. Lack of audible
release is indicated in phonetic transcription by the symbol [̚], e.g.
schwankt [ʃvaŋk ̚tʰ], *Abgabe* [ˈap ̚gaːbə], *frag Peter* [fraːk ̚ ˈpheːtʰɐ], etc.
When two plosives with the same place of articulation occur together,
both the release stage of the first and the closing stage of the second are
missing, so that these combinations of consonants differ from a single
consonant only in the length of the hold stage, e.g. *Stadttor* [ˈʃtat ̚tʰoːɐ],
Schreibpapier [ˈʃraɪp ̚pʰapʰiːɐ], *ein Stück Kuchen* [aɪn ˈʃtʏk ̚ ˈkhuːxn̩]. In
combinations of three plosives, the middle one usually has no closing or
release stages, and so the only clue to its presence is a slightly longer hold
stage than there would be if there were only two consonants. Examples
of clusters of three consonants are: *Hauptbahnhof* [ˈhaʊp ̚t ̚baːnhoːf],
er schreibt besser [ɛɐ ˈʃraɪp ̚t ̚ ˈbɛsɐ].

3.2.1   /p/ and /b/

(a)   *Description*

For /p/ and /b/ the lips are pressed firmly together so that no air can
escape. The soft palate is raised, and as the tongue is not involved in the
closure it is free to take up the position of the following sound. Both
these consonants have the same place of articulation, the upper and lower
lips together, and are thus known as **bilabial plosives.** The difference
between them is that /p/ is voiceless and fortis, whereas /b/ is voiced and
lenis.

/p/
fortis
bilabial
plosive

/b/
lenis
bilabial
plosive

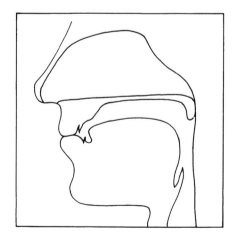

Fig. 3: /p/ and /b/

(b) *Distribution and examples*

/p/

Spelling: ⟨p⟩, ⟨pp⟩, final ⟨b⟩

/p/ occurs in the initial, medial and final positions:

initial: *Paß* [pas], *Papier* [pa'pi:ɐ], *Platz* [plats], *Preis* [praɪs], *Psychologie* [psyçolo'gi:]

initial clusters: *Sprache* ['ʃpra:xə], *Specht* [ʃpɛçt]

medial: *Hupe* ['hu:pə], *Stempel* ['ʃtɛmpl̩], *Lippe* ['lɪpə], *kaputt* [ka'pʊt]

final clusters: *Haupt* [haʊpt], *Abt* [apt]

final: *plump* [plʊmp], *Galopp* [ga'lɔp], *Dieb* [di:p], *Lob* [lo:p], *gab* [ga:p]

/b/

Spelling: ⟨b⟩, ⟨bb⟩

/b/ occurs in the initial and medial positions, but not finally:

initial: *Baum* [baʊm], *Bus* [bʊs], *bitte* ['bɪtə], *Blatt* [blat], *braun* [braʊn]

medial: *Hebel* ['he:bl̩] *dabei* [da'baɪ], *Taube* ['taʊbə], *Ebbe* ['ɛbə]

3.2.2 /t/ **and** /d/

(a) *Description*

The second pair of plosives is /t/ and /d/, which are pronounced with the blade (or for some people the tip) of the tongue pressed against the alveolar ridge and the sides of the tongue against the sides of the hard palate, forming a closure. The soft palate is raised so that no air can escape through the nose. As they are pronounced with the tongue pressed against the alveolar ridge, these consonants are known as **alveolar plosives.** The relationship between these consonants is exactly the same as between /p/ and /b/: /t/ is the voiceless, fortis member of the pair and /d/ is voiced and lenis.

/t/
fortis
alveolar
plosive

/d/
lenis
alveolar
plosive

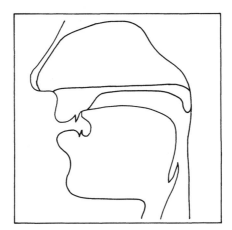

Fig. 4: /t/ and /d/

(b) *Distribution and examples*

/t/

Spelling: ⟨t⟩, ⟨th⟩, ⟨tt⟩, ⟨dt⟩, final ⟨d⟩

/t/ occurs in the initial, medial and final positions:

🎧 **initial:** *Tag* [taːk], *Tür* [tyːɐ], *toll* [tɔl], *Theater* [teˈaːtɐ], *Thron* [troːn]
initial clusters: *stehen* [ˈʃteːən], *Straße* [ˈʃtraːsə]
medial: *Miete* [ˈmiːtə], *heute* [ˈhɔʏtə], *Schwester* [ˈʃvɛstɐ], *Mutter* [ˈmʊtɐ], *Städte* [ˈʃtɛtə]
final clusters: *Rutsch* [rʊtʃ], *Kitsch* [kɪtʃ]
final: *laut* [laʊt], *Spott* [ʃpɔt], *nett* [nɛt], *Leid* [laɪt], *bald* [balt]

/d/

Spelling: ⟨d⟩, ⟨dd⟩

/d/ occurs in the initial and medial positions, but not finally:

🎧 **initial:** *Dach* [dax], *Ding* [dɪŋ], *dürfte* [ˈdʏrftə], *draußen* [ˈdraʊsn̩], *drängen* [ˈdrɛŋən]
medial: *leider* [ˈlaɪdɐ], *Hände* [ˈhɛndə], *niedrig* [ˈniːdrɪç], *Adler* [ˈaːdlɐ], *paddeln* [ˈpadl̩n]

3.2.3 /k/ and /g/

(a) *Description*

The plosives /k/ and /g/ are formed with the soft palate raised and a closure in the oral passage further back than for /t/ and /d/. These consonants are known as **velar plosives**, as a typical articulation is with the back of the tongue pressed against the soft palate or velum. However, the exact place of articulation varies greatly depending on the neighbouring sounds (particularly the following sound): before a back vowel like /ɔ/ the closure is made towards the front of the soft palate, but before a front vowel like /iː/ it is made with the front of the tongue pressed against the middle of the hard palate. You can test this by saying works like *Koch* and *Kiel* in succession and noting the position of the closure for each. You will feel the position of your tongue more easily if you move it slightly from side to side. /k/ is the voiceless, fortis member of the pair and /g/ is voiced and lenis. The diagram depicts a relatively central position for the velar closure before /aː/ as in *kam* or *Gas*.

/k/
fortis
velar
plosive

/g/
lenis
velar
plosive

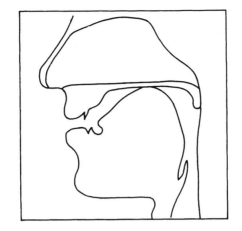

Fig. 5: /k/ and /g/

(b) *Distribution and examples*
/k/
Spelling: ⟨k⟩, ⟨ck⟩, ⟨kk⟩, final ⟨g⟩, ⟨c⟩, ⟨ch⟩, ⟨x⟩ (= [ks]), ⟨q⟩ (in the combination ⟨qu⟩)
/k/ occurs in the initial, medial and final positions:
▣ **initial:** *Kind* [kɪnt], *klein* [klaɪn], *knapp* [knap], *Kreis* [kraɪs], *Café* [ka'fe:], *Chor* [ko:ɐ̯], *Qual* [kva:l]
initial clusters: *Skandal* [skan'da:l], *Skelett* [ske'lɛt]
medial: *Zucker* ['tsʊkɐ], *Paket* [pa'ke:t], *Werke* ['vɛrkə], *Mokka* ['mɔka], *Hexe* ['hɛksɔ]
final clusters: *Keks* [ke:ks], *Markt* [markt]
final: *Streik* [ʃtraɪk], *Lack* [lak], *zog* [tso:k], *Krug* [kru:k]

/g/
Spelling: ⟨g⟩, ⟨gg⟩
/g/ occurs in the initial and medial positions, but not finally:
▣ **initial:** *gut* [gu:t], *gestern* ['gɛstɐn], *Glaube* ['glaʊbə], *Grab* [gra:p], *Gnade* ['gna:də]
medial: *Liege* ['li:gə], *Flagge* ['flagə], *tragisch* ['tra:gɪʃ], *Hügel* ['hy:gl], *Vogel* ['fo:gl]

Note that the ⟨ng⟩ in words like *lang*, *hing*, *Endung* represents the
phoneme /ŋ/, so that these words do not have a final /k/, but are pronounced [laŋ], [hɪŋ], [ˈɛnduŋ] (see section 3.4.3). For the pronunciation
of final ⟨g⟩, see also section 3.3.4(d).

(c)   *Problems for English-speaking learners*

The German plosives are similar to their counterparts in SBS, so that
most English speakers have no problems with the articulation of these
sounds. The one exception is /t/, which has a number of regional variants
in English. Especially in the south of England, but also elsewhere, e.g.
Liverpool, /t/ can be affricated (= [tˢ]), e.g. *told* [tˢəuld]. This pronunciation is unacceptable for German /t/, not least because it could
cause confusion with the affricate [ts]. In German it is essential to distinguish between words like *Teig* [taɪk] and *zeig* [tsaɪk]. Speakers who
have this pronunciation in English should make sure that their German /t/
is pronounced without affrication.

The realisation of /t/ as a glottal stop, as occurs in many regional
accents of English (London, some Scottish accents, etc.), e.g. *bottle*
[ˈbɔʔl], is not acceptable in German.

The variations in the degree of aspiration of the fortis plosives are very
similar in the two languages and do not generally cause problems.

Finally, initial plosives are pronounced in some contexts in German in
which they are omitted in English. In English,

initial ⟨p⟩ is silent before ⟨s⟩, ⟨t⟩ or ⟨n⟩,
initial ⟨k⟩ is silent before ⟨s⟩ and ⟨n⟩, and
initial ⟨g⟩ is silent before ⟨n⟩.

In German, however, /p/, /k/ and /g/ are pronounced in these positions:

	English	*German*
⟨ps⟩	*psychology* [saɪˈkɔlədʒɪ]	*Psychologie* [psyçoloˈgiː]
⟨pt⟩	*Ptolemy* [ˈtɔlɪmɪ]	*Ptolemäus* [ptoleˈmɛːʊs]
⟨pn⟩	*pneumatic* [njuːˈmætɪk]	*pneumatisch* [pnɔyˈmaːtɪʃ]
⟨x⟩	*xenophobia* [zenəˈfəubɪə]	*Xenophobie* [ksenofoˈbiː]
⟨kn⟩	*knave* [neɪv]	*Knabe* [ˈknaːbə]
⟨gn⟩	*gnat* [næt]	*Gnade* [ˈgnaːdə]

(d)   *Regional variation*

In some central and southern German varieties, the fortis plosives are
either very weakly aspirated or completely unaspirated and are thus not
differentiated from the weak voiced plosives, leading to homophones
(identical pronunciations) such as *Pein–Bein* [p⁼aɪn]–[b̥aɪn], *Torf–*
Dorf [t⁼ɔrf]–[d̥ɔrf], etc. This pronunciation is not standard and should be
avoided by foreign learners.

In some northern and central varieties, voiceless plosives, especially /t/, are voiced intervocalically (i.e. between vowels), e.g. *weiter* [ˈvaɪdɐ], *bitte* [ˈbɪdə], This pronunciation is also non-standard.

3.3 Fricatives

The fricatives are the largest group of German consonants, numbering nine phonemes in all: /f, v, s, z, ʃ, ʒ, x, j, h/. The first six of these occur in three pairs of fortis/lenis consonants. The fricatives are formed by bringing the organs of speech very close to one another at some point so that a narrow channel is formed. Just as the water in a river flows faster at narrow parts, so the air escaping from the lungs is forced to travel faster through the narrowing formed by the organs of speech. On exit this rapid airflow causes turbulence which results in a rubbing sound or friction, from which this group of consonants gets its name.

We will start our description with the fricatives that occur in fortis/lenis pairs.

3.3.1 /f/ and /v/

(a) *Description*
For /f/ and /v/ the lower lip and the upper front teeth (incisors) are brought together to form a narrowing, through which the airstream travels rapidly, causing turbulence. Because both the lower lip and the upper teeth are involved in making these sounds, they are known as **labio-dental fricatives** (G. *der labiodentale Reibelaut*). /f/ is the voiceless, fortis member of the pair and /v/ is voiced and lenis.

/f/
fortis
labio-dental
fricative

/v/
lenis
labio-dental
fricative

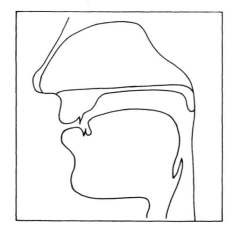

Fig. 6: /f/ and /v/

(b) *Distribution and examples*
/f/
Spelling: ⟨f⟩, ⟨ff⟩, ⟨v⟩, ⟨ph⟩
/f/ occurs in the initial, medial and final positions:
🖵 **initial:** *Fuß* [fu:s], *frei* [fraɪ], *Vater* [ˈfaːtɐ], *phantastisch* [fanˈtastɪʃ], *Philipp* [ˈfɪlɪp]
medial: *laufen* [ˈlaʊfn̩], *Hafen* [ˈhaːfn̩], *Seife* [ˈzaɪfə], *hoffen* [ˈhɔfn̩], *Strophe* [ˈʃtroːfə]
final: *auf* [aʊf], *tief* [tiːf], *Stoff* [ʃtɔf], *Wolf* [vɔlf], *Senf* [zɛnf], *Nerv* [nɛrf]

/v/
Spelling: ⟨w⟩, ⟨v⟩, ⟨u⟩ (in the combination ⟨qu⟩)
/v/ occurs initially and medially, but not finally:
🖵 **initial:** *Wein* [vaɪn], *Wind* [vɪnt], *Veto* [ˈveːto], *Vase* [ˈvaːzə], *wringen* [ˈvrɪŋən], *Wien* [viːn]
initial clusters: *Schweiß* [ʃvaɪs], *zwei* [tsvaɪ], *zwar* [tsvaːɐ], *Quatsch* [kvatʃ]
medial: *Klavier* [klaˈviːɐ], *November* [noˈvɛmbɐ], *Universität* [univɛrziˈtɛːt], *Lawine* [laˈviːnə], *Aquarium* [aˈkvaːri̯ʊm]

(c) *Problems for English-speaking learners*
These German sounds are very straightforward for speakers of English, as the corresponding English sounds can be used in German. The only problems are caused by the spelling of Modern German:

> /v/ is most frequently represented by ⟨w⟩: *warum, wann, Wein,* etc.
> ⟨v⟩ represents /f/ in native German words: *Vater, vier, verlieren* (and in some old, well-established loan words: *Vers, Vesper, Veilchen*).
> ⟨v⟩ represents /v/ in newer loan words: *Vase, privat, Klavier,* etc.
> In a few cases there are two possible pronunciations: *Eva* [ˈeːva] or [ˈeːfa], *David* [ˈdaːvɪt] of [ˈdaːfɪt].

(d) *Regional variation*
Some speakers have a bilabial, rather than a labio-dental pronunciation of these sounds, especially /v/, which is realised as [β]. The bilabial fricative is less forceful than the labio-dental one. It is not to be recommended to English learners because of the danger that they may produce something too close to the English /w/, which is a bilabial approximant rather than a fricative, and which is pronounced with rounded lips rather than the spread lips required for German [β].

3.3.2 /s/ **and** /z/

(a) *Description*
The narrowing of the organs of speech for /s/ and /z/ is made by placing

the blade of the tongue very close to the alveolar ridge. The lips are loosely spread, the upper and lower teeth are close together, the sides of the tongue are in contact with the upper teeth and the tongue is grooved, i.e. it is lower in the middle than at the sides, which means that the air is channeled out through the middle of the mouth. This can be felt by putting the tongue in position for an [s] and breathing in; the cold air can be felt in the groove down the middle of the tongue. For some speakers in both English and German the narrowing is made between the tip of the tongue and the alveolar ridge. As both articulations are possible in both languages, it does not matter which you use, particularly as the difference between them is barely audible in many cases. /s/ is the voiceless, fortis member of the pair and /z/ is voiced and lenis.

/s/
fortis
alveolar
fricative

/z/
lenis
alveolar
fricative

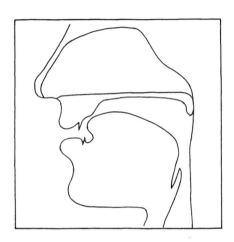

Fig. 7: /s/ and /z/

(b)   *Distribution and examples*
/s/
Spelling: ⟨s⟩, ⟨ss⟩, ⟨ß⟩, ⟨x⟩ (= [ks])
/s/ occurs in medial and final position and initially before consonants:
initial before consonant: *Skizze* [ˈskɪtsə], *Szene* [ˈstseːnə], *Skandinavien* [skandiˈnaːvjən]
initial clusters: *Psychologie* [psyçoloˈgiː], *Xaver* [ˈksaːvɐ]
medial: *wissen* [ˈvɪsn̩], *heißen* [ˈhaɪsn̩], *Fenster* [ˈfɛnstɐ], *wußte* [ˈvʊstə], *Rätsel* [ˈrɛːtsl̩]
final: *weiß* [vaɪs], *lies* [liːs], *Mannes* [ˈmanəs], *Hals* [hals], *rechts* [rɛçts], *Max* [maks]
final clusters: *Hast* [hast], *Axt* [akst]

/z/

Spelling: ⟨s⟩

/z/ occurs initially before vowels and in medial position, but not finally:

🙂 **initial before vowel:** *See* [ze:], *sein* [zaɪn], *sechs* [zɛks], *Summe* ['zʊmə], *singen* ['zɪŋən]

medial: *Rose* ['ro:zə], *lesen* ['le:zn̩], *Esel* ['e:zl̩], *langsam* ['laŋza:m]

(c) *Problems for English-speaking learners*

Once again these sounds, as such, do not cause any problems for English-speaking learners of German, as they can simply use the corresponding English sounds, even though the German /s/ and /z/ tend to be slightly more grooved than their English counterparts.

Problems for English learners are much more likely to arise because of the different distribution of these sounds in English and German. In German, initial ⟨s⟩ before a vowel represents /z/, e.g. *sieben* ['zi:bən], *Summe* ['zʊmə], whereas in English it represents /s/, e.g. *seven* ['sevən], *sum* [sʌm]. Final ⟨s⟩, on the other hand, **always** represents /s/ in German, e.g. *Mannes* ['manəs], *Autos* ['aʊtos], whereas in English it can represent both /s/ and /z/, e.g. *hats* [hæts], *man's* [mænz], *cars* [kɑːz], *pieces* ['pi:səz]. Because of the differences in distribution, English learners should exercise special care in the pronunciation of German words containing ⟨s⟩, especially those with genitive and plural endings in ⟨s⟩.

(d) *Regional variation*

In many southern varieties /z/ is devoiced and thus not very clearly distinguished from /s/, e.g. *setzen* ['zɛtsn̩], *Rose* ['ro:z̥ə].

In other areas, /s/ tends to be voiced intervocalically, e.g. *besser* ['bɛzɐ], *Soße* ['zo:zə]. Neither of these pronunciations is standard and they should not be imitated.

3.3.3 /ʃ/ **and** /ʒ/

(a) *Description*

The narrowing of the organs of speech for /ʃ/ and /ʒ/ is further back than for /s/ and /z/, stretching from about the middle of the alveolar ridge to the front part of the hard palate. The place of articulation is known as **palato-alveolar**. /ʃ/ is a voiceless, fortis consonant and /ʒ/ is voiced and lenis. The difference in position between the alveolar and palato-alveolar fricatives can be felt either by saying the sounds in alternation [sʃsʃsʃsʃ], or by first making an [s], leaving the tongue in position and breathing in sharply, then repeating the process for [ʃ]. The cold air entering the mouth can be felt most strongly at the narrowing. In contrast to /s/ and /z/, the lips are quite strongly rounded for German /ʃ/ and /ʒ/, and the groove in the tongue is broader.

/ʃ/
fortis
palato-alveolar
fricative

/ʒ/
lenis
palato-alveolar
fricative

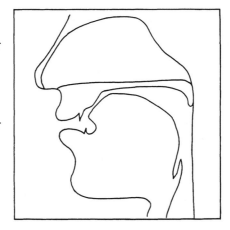

Fig. 8: /ʃ/ and /ʒ/

(b) *Distribution and examples*

German /ʃ/ is extremely common and occurs in all positions, whereas /ʒ/ is rare, occurring only in words of French and Italian origin. This pattern of occurrence is very similar to that in English, the only difference being that /ʒ/ is rather more common in English than in German.

/ʃ/

Spelling: ⟨sch⟩, ⟨s⟩ (in initial ⟨sp⟩, ⟨st⟩), ⟨ge⟩ (in final position in French loan words)

/ʃ/ occurs in initial, medial and final position:

initial before vowel: *Schein* [ʃaɪn], *Schuh* [ʃuː], *schön* [ʃøːn], *scheu* [ʃɔʏ]
initial before consonant: *Schnee* [ʃneː], *schlafen* [ˈʃlaːfn̩], *Schnupfen* [ˈʃnʊpfn̩], *Schrift* [ʃrɪft], *Stein* [ʃtaɪn]
medial: *Asche* [ˈaʃə], *mischen* [ˈmɪʃn̩], *rutschen* [ˈrʊtʃn̩], *falsche* [ˈfalʃə]
final: *Tisch* [tɪʃ], *deutsch* [dɔʏtʃ], *Wunsch* [vʊnʃ], *Marsch* [marʃ], *beige* [beːʃ], *rouge* [ruːʃ].

/ʒ/
Spelling: ⟨g⟩, ⟨j⟩
/ʒ/ occurs in initial and medial position, but not finally:

⊡ **initial:** *Genie* [ʒeˈniː], *Gelee* [ʒeˈleː], *Journalist* [ʒʊrnaˈlɪst], *Jalousie* [ʒaluˈziː]
medial: *Regime* [reˈʒiːm], *Regisseur* [reʒɪˈsøːʁ], *leger* [leˈʒeːʁ], *Etage* [eˈtaːʒə]

(c) *Problems for English-speaking learners*

For most learners these sounds do not generally cause any great problems. However, there are some speakers of English who have very little lip-rounding for /ʃ/ and /ʒ/; such speakers should make sure that these sounds are produced with the lips well rounded and even protruding a little. Lip-rounding is both more common and more pronounced in German than in English, as we shall also see later with the vowels.

(d) *Regional variation*

Some North German accents (e.g. Hamburg, Hannover) have initial [sp] and [st] instead of the standard [ʃp], [ʃt]: *Spiel* [spiːl], *Stein* [staɪn].

On the other hand, some south-western accents (e.g. Swabian, Alemannic) have [ʃp] and [ʃt] for ⟨sp⟩ and ⟨st⟩ in medial and final position as well, e.g. *Wespen* [ˈvɛʃpm̩], *jüngste* [ˈjʏŋʃtə], *Durst* [dʊrʃt], *Nest* [nɛʃt].

These regional forms should be avoided by the learner, as they are not regarded as standard.

Many German-speakers tend not to use the lenis /ʒ/ at all, replacing it with the fortis /ʃ/ in all positions, e.g. *Jalousie* [ʃaluˈziː]. This pronunciation is not standard, but it is widespread.

3.3.4 /x/

(a) *Description*

The German phoneme /x/ consists of two quite distinct allophones: [x] and [ç], both of which are voiceless, fortis fricatives, but which differ in their place of articulation.

[x] (referred to in German as the 'ach-Laut') is a **velar fricative**, which is formed with the back of the tongue raised towards the soft palate and the sides of the back of the tongue touching the upper molars. As is usual with velar consonants (cf. the velar plosives /k/ and /g/), the place of articulation for [x] varies according to the neighbouring sounds, ranging from the back of the hard palate/front of the soft palate following /uː/ and /ʊ/ to the back of the soft palate following /ɔ/ and /a/.

[ç] (the 'ich-Laut') is a **palatal fricative**, i.e. the narrowing of the organs of speech takes place between the front of the tongue and the hard palate. The tip of the tongue is considerably further forward than for /ʃ/ and /ʒ/, with the tip touching the lower front teeth and the sides of the front of the tongue touching the upper molars. The narrowest point is between the front of the tongue and the hard palate, but tongue and palate are not quite as close as for the palato-alveolar fricatives; in fact the tongue is in the same position as for the vowel [iː]. The tongue is also not grooved but slightly rounded, and the lips are loosely spread.

[x]
fortis
velar
fricative

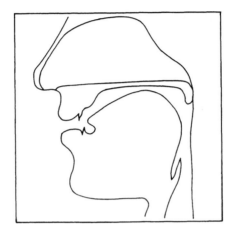

Fig. 9: [x]

[ç]
fortis
palatal
fricative

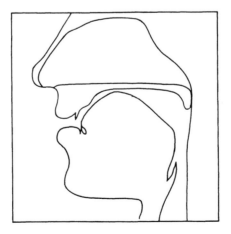

Fig. 10: [ç]

(b)   *Distribution and examples*

[x]

Spelling: ⟨ch⟩

[x] occurs medially and finally after the vowels /a/, /aː/, /oː/, /ɔ/, /uː/, /ʊ/ and /au/ (in other words after the vowels spelt ⟨a, o, u, au⟩). It does not occur initially except in learned pronunciation of a small number of loan words (especially from Slavonic languages) and some foreign place-names:

medial: *Buche* [ˈbuːxə], *mochte* [ˈmɔxtə], *lachen* [ˈlaxn̩], *brauchen* [ˈbrauxn̩]
final clusters: *Bucht* [bʊxt], *acht* [axt]
final: *Bach* [bax], *doch* [dɔx], *hoch* [hoːx], *Tuch* [tuːx], *Rauch* [raux]

[ç]

Spelling: ⟨ch⟩, ⟨g⟩ (in the ending *-ig*)

[ç] occurs in the initial position and medially and finally following front vowels:

initial: *Chemie* [çeˈmiː], *Chemiker* [ˈçeːmikɐ], *China* [ˈçiːna], *Chinese* [çiˈneːzə], *Chirurg* [çiˈrʊrk]
medial: *Becher* [ˈbɛçɐ], *riechen* [ˈriːçn̩], *fechten* [ˈfɛçtn̩], *Mädchen* [ˈmɛːtçən], *Hähnchen* [ˈhɛːnçən]
final clusters: *Licht* [lɪçt], *feucht* [fɔʏçt], *höchst* [høːçst]
final: *ich* [ɪç], *reich* [raɪç], *Milch* [mɪlç], *durch* [dʊrç], *möglich* [ˈmøːklɪç], *eilig* [ˈaɪlɪç], *fertig* [ˈfɛrtɪç]

The pattern of occurrence of the consonants [ç] and [x] in German is one of **complementary distribution**, i.e. they occur in phonetic environments which are mutually exclusive:

> The **palatal fricative [ç]** occurs
> initially
> after front vowels
> after consonants
>
> The **velar fricative [x]** occurs
> medially and finally after back and open vowels

Because the occurrence of [x] and [ç] is determined by the phonetic environment, these consonants alternate in different forms of the same word if the phonetic environment changes. This is the case with 'Umlaut' (or 'i-mutation'), in which a back vowel is changed into a front one in certain grammatical forms of a word (e.g. noun plurals, third person singular in the present tense of verbs). If the original back vowel is followed by [x], this must be replaced by [ç] in the forms containing Umlaut:

Dach [dax]   – *Dächer* [ˈdɛçɐ]
Loch [lɔx]   – *Löcher* [ˈlœçɐ]
Buch [buːx]   – *Bücher* [ˈbyːçɐ]
Brauch [braux] – *Bräuche* [ˈbrɔʏçə]

[x] and [ç] can never serve to distinguish words on their own, since they occur in complementary distribution. This means that there must always be at least one other difference between two words containing these sounds, that is the difference in environment (back vowel versus front vowel) which is responsible for the alternation between [x] and [ç]. They are also closely related sounds, as both are fortis fricatives, differing only in the part of the palate at which they are articulated. For these reasons, it is usual, in a phonemic analysis of German, to regard [ç] and [x] as variants, or allophones, of a single phoneme /x/. In a phonemic transcription we can simply write: *Dach* /dax/, *Dächer* /ˈdɛxər/, *Buch* /buːx/, *Bücher* /ˈbyːxər/, and our knowledge of the environments in which [x] and [ç] occur will tell us which of the variants is present in a given word. However, there are a small number of cases in which this description runs into problems:

(a) The diminutive ending *-chen* is always pronounced [çən], regardless of whether it is preceded by a back or front vowel. We thus have words like *Kuhchen* (little cow), which is pronounced [ˈkuːçən], in contrast with *Kuchen* (cake), pronounced [ˈkuːxən].
(b) There are a few words of foreign origin which have a learned pronunciation with initial [x], e.g. *Chassidismus* [xasiˈdɪsmʊs], 'Hasidism'.

However, the number of these cases is very small and they are all marginal words (like our example *Kuhchen*, which is hardly ever used in real conversation). The analysis of [x] and [ç] as belonging to a single phoneme can also be justified by pointing to differences in word structure between *Kuchen* and *Kuhchen*. In the latter case, *-chen* is a separate morpheme, i.e. a separate grammatical unit with a meaning of its own, and [ç] is actually in the initial position in this morpheme. This is not the case in *Kuchen*, which is a single morpheme, in which [x] occurs in medial position. The words with initial [x] can be regarded as following the pronunciation rules of languages other than German; they are of so recent origin or so marginal importance that they have not been adapted to the normal rules of German. In spite of these problems, therefore, we will continue to regard [x] and [ç] as allophones of a single phoneme /x/. This is, of course, more a theoretical than a practical question, as the use of [x] and [ç] is indicated in a broad allophonic transcription such as is used in this book (and in all the pronouncing dictionaries of German).

(c) *Problems for English-speaking learners*

Most speakers of English do not have the sound [x] in their native language, and therefore need quite a lot of practice before they get it exactly right. The sound is not totally unfamiliar, however, as there is a rather similar sound in Scottish English, also well-known to speakers of other varieties of English in the word *Loch* (*Ness* etc.). The exact place of the narrowing of the organs of speech depends on the vowel preceding [x]. Many learners seem to find it easier to start practising this sound when it is articulated towards the back of the soft palate after the vowels [ɔ] and [a], e.g. *Loch*, *kochen*, and *Bach*, *lachen*. Learners who have problems with this sound can start with an o-sound and raise the back of the tongue towards the soft palate until friction becomes audible. This should produce an acceptable [ɔx]-sound. The same can then be tried for [x] following [a]. The articulation of [x] is rather further forward following [uː] and [ʊ], and this seems to create more problems, the most common mistake being pronunciations like [ˈzuːçn̩] for *suchen*. This is probably due to the vowel being pronounce too far forward under the influence of English habits. Once the correct tongue position for German /uː/ and /ʊ/ has been learnt – further back and closer than the corresponding SBS vowels – the correct pronunciation for words like *suchen* [ˈzuːxn̩] and *Sucht* [zʊxt] will not be difficult to achieve. [x] should be articulated forcefully, as the friction is clearly audible when it is pronounced correctly.

The consonant [ç] is also one of the main pronunciation problems for learners, as it is very common in German and does not exist as a single sound in English. Contrary to popular belief, though, SBS does have a combination of sounds which is very similar to the German [ç], namely the initial consonants in words like *huge* and *human*, which are transcribed in English as [hj]. If learners have a problem with the German [ç], they can start off with these English words, pronouncing the initial consonants very vigorously, then leaving out the rest of the word until they are just pronouncing a strong [hj]-sound. This is quite an acceptable substitute for the German fortis palatal fricative, and they then ought to be able to pronounce German words with an initial [ç] without any problems. Once the sound has been mastered in the initial position, where it is rather rare in German, the learner can go on to the much more common medial and final positions. Some speakers of English do not have [hj] in words like *human*: some do not have a [j] in this position (e.g. East Anglian), others do not have an [h] (h-dropping accents). For these speakers it is best to start with the sound [j] as in *yes*, prolong it – [jjjjjjjj] – and then try to say it without voice (e.g. whispering) and with greater strength. Once again, this should lead to an acceptable German [ç] in initial position, and the sound can then be practised in other positions.

(d) *Regional variation*

Dialects in the extreme south-west of Germany and throughout Switzerland do not have the sound [ç] and use [x] in all environments, e.g. *ich* [ɪx], *nicht* [nɪxt], *Bücher* [ˈbyːxɐ]. These dialects do not have the diminutive suffix *-chen*, using a variant of *-lein* (*-li*, *-le*, *-l*) instead, but if it is borrowed from Standard German it is pronounced with the velar fricative [x]. This use of [x] should be avoided by the learner, as it occurs only in a small part of the German-speaking area and is not regarded as standard. If an English speaker were to use [x] in this way, it would probably be interpreted by Germans as ignorance of the rules governing the distribution of [x] and [ç].

Many Austrians and Bavarians do distinguish between [x] and [ç], but differ from standard German in that they have [x] instead of [ç] after /r/, e.g. *durch* [dʊrx], but this again is a non-standard pronunciation.

In some central German dialects, e.g. in the Rhineland, Saarland, Upper Saxony, [ç] is regularly replaced by [ʃ], e.g. *ich* [ɪʃ], *Kirche* = *Kirsche* [ˈkɪrʃə]. These dialectal forms should also be avoided by learners, as should North German (originally Low German) forms in which [ç] is replaced by [k] (the best-known is the Berlin pronunciation of *ich* as [ɪk]).

On the other hand, the pronunciation of initial [ç] as [k], e.g. *China* [ˈkiːna], *Chemie* [keˈmiː], which is prevalent throughout the southern part of the German-speaking area, is regarded as an acceptable variant of standard pronunciation.

In fact, the fricatives [x, ç] and the plosive [k] alternate widely as the pronunciation for a **final** ⟨g⟩, along the lines of a north–south division:

			North	South
1	After back vowel	*Tag*	[taːx]	[taːk]
2	After front vowel	*Sieg*	[ziːç]	[ziːk]
3	After consonant	*Burg*	[bʊrç]	[bʊrk]
4	In the ending *-ig*	*einig*	[ˈaɪnɪç]	[ˈaɪnɪk]

The German pronouncing dictionaries, following Siebs, have adopted a standard pronunciation which follows the southern pronunciation except for the ending *-ig*, for which they follow the northern pronunciation. There are no reasons why learners should not adopt this mixed pattern, but it must be said that millions of German-speakers whose pronunciation is otherwise perfectly standard consistently use either the northern or the southern pronunciations in all four cases, and it is therefore hard to see any objections to foreign learners doing the same.

3.3.5 /j/

(a) *Description*
The tongue position for /j/ is the same as for [ç], with the front of the tongue raised towards the hard palate, but, whereas [ç] is fortis and voiceless, /j/ is lenis and voiced. The amount of friction is always less than for [ç], but sometimes it is so reduced that the sound is not a fricative but an approximant, i.e. the organs of speech are brought together, but the narrowing is not close enough, or the force of articulation is not great enough, to cause friction. For an illustration, see figure 10.

(b) *Distribution and examples*
Spelling: ⟨j⟩, ⟨y⟩, ⟨l⟩ (in ⟨-ll-⟩ in French and Spanish loan words)
/j/ occurs in initial and medial position, but not finally:
initial: *jung* [jʊŋ], *jetzt* [jɛtst], *Januar* [ˈjanuaːɐ̯], *Jäger* [ˈjɛːgɐ], *Jubel* [ˈjuːbl̩], *jüdisch* [ˈjyːdɪʃ]
medial: *Boje* [ˈboːjə], *Majonaise* [majoˈnɛːzə], *Injektion* [ɪnjɛkˈtsi̯oːn], *loyal* [lo̯aˈjaːl], *brillant* [brɪlˈjant]

(c) *Problems for English-speaking learners*
The voiced consonant /j/ causes no problems for speakers of English, as the corresponding English sound (as in *yes, yonder,* etc.) can be used.

(d) *Regional variation*
In some areas of Germany (e.g. Berlin, the Rhineland), /j/ is used in words which contain initial and intervocalic /g/ in Standard German, e.g. *gerade* [jəˈraːdə], *gemacht* [jəˈmaxt], *Wege* [ˈveːjə].

3.3.6 /h/

(a) *Description*
For the last of the fricatives, /h/, there is a slight narrowing of the vocal cords, so that the airstream causes friction as it passes through the glottis. /h/ is an unusual consonant, in that there is no definite position for the tongue and the lips, which are thus free to take up the position for the following vowel. This means that there are as many h-sounds as there are vowels in a language, and it would in fact be possible to describe /h/ as a voiceless vowel of the same quality as the following vowel, using the transcription [o̥ːx] for *hoch*, [ˈɪ̥ntɐ] for *hinter*, etc. However, as

the different tongue and lip positions for the different variants of /h/ are produced perfectly naturally according to the following vowel, it is not necessary to indicate them in transcription and we will simply use the symbol [h] in all positions. The narrowing of the organs of speech for /h/ takes place in the glottis, and it is thus known as the **glottal fricative**.

fortis
glottal
fricative

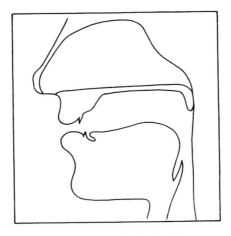

Fig. 11: /h/ (as in [ha:])

(b) *Distribution and examples*

Spelling: ⟨h⟩
/h/ occurs initially and medially before vowels, but not before consonants or in final position. The letter ⟨h⟩ is used before /ə/, unstressed /ɪ/ or /ʊ/, before consonants and finally to indicate a long vowel: *sehen, ruhig, Verzeihung, nehmen, sah.* /h/ is not pronounced in these positions, nor following a consonant in the same syllable: *Therapie, Rhythmus.*

initial before vowels: *Haus* [haʊs], *Hut* [huːt], *hart* [hart], *heißen* [ˈhaɪsn̩], *Hülle* [ˈhʏlə]
medial before vowels: *Gehalt* [gəˈhalt], behilflich [bəˈhɪlflɪç], *Unheil* [ˈlʊnhaɪl], *Ahorn* [ˈaːhɔrn] ('maple')

(c) *Problems for English-speaking learners*
The German /h/ is exactly the same as the corresponding sound in English, so it does not cause problems for speakers of SBS. However, many dialects throughout England (though not in Scotland and Ireland) have the phenomenon known as h-dropping, i.e. in their most extreme forms they do not have any h's at all. This phenomenon does not occur in

German, even in dialect or colloquial speech, and so speakers of English who have this habit must learn to pronounce /h/ in German.

(d) *Regional variation*
There is no significant variation in the pronunciation of /h/ in the German-speaking area.

3.4 Nasals

The nasals are similar to the plosives in that they are formed with a total closure of the organs of speech in the mouth, but the soft palate is lowered so that air can escape through the nose. You can demonstrate to yourself the fact that air escapes only through the nose for nasals by pronouncing a long [mmmmm] and pressing your finger and thumb firmly against your nose. The sound will suddenly be cut off as the air cannot escape through the mouth.

In German and English there are three nasal consonants. They do not form fortis–lenis pairs in the same way as the plosives, but are all voiced. The places of articulation are those of the three pairs of plosives.

3.4.1 /m/

(a) *Description*
The closure for /m/ is made in the same place as for /p/ and /b/, with the lips pressed firmly together. It is thus known as the **bilabial nasal**. As for all the nasals, the soft palate is lowered. The tongue, which is not involved in the closure, is free to take up the position of the following sound.

voiced
bilabial
nasal

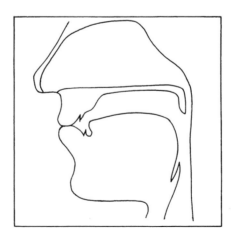

Fig. 12: /m/

(b) *Distribution and examples*

Spelling: ⟨m⟩, ⟨mm⟩

/m/ occurs in the initial, medial and final positions:

🖂 **initial:** *Mann* [man], *mehr* [meːɐ̯], *März* [mɛrts], *malen* [ˈmaːlən]

initial clusters: *schmal* [ʃmaːl], *Gmünd* [gmʏnt]

medial: *immer* [ˈɪmɐ], *Name* [ˈnaːmə], *Sommer* [ˈzɔmɐ], *nehmen* [ˈneːmən]

final clusters: *Hemd* [hɛmt], plump [plʊmp]

final: *Baum* [baʊm], *langsam* [ˈlaŋzaːm], *angenehm* [ˈangəneːm], *warm* [varm], *Helm* [hɛlm]

3.4.2 /n/

(a) *Description*

For /n/ the soft palate is lowered and the tongue is in the same position in German and English as for /t/ and /d/, i.e. the blade (or the tip) of the tongue is pressed firmly against the middle of the alveolar ridge. Test this for yourself by pronouncing the sounds [n] and [d] in succession: [ndndndnd]. You will find that after pronouncing the [n] your tongue is in exactly the right position for [d]. /n/ is therefore known as the **alveolar nasal**.

voiced
alveolar
nasal

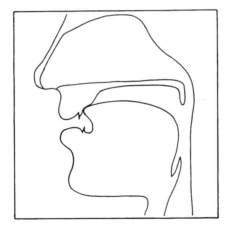

Fig. 13: /n/

(b) *Distribution and examples*

Spelling: ⟨n⟩, ⟨nn⟩

/n/ occurs in the initial, medial and final positions:

🖂 **initial:** *Nuß* [nʊs], *nicht* [nɪçt], *neu* [nɔʏ], *nötig* [ˈnøːtɪç], *niemand* [ˈniːmant]

initial clusters: *schneiden* [ˈʃnaɪdn̩], *Knie* [kniː]

medial: *genug* [gə'nu:k], *Anfang* ['anfaŋ], *Fenster* ['fɛnstɐ], *warnen* ['varnən]

final clusters: *Grund* [grʊnt], *fünf* [fʏnf], *Hans* [hans]

final: *waschen* ['vaʃn̩], *tun* [tu:n], *schön* [ʃøːn], *modern* [mo'dɛrn], *handeln* ['handln̩]

3.4.3 /ŋ/

(a) *Description*

The nasal consonant /ŋ/, as in *lang* [laŋ], *Hunger* ['hʊŋɐ], *Menge* ['mɛŋə], is formed with the soft palate lowered and the tongue in the same position as for /k/ and /g/, with the back of the tongue pressed against the soft palate. You can feel this for yourself by pronouncing the sounds [g] and [ŋ] in succession: [ŋgŋgŋgŋgŋg]. /ŋ/ is known as the **velar nasal**. As with the other velar consonants, the exact place of the oral closure varies from palatal following the front vowels (e.g. *hing* [hɪŋ]) to the middle of the soft palate following back vowels (e.g. *Gong* [gɔŋ]). /ŋ/ does not have a letter of its own in the alphabet and is represented in writing by ⟨ng⟩ or ⟨n⟩.

voiced
velar
nasal

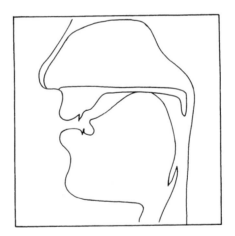

Fig. 14: /ŋ/ (as in [laŋ])

(b) *Distribution and examples*

Spelling: ⟨ng⟩, ⟨n⟩ before /k/, /g/ (except in compounds, e.g. *Weingut, einkaufen*, which retain /n/)

/ŋ/ occurs in medial and final position, but not initially:

medial before vowel: *hingen* [ˈhɪŋən], *länger* [ˈlɛŋɐ], *abhängig* [ˈaphɛŋɪç], *Bedingung* [bəˈdɪŋʊŋ]
before /k/: *trinken* [ˈtrɪŋkən], *Anker* [ˈaŋkɐ], *Enkel* [ˈɛŋkl̩]
before /g/: *Ungarn* [ˈʊŋgarn], *Kongo* [ˈkɔŋgo], *fingiert* [fɪŋˈgiːɐ̯t] ('fictitious'), *Kontingent* [kɔntɪŋˈgɛnt], *evangelisch* [evaŋˈgeːlɪʃ], Linguistik [lɪŋˈgu̯ɪstɪk]
final clusters: *Punkt* [pʊŋkt], *längst* [lɛŋst], *Bank* [baŋk]
final: *lang* [laŋ], *Ring* [rɪŋ], *Hoffnung* [ˈhɔfnʊŋ], *Frühling* [ˈfryːlɪŋ], *streng* [ʃtrɛŋ]

It will be noted that /ŋ/ usually corresponds to ⟨ng⟩ in writing, with the exception that it is also used in place of /n/ before /k/ and /g/. Historically this is a case of assimilation of /n/ to a following velar consonant. In formal pronunciation, /n/ is preserved before /k/ and /g/ when they belong to separate elements in compounds, e.g. *ungern* [ˈʊngɛrn], *hingehen* [ˈhɪngeːən], but in conversational pronunciation /ŋ/ occurs in these positions too: [ˈʊŋgɛɐ̯n], [ˈhɪŋgeːən] (see section 6.1.1).

/ŋ/ is also commonly used to replace nasal vowels in words of foreign (mainly French) origin, e.g. *Beton* [beˈtɔŋ] and *Balkon* [balˈkɔŋ].

(c) *Problems for English-speaking learners*
Although the articulation of this consonant is the same in English and German, there are some differences in its use which can cause problems for speakers of English.

1 In most varieties of English a distinction is made between forms derived from verbs like *singing* [ˈsɪŋɪŋ], *longing* [ˈlɔŋɪŋ], etc., which have medial /ŋ/, and non-verbal forms like *longer* [ˈlɔŋgə], *finger* [ˈfɪŋgə], *anger* [ˈæŋgə], which have /ŋg/. As a result of this, *singer* and *finger* do not rhyme in English, and *longing* (verb) and *longer* (adjective) have different pronunciations. This difference is absent in German, which does not have the extra /g/ in words like *Hunger* [ˈhʊŋɐ], *Finger* [ˈfɪŋɐ], so English speakers must change their pronunciation habits with these words. The combination /ŋg/ is present in German only in a small number of words of foreign origin (see examples above).

2 Some north-western and Midlands dialects always have /ŋg/ in place of SBS /ŋ/ before vowels and at the end of words. For these speakers, the English word *singer* [ˈsɪŋgə] rhymes with *finger* [ˈfɪŋgə]. Speakers who have this feature in their English must pay even more attention to the pronunciation of German words containing /ŋ/, and must learn to omit the [g].

(d) *Regional variation*

Many northern and south-eastern forms of German have [ŋk] in place of
final /ŋ/, e.g. *jung* [jʊŋk], *Ring* [rɪŋk], but this is regarded as substandard
pronunciation. The same phenomenon also occurs in English regional
speech, for instance in the forms *anything* ['enɪθɪŋk], *nothing* ['nʌθɪŋk],
etc.

3.4.4   **Nasal plosion**

Plosives are not released in the normal way when they are followed by a
homorganic nasal. **Homorganic** (G. *homorganisch*) is the technical term
for sounds which have the same place of articulation, e.g. /t, d, n/ are all
alveolar consonants, /p, b, m/ are bilabials, and /k, g, ŋ/ are velars. When
followed by a homorganic nasal, e.g. [tn] or [pm], the closure of the
plosive is not released by removing the tongue or lips and allowing the air
to escape out of the mouth, but by lowering the soft palate and allowing
air to escape through the nose. Because the plosive and the following
nasal are homorganic, lowering the soft palate is all we need to do to
form the nasal and is obviously a more economic way of pronouncing
this sequence of consonants than if we had to move the tongue or lips
as well. This form of release is known as **nasal plosion**. (G. *nasale
Verschlußlösung*, *nasale Plosion* or *Nasalsprengung*).

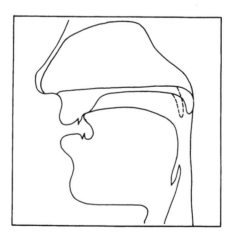

Fig. 15: Nasal plosion ([tn])

Nasal plosion occurs both within words and across word boundaries, e.g.:

[tn] *Bildnis, Rentner, er fährt nicht*
[pm] *abmelden, Grabmal, gib mal*

A similar phenomenon occurs with sequences of non-homorganic plosives and nasals. Here the oral closure for the nasal is formed before the release of the preceding plosive, and so once again the air escapes through the nose rather than through the mouth. Examples are: [k + n] *wegnehmen* [ˈvɛkneːmən], [p + n] *Abnahme* [ˈapnaːmə], [t + m] *Windmühle* [ˈvɪntmyːlə].

3.4.5 Syllabic nasals

The nasal consonants can occur not only in the normal positions for consonants at the beginning or end of a syllable, but also in the middle, or filling out the syllable on their own, positions normally reserved for vowels. They are then referred to as **syllabic nasals** (G. *der silbische Nasal*), and can be indicated in phonetic transcription by means of a dash underneath the consonant in question: [n̩], [m̩] (or above the consonant in the case of [ŋ̍]).

Syllabic /n/ is frequent enough in English – *sudden* [ˈsʌdn̩] rather than [ˈsʌdən], *flatten* [ˈflætn̩] rather than [ˈflætən] – and syllabic /ŋ/ and /m/ are possible in words like *taken* [ˈteɪkŋ̍] (for [ˈteɪkən]) and *happen* [ˈhæpm̩]. In German the tendency to use syllabic nasals is **considerably stronger** than in English, especially in conversational pronunciation, so the English-speaking learner should pay close attention to the pronunciation of these sounds (see also section 6.2.1).

Syllabic /n/ is used for ⟨en⟩ in final position and before consonants:

(a)   after plosives: *wetten* [ˈvɛtn̩], *leiden* [ˈlaɪdn̩], *jeden* [ˈjeːdn̩], *bildende* [ˈbɪldn̩də], *bedeutende* [bəˈdɔytn̩də];
following /p, b/ the /n/ is assimilated to /m/: *haben* [ˈhaːbm̩], *Wappen* [ˈvapm̩];
following /k, g/ the /n/ is assimilated to /ŋ/: *wecken* [ˈvɛkŋ̍], *Regen* [ˈreːgŋ̍], *streikende* [ˈʃtraɪkŋ̍də].
(b)   after fricatives: *hoffen* [ˈhɔfn̩], *küssen* [ˈkʏsn̩], *rauchen* [ˈraʊxn̩], *tauschen* [ˈtaʊʃn̩], *Reisende* [ˈraɪzn̩də], *Vorsitzende* [ˈfoːɐ̯zɪtsn̩də], *fluchende* [ˈfluːxn̩də].

3.5 **Laterals**

3.5.1   /l/

(a) *Description*

For the lateral consonant /l/ contact is made between the blade (or for some people the tip) of the tongue and the centre of the alveolar ridge, but a gap remains between the sides of the tongue and the sides of the palate, through which air can escape. You can test this for yourself by forming an [l] and breathing in sharply – the cold air can be felt on the sides of the tongue and palate. The place of articulation is the same as for /t, d, n/, with contact between the blade of the tongue and the alveolar ridge, and thus /l/ is known as the **alveolar lateral**, although since there is only one lateral consonant in German it is usually simply referred to as the lateral. /l/ is voiced, as you can feel if you place your finger and thumb on your larynx while pronouncing it.

voiced
alveolar
lateral

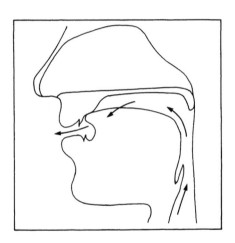

Fig. 16: /l/

(b) *Distribution and examples*

Spelling: ⟨l⟩, ⟨ll⟩

/l/ occurs in initial, medial and final position:

initial before vowels: *Luft* [lʊft], *Land* [lant], *liegen* [ˈliːɡən], *Lüge* [ˈlyːɡə]

initial clusters: *Pflug* [pflu:k], *blaß* [blas], *schlafen* [ˈʃlaːfn̩]
medial: *Schule* [ˈʃuːlə], *füllen* [ˈfʏlən], *Fräulein* [ˈfrɔʏlaɪn], *halten* [ˈhaltn̩]
final clusters: *Hals* [hals], *Pilz* [pɪlts], *halb* [halp]
final: *Stuhl* [ʃtuːl], *wohl* [voːl], *hell* [hɛl], *Zoll* [tsɔl], *Ball* [bal], *Saal* [zaːl]

(c) *Problems for English-speaking learners*

The German /l/ causes problems for many English speakers, because most varieties of English have two different l-sounds: a clear [l] before vowels and /j/ and a dark [ɫ] in all other positions, i.e. before all consonants except /j/ and in final position.

> **English clear l:** *live, laugh, hillock, colon, prelude*
> **English dark l:** *hill, coal, cold, health, bottle, pickle*

The English dark l is formed by raising the back of the tongue to about the position required for the vowel [uː], which is why it is sometimes referred to as a 'u-coloured' l (e.g. Siebs, 1969).

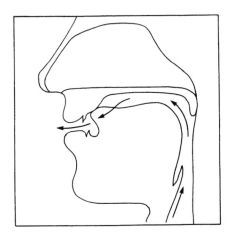

Fig. 17: English dark [ɫ]

The Standard German /l/, on the other hand, is always clear. This means that English-speakers must learn to produce a clear [l] in all

environments and must learn not to use the dark [ɫ] in German. For
speakers of SBS and other varieties which have both a clear and a dark l,
the best way of achieving this is to make use of the habit of producing a
clear [l] before vowels in an exercise consisting of five steps:

A1   Practise saying words with an /l/ before a final vowel: *viele, Felle,
     heile, Weile, Wille*, etc. (speakers of SBS will naturally have a clear l
     in this position).
A2   Say the words again, this time holding the [l] for three or four
     seconds. This will give you a chance to feel the position of the
     tongue for the clear l: *vielllllle, Felllllle*, etc.
A3   Say the words again as in A2, this time leaving out the final vowel.
     Make sure your tongue position is the same as for A2: *vielllll,
     Felllll, heilllll*, etc.
A4   Say the words in the same way again, this time adding a suitable
     consonant (or consonant combination) at the end: *hielllllt, hälllllt,
     weilllllt, willlllst*, etc.
A5   Now reduce the length of the l in these words, making sure that the
     tongue position remains the same as before: *viel, Fell, Heil, weil;
     hielt, hält, weilt, willst*

Exercises like these will not help all speakers, however, as there are
some varieties of English which have a dark (or at any rate fairly dark)
[ɫ] in all positions (many Americans, some Scottish and northern
English speakers). These speakers need to learn to make a clear [l], and it
is best to start from the position which is easiest for them. This will
probably be an /l/ adjacent to the palatal consonant /j/ or a close front
vowel /iː/ or /ɪ/. The exercises are as follows:

B1   [iːl]: While pronouncing the words *viel, Kiel, Nil*, the tongue
     position of the vowel should be kept until the end of the word, with
     only the blade of the tongue raised to touch the alveolar ridge.
B2   [lj]: Most speakers have a fairly clear l before /j/ in words like
     million, billion, etc. They can practise the [l] by lengthening it, and
     then by leaving out the part of the word following it: *millllllljən,
     billllljən, millllll, billlll*.
B3   [liː] or [lɪ]: Start by pronouncing the combination [iːt], making the
     vowel very long. Once you have got used to the correct tongue
     position for /iː/, add an /l/ to the beginning of the word: [liːt] *Lied*.
     Other words: *lieb* [liːp], *lies* [liːs], *lief* [liːf], *Lieder* ['liːdɐ]. Once
     these speakers have mastered a clear [l] in one position, the
     exercises A2–A5 above can be used to practise it in other positions.

It should be mentioned that there are some varieties of English which have clear [l] in all positions, e.g. Irish English; speakers of these varieties obviously do not have any problems with the clear German /l/.

The German /l/ is normally a voiced consonant, but following an initial strong plosive it is devoiced, as in English, e.g. German: *Platz* [pl̥ats]; *Klage* [ˈkl̥aːgə]; English: *place* [pl̥eɪs], *clan* [kl̥æn].

(d)   *Regional variation*

The dark [ɫ] is not completely foreign to German, as it can be heard in some dialects, e.g. Rhineland (Cologne) and some parts of Switzerland. However, it is not regarded as standard and should be avoided by English-speaking learners, since it is one of the principal signs of an English accent in German.

3.5.2   **Lateral plosion**

When /l/ follows the alveolar plosives /t/ or /d/, as in *deutlich*, *Adler*, the blade (or tip) of the tongue can remain pressed against the alveolar ridge during the transition from plosive to lateral, and the /l/ is formed simply by lowering the sides of the tongue to let the stream of air escape laterally. This form of release of the plosive is known as *lateral plosion*. A similar transition is also used for combinations of /n + l/, as in *Anlaß*, *einladen*, but in this case we cannot speak of plosion, of course. The blade of the tongue remains in position against the alveolar ridge and the sides of the tongue are lowered to allow the lateral release of air, but in this transition the soft palate must also be raised to form the /l/.

3.5.3   **Syllabic /l/**

As with the nasals, the lateral can also occur on its own in a syllable, position which is normally reserved for vowels. This is known as **syllabic** /l/ (G. *silbisches l*), and can be indicated by means of a dash underneath the symbol: [l̩].

Syllabic /l/ occurs in place of /əl/ in the final position and before consonants:

(a)   after plosives: *Mittel* [ˈmɪtl̩], *Handel* [ˈhandl̩], *Spiegel* [ˈʃpiːgl̩], *vermitteln* [fɛɐˈmɪtl̩n], *wackeln* [ˈvakl̩n], *handeln* [ˈhandl̩n];
(b)   after fricatives: *Schlüssel* [ˈʃlʏsl̩], *lächeln* [ˈlɛçl̩n], *Äpfel* [ˈapfl̩], *wechseln* [ˈvɛksl̩n], *Kartoffeln* [karˈtɔfl̩n];

(c)   after nasals: *Dschungel* [ˈdʒʊŋ!̩], *Himmel* [ˈhɪml̩], *Engel* [ˈɛŋ!̩], *angeln* [ˈaŋl̩n].

The use of syllabic /l/ in German is similar to English as in *cattle*, *middle*, but in English the syllabic /l/ is the dark [ɫ], whereas in German it is, of course, a clear [l].

3.6   /r/

(a)   *Description*

/r/ is the most varied of German consonants, for not only are there regional differences, but there are also numerous positional and stylistic variants. Unfortunately, all the German r-sounds are different from the common pronunciations in English (e.g. SBS or American English), so the German /r/ typically causes problems for English-speaking learners. Thus, although speakers of English can to a certain extent choose which type of German /r/ they wish to learn, they should be prepared to spend some time and energy practising the German sounds, since the /r/ is one of the most obvious signs of an English accent in German.

The basic distinction in German is between consonantal and vocalic types of /r/. Within the first of these categories, the consonantal type, there are a number of different manners of articulation: **rolls** (G. *der Vibrant*, that is a sound produced by one of the organs of speech vibrating against a neighbouring one); **flaps** (G. *der Anschlag*, *der Zungenschlag*, that is a sound produced by a single very rapid contact between two organs of speech), a **fricative** and an **approximant**. Each of these types will be described in detail in the following sections.

3.6.1   **The uvular roll**

The uvular roll (G. *das Zäpfchen-r*) is formed by raising the back of the tongue towards the uvula so that a narrow passage is created. The force of the airstream passing through this narrow passage is so great that the uvula is moved against the back of the tongue, making contact either once (uvular flap) or several times (uvular roll). The phonetic symbol for the uvular roll is [ʀ].

voiced
uvular
roll

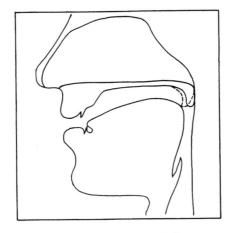

Fig. 18: Uvular roll ([ʀ])

There is no sound like this in English (with the exception of the so-called 'Northumbrian burr' in a small area in the north-east of England), and English-speakers often find the uvular [ʀ] difficult to pronounce. A good starting-point for learners who have problems with this sound is a non-linguistic activity: gargling, which is a very strong form of uvular roll. Try gargling for a few seconds to get used to the feeling of the uvula vibrating against the back of the tongue. If the same sound can be greatly reduced, both in force and in duration, the result will be the German uvular [ʀ].

3.6.2 The uvular fricative

The position of the organs of speech for the uvular fricative (G. *das Reibe-r*) is almost the same as for the uvular-r: the back of the tongue is raised towards the uvula or the back of the soft palate forming a narrow passage, but there is no contact between the uvula and the back of the tongue, and no vibration, only the turbulence associated with fricative consonants. The phonetic symbol for this uvular fricative is [ʁ]. The uvular fricative is especially common in relaxed, colloquial pronunciation and in less strongly stressed positions, but even in the careful pronunciation of trained radio and television announcers it is now the most common pronunciation of /r/.

voiced
uvular
fricative

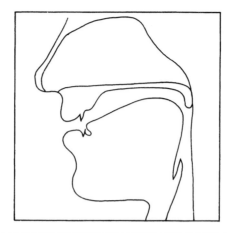

Fig. 19: Uvular fricative ([ʁ])

This type of r is quite similar to the velar fricative [x], and those who can produce a satisfactory German [x] can use this as a starting-point for practising the uvular [ʁ]. Try articulating [x] as far back in the mouth as possible: if this is done and then voicing (i.e. vibrations of the vocal cords) added at the same time, the result will be a perfectly acceptable German uvular fricative [ʁ]. Of course, this method of learning [ʁ] is of no use to those who have problems with [x], so it is advisable to practise this latter sound thoroughly before attempting the voiced uvular fricative [ʁ].

Like other voiced consonants in German, [ʁ] is also subject to devoicing, with the result that in certain environments this sound is practically identical with the velar fricative [x]. This happens most obviously following back vowels and preceding fortis plosives, and it means that some pairs of words are often not distinguished by speakers who use the fricative [ʁ], e.g.: *dort/Docht* ('wick') [dɔxt]. Other pairs are: *warte/ wachte, scharrt/Schacht, fort/focht, surrt/Sucht*. To avoid misunderstandings, German speakers can, of course, use a uvular roll in place of the fricative [ʁ] in these words.

The devoicing of [ʁ] also takes place in other environments, e.g. after front vowels (*wirken, türkisch*), and following fortis plosives (*prächtig, tragen*), but here there is no danger of confusion with [x], which does not occur in these environments.

Especially in conversational pronunciation, this uvular fricative is frequently weakened to a frictionless approximant (phonetic symbol [ʁ̞]), in which the organs of speech are in the same position as for the fricative, but the force of articulation is not sufficient to cause friction (see also section 6.4.1).

The uvular r is now the more common variety of German /r/ and is the obvious choice for English learners to adopt, but, if you have great difficulty learning it, the apical r described below is an acceptable alternative.

3.6.3 The apical roll

The apical roll (G. *das gerollte Zungenspitzen-r*) is articulated by tapping the tip of the tongue very quickly two or three times against the alveolar ridge. Many people can produce this sound quite easily, but if you have problems a good way to start practising it is with the common non-linguistic gesture expressing cold, usually written *brrrr*, which is in fact a very vigorous pronunciation of a bilabial plosive followed by an extended apical roll: [brrrrr]. Say this and feel how the tip of the tongue is forced away from the alveolar ridge as the air pressure builds up behind the closure. When the air escapes, the tip of the tongue returns to its original position against the alveolar ridge, thus re-forming the closure, and the process is repeated. Once you have got used to the way in which this sound is made, you can practise articulating it much more gently in German words.

voiced
apico-alveolar
roll

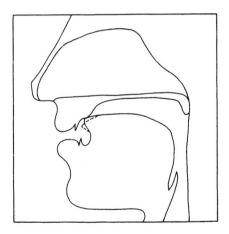

Fig. 20: Apical roll ([r])

In weakly stressed positions the apical roll is reduced to a **flap**, in which the tip of the tongue makes contact only once with the alveolar ridge. This sound is similar to very quick /d/, or to the /t/ as it is pronounced by American speakers in words like *writer*, *city*. The phonetic symbol for this apical flap is [ɾ].

3.6.4 **Vocalic r**

The final type of German r is so reduced that it is no longer pronounced as a consonant, but as a vowel [ɐ], which is described more fully in the chapter on vowels, pp. 100–2. The use of vocalic /r/ (G. *vokalisches r*) is much more common in areas which have a uvular r [ʀ, ʁ] than in those with an apical r [r], where a consonantal pronunciation is frequently maintained in all positions. The general rule is that vocalic r is used after long vowels in final position and before consonants, for final *-er*, and in the prefixes *er-*, *her-*, *ver-*, *zer-*, and that a consonantal pronunciation of /r/ should be used in all other positions, i.e. before vowels and before consonants after short vowels. However, at least in conversational pronunciation the vocalic r is also commonly used after short vowels in final position and before consonants, e.g. *Herr*, *wird* (see also section 6.4.1).

(b) *Distribution and examples*
Spelling: ⟨r⟩, ⟨rr⟩, ⟨rh⟩
/r/ occurs in initial, medial and final position

consonantal r (uvular or apical r)
▦ **initial:** *rot* [roːt], *Runde* [ˈrʊndə], *reden* [ˈreːdn̩], *Rat* [raːt], *rühmen* [ˈryːmən], *Römer* [ˈrøːmɐ], *Rhein* [raɪn]
initial clusters: *Straße* [ˈʃtraːsə], *Preis* [praɪs], *Schrift* [ʃrɪft]
medial before vowels: *hören* [ˈhøːrən], *Lehrer* [ˈleːrɐ], *gerade* [ɡəˈraːdə]
before consonants after short vowels: *warten* [ˈvartn̩], *Firma* [ˈfɪrma], *fort* [fɔrt], *kurz* [kʊrts], *hart* [hart], *Gehirn* [ɡəˈhɪrn], *Berg* [bɛrk]
final after short vowels: *Herr* [hɛr], *wirr* [vɪr], *Narr* [nar], *Geschirr* [ɡəˈʃɪr], *dürr* [dʏr]

vocalic r
▦ **after long vowels before consonants:** *führte* [ˈfyːɐtə], *Pferd* [pfeːɐt]
after long vowels in final position: *Uhr* [uːɐ], *mehr* [meːɐ]
in final -er: *Lehrer* [ˈleːrɐ], *Kinder* [ˈkɪndɐ], **even when followed by a case ending:** *Lehrers* [ˈleːrɐs], *Kindern* [ˈkɪndɐn]
in the unstressed prefixes er-, her-, ver-, zer-: *erzählen* [ɛɐˈtsɛːlən], *hervor* [hɛɐˈfoːɐ], *verteidigen* [fɛɐˈtaɪdɪɡən], *zerstören* [tsɛɐˈʃtøːrən] (for further examples, see section 4.3.17).

(c) *Problems for English-speaking learners*
German /r/ is one of the greatest problems for learners, as it differs from the common pronunciations of English /r/ in both articulation and distribution. The following points should be observed:

1   A great effort should be made to avoid the use of the English r (post-alveolar approximant) in German, as it is one of the main features of an English accent.

2   As a general rule, foreign learners should aim for a uvular r in German, either fricative or roll, unless these cause them great problems, in which case the apical r is a perfectly acceptable alternative. The reason for this is that the uvular r is the more common pronunciation in German and is gaining ground all the time. For English-speaking learners it is also worth noting that interference from the habits of their native tongue is less likely if they learn the uvular r, because this is completely different from the English r.

3   In SBS and most accents of England, /r/ has been dropped before consonants and in the final position with compensatory lengthening of a preceding short vowel e.g. English *fort* [fɔːt], *before* [bɪˈfɔː]. A similar tendency is not unknown in relaxed conversational speech in German, but it is very much weaker than in English (where it is the accepted pronunciation in SBS). English-speaking learners are strongly recommended to learn the formal pronunciation, in which the distribution of consonantal and vocalic r is as described above, first and only when they are fully familiar with this to copy models of German speech in which r's are dropped. Otherwise, the danger is that learners will carry over their pronunciation habits for r from English to German, which can only lead to a marked English accent.

4   In English, an /r/ which is omitted in final position is pronounced as a 'linking r' when the following word begins with a vowel, e.g. *before eight* [bɪˈfɔːr eɪt], *their* [ðeə] but *their own* [ðeər əʊn]. This 'linking r' does not exist in German, and in fact many words which begin with a vowel in German spelling are actually pronounced with an initial glottal stop (i.e. a consonant), and thus cut off from, rather than linked to the preceding word. This point is discussed in greater detail in section 3.8.

(d)   *Regional variation*

All the r-sounds described here are accepted as standard pronunciation in German. Their regional distribution can be summarised as follows:

1   Uvular r predominates in northern, central and south-western parts of the German-speaking area, apical r in south-eastern parts (Bavaria and Austria), but also in Schleswig-Holstein in the extreme north.

2   Uvular r is on the increase at the expense of apical r; in particular its use is increasing in the cities in areas which traditionally use apical r.

3   The use of vocalic r is much more common with speakers who have uvular r; speakers who have apical r frequently preserve it in all positions.

The pattern is actually much more complicated than this, and exceptions to the general rule stated above do occur. Because of the great variety of acceptable realisations of /r/ we will not attempt to indicate the precise allophones in our transcriptions in the remainder of this book, but will just distinguish between [r] (= any consonantal variant of /r/) and [ɐ] (= vocalic r).

3.7 **Affricates**

Affricates combine features of plosives and fricatives. In articulatory terms they can be described as plosives in which the closing and hold stages are performed normally, but, instead of the usual quick explosive release, the closure is released slowly, resulting in a fricative phase, e.g. [pf], [ts]. There has been a great deal of discussion among phonologists as to whether affricates are to be regarded as single phonemes or as combinations of two separate phonemes. Arguments can be brought for both points of view, but the evidence is hardly conclusive. As the question of their phoneme status does not affect the pronunciation of the German affricates, we will not go into this question in any detail here and will simply adopt a common view in German phonology and regard affricates as combinations of phonemes (plosive + fricative) rather than single units.[2]

In this section we will concentrate on the two most common German affricates: [ts] and [pf]. Others do occur in German – [tʃ] (not common in spite of occurring in the word *deutsch*) and [dʒ] (occurring only in loan words, principally from Italian, e.g. *Adagio*) – but these can be ignored, as they are familiar to speakers of English.

3.7.1 **[pf]**

(a) *Description*
The closing and hold stages of the plosive /p/ are formed in the normal way, but, instead of the lips being opened to release the air explosively, the closure is released slowly and a narrow passage is formed between lower lip and upper teeth, through which the air escapes causing the friction associated with the labio-dental fricative /f/.

---

[2] See 'Sources and further reading' for literature on this point.

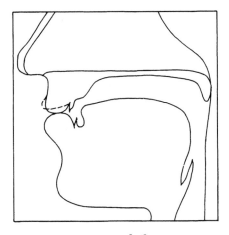

Fig. 21: [pf]

(b) *Distribution and examples*
Spelling: ⟨pf⟩
[pf] occurs in initial, medial and final position:

initial: *Pfeil* [pfaɪl], *Pfanne* [ˈpfanə], *Pfosten* [ˈpfɔstn̩], *Pflanze* [ˈpflantsə], *pflegen* [ˈpfleːgən]

medial: *Apfel* [ˈapfl̩], *Kupfer* [ˈkʊpfɐ], *schimpfen* [ˈʃɪmpfn̩], *Opfer* [ˈɔpfɐ], *Köpfe* [ˈkœpfə]

final: *Kopf* [kɔpf], *Kampf* [kampf], *Strumpf* [ʃtrʊmpf], *Geschöpf* [gəˈʃœpf]

3.7.2 [ts]

(a) *Description*
The first two stages, the closing and hold stages, of the plosive /t/ are performed normally, but, instead of taking the tongue right away from the alveolar ridge in the release stage, the blade or tip of the tonge is removed slowly and the hissing noise of the alveolar fricative can be heard as the air escapes from the mouth.

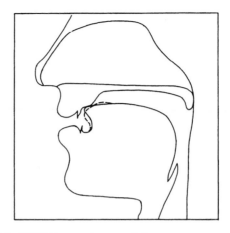

Fig. 22: [ts]

(b) *Distribution and examples*
Spelling: ⟨z⟩, ⟨zz⟩, ⟨tz⟩, ⟨ts⟩, ⟨c⟩, ⟨t⟩ (before i + vowel in words of Latin origin)
[ts] occurs in initial, medial and final position:

initial: *Zahl* [tsaːl], *zu* [tsuː], *Zoll* [tsɔl], *zwei* [tsvaɪ], *zwischen* [ˈtsvɪʃn̩], *Celsius* [ˈtsɛlzi̯ʊs]
medial: *heizen* [ˈhaɪtsn̩], *Mozart* [ˈmoːtsart], *Skizze,* [ˈskɪtsə], *schwitzen* [ˈʃvɪtsn̩], *Nation* [naˈtsi̯oːn], *Faszination* [fastsinaˈtsi̯oːn]
final: *Holz* [hɔlts], *Tanz* [tants], *Schweiz* [ʃvaɪts], *Schutz* [ʃʊts], *nichts* [nɪçts]

(c) *Problems for English-speaking learners*
[pf] and [ts] are not usually regarded as affricates in English, but combinations of both [p + f] and [t + s] occur in English compounds, and the combination of [t + s] is very common in final position because of plurals, genitives and third person singular endings. Thus we have in English:

[p + f] **medial**: *cupful, hopeful, stepfather*
[t + s] **medial**: *outside, footsore, Watson, fatso*
[t + s] **final**: *let's, gets, minutes, abbot's*

So English-speakers do not have problems articulating the German affricates, yet a surprising number of people find it difficult to pronounce them when they occur in unfamiliar positions, particularly at the beginning of words. With [ts] this problem sometimes seems to be caused by the different pronunciations of the letter ⟨z⟩ in English and German: the strong English habit interferes with the German pronunciation. If this is the case, regular practice of words containing ⟨z⟩ will help establish the German pronunciation [ts] for ⟨z⟩ and help overcome the interference from English pronunciation. If you do have problems with the actual articulation of affricates, start by practising them in familiar positions: say a word like *Netz* slowly several times, concentrating on feeling how the final affricate is formed. Once you have done this, you can go on to saying words with initial affricates, like *Zahl* and *zeigen*. The same method can be used for [pf].

(d) *Regional variation*

There is a widespread tendency to simplify [pf] to [f] in the initial position and after consonants: *Pferd* [feːɐ̯t], *Kampf* [kamf], especially in rapid conversational speech. In formal pronunciation the affricate is retained.

In northern (formerly Low German-speaking) areas the pronunciation [p] can be found for [pf] following vowels: *Kopf* [kɔp], *Schnupfen* [ˈʃnʊpm̩]. This pronunciation is of Low German origin and is not to be recommended to learners.

There is very little regional variation associated with the affricate [ts] in German.

3.8 The glottal stop

In addition to the six plosive phonemes described in section 3.2 above, there is a further plosive which does not have phoneme status in German, but which is very characteristic of German pronunciation. This is the **glottal stop** or **glottal plosive** (G. *der Glottisverschluß* or *der Glottisschlag*), which is formed by a complete closure of the vocal cords, thus cutting of the airstream at the glottis. Phonetically it can be described as a voiceless glottal plosive. To hear what the glottal stop sounds like, pronounce a long [aː] sound and interrupt this by cutting off the air at the glottis: [aːʔaːʔaːʔaːʔaːʔ]. This consonant is used in some varieties of English (Cockney, some Scottish accents) as an allophonic variant of certain plosives (esp. /t/), e.g. *bottle* [ˈbɒʔl̩], *Scotland* [ˈskɒʔlənd]. It plays a completely different and altogether more significant role closely connected with the pronunciation of vowels in German, where **any vowel at the beginning of a word or a stressed syllable within a word may be preceded by a glottal stop**: *aber* [ˈʔaːbɐ], *ewig* [ˈʔeːvɪç] *Uhr* [ˈʔuːɐ̯], *beachten* [bəˈʔaxtn̩], *verantworten* [fɛɐ̯ˈʔantvɔrtn̩], *erinnern* [ʔɛɐ̯ˈʔɪnɐn].

This is usually referred to as *harter Vokaleinsatz* in German, and it has the effect of interrupting the flow of air and cutting off words beginning with a vowel from the preceding word. This is the opposite tendency to

the usual pronunciation in English, which has a rather smooth airflow and
tends to link words together in utterances, particularly by means of the
'linking r' in SBS and other varieties of English which do not have post-
vocalic r. Compare the following phrases in English and German:

> *our other uncle* [aʊrˈʌðərˈʌŋkl̩]
> *unser anderer Onkel* [ˈʔʊnzɐˈʔandərɐˈʔɔŋkl̩]

The glottal stop is not used universally before initial vowels in German. It
is most common before vowels at the beginning of utterances and within
utterances before stressed initial vowels.

> *Er hat die anderen beeindruckt*
> [ʔɛɐ hat di ˈʔandərən bəˈʔaindrʊkt]

It is much less commonly used before unstressed vowels; in particular it is
almost never used before unstressed pronouns following the verb (e.g.
muß ich, hab' ich, weiß er, habt ihr):

> *die Etage* [di eˈtaːʒə] (cf. *der Esel* [dɛɐ ˈʔeːzl̩])
> *die Übersetzung* [di yːbɐˈzɛːtsʊŋ] (cf. *der Überfall* [dɛɐ ˈʔyːbɐfal)
> *Muß er uns an das Geld erinnern?* [ˈmʊs ɛɐ ʊns ans ˈgɛlt ɛɐˈʔinɐn]

It follows from what was said above that if a pronoun, etc., is stressed for
emphasis (contrastive stress) the glottal stop is used:

> *Muß ich gehen?* [mʊs ˈʔiç ˈgeːən]
> *Sie saß auf dem Auto.* [zi zaːs ˈʔaʊf dem ˈʔaʊto]

3.9 Summary and comparison of German and English consonant articulations

The consonant articulations can be displayed in a chart arranged according to place and manner of articulation. A second chart is provided with
the main consonant articulations of English (SBS) for comparison.

Table 1. **The German consonants**

	Place of articulation							
Manner of articulation	Bilabial	Labio-dental	Alveolar	Palato-alveolar	Palatal	Velar	Uvular	Glottal
Plosive	p b		t d			k g		ʔ
Fricative	β	f v	s z	ʃ ʒ	ç j	x ɣ	ʁ	h
Nasal	m		n			ŋ		
Lateral			l					
Approximant					j		ʁ̞	
Roll			r				ʀ	
Flap			ɾ					

Table 2. **The English (SBS) consonants**

	Place of articulation							
Manner of articulation	Bilabial	Labio-dental	Dental	Alveolar	Palato-alveolar	Palatal	Velar	Glottal
Plosive	p b			t d			k g	ʔ
Fricative		f v	θ ð	s z	ʃ ʒ			h
Affricate					tʃ dʒ			
Nasal	m			n			ŋ	
Lateral				l			(ɫ)	
Approximant	w			ɹ		j		

4

The German vowels

4.1   **The description of vowels**

In contrast to consonants, vowels are articulated without a closure or narrowing of the organs of speech sufficient to cause audible friction as the airstream escapes from the mouth. The differences between the vowels depend on the size and shape of the resonance chamber formed by the mouth when they are produced. Three factors are important in determining this:

1   the position of the tongue;
2   the position of the lips;
3   the position of the soft palate.

Although the position of the lips and the soft palate can be described in the same way as for the consonants, the description of tongue position for vowels presents a problem, because there is no contact or close proximity between the tongue and the palate which could be felt as there is in the case of the consonants. It is possible to feel pronounced movements of the tongue (e.g. between [iː] and [aː]), but even here it is much more difficult to give the precise position of the tongue than for consonants. Also, vowels are often distinguished by very small differences in tongue position, which makes them difficult to describe in articulatory terms or to represent on the diagram that was used for the consonants. For this reason a special diagram has been developed to represent the vowel area, i.e. the area in the mouth in which vowel sounds can be formed. This area is limited at the bottom by the lowest natural position of the tongue, and at the top by the fact that if the tongue is too close to the palate a narrow channel will be formed and the result will be a fricative rather than a vowel; see figure 23.

This area with its curved lines is difficult to reproduce accurately in diagrams, so it has been simplified to figures with straight lines, first the rather irregular quadrilateral in figure 24, and then the more regular form

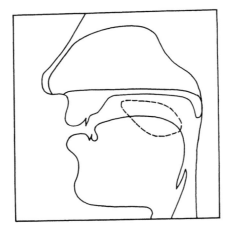

Fig. 23: The vowel area

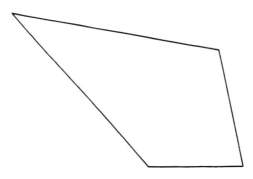

Fig. 24: Vowel diagram (irregular)

in figure 25. The diagram in figure 24 is a more accurate representation of the vowel area and is still sometimes used, but the diagram in figure 25 has the advantage of being simpler to reproduce accurately and is far more common nowadays. Whenever using the vowel diagram it is important to remember that it is a stylised version of the vowel area in the mouth. The tongue position for any vowel sound can be represented in this diagram by means of a dot indicating **the highest point of the tongue** for the vowel in question. The terms used to describe tongue position are **close** (G. *geschlossen*) for vowels pronounced with a tongue position close to the palate, **open** (G. *offen*) for vowels pronounced with a low tongue position, and **half-close** (G. *halbgeschlossen*) and **half-open** (G. *halboffen*) for points in between. The terms **front**, **central** and **back** are used to indicate where the highest point of the tongue is

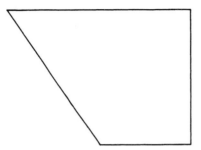

Fig. 25: Vowel diagram (regular)

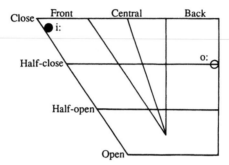

Fig. 26: German /i:/ and /o:/

along the horizontal axis (G. *Vorderzungenvokal, Mittelzungenvokal, Hinterzungenvokal*; the terms *palatal* and *velar* are also sometimes used in German to describe front and back vowels respectively). Thus we can describe German /i:/ as a close front vowel, and German /o:/ as a half-close back vowel, and indicate their positions in the vowel diagram as in figure 26.

The second important factor in determining vowel sounds is the positions of the lips, which can be either **spread** (G. *gespreizt*) or **rounded** (G. *gerundet*). There are various degrees of both spreading and rounding and a **neutral** position in between. Examples are English and German /i:/, pronounced with spread lips, and German and French /u:/, pronounced with close rounded lips. Lip-rounding for vowels can be indicated on the vowel diagram by the use of a circle rather than a dot for vowels pronounced with rounded lips, as in figure 26 for German /o:/.

The soft palate is raised for all the native German vowels, which are thus **oral**, i.e. the airstream can escape only through the mouth. Vowels pronounced with the soft palate lowered, thus allowing the airstream to escape through the nasal cavity as well, are known as **nasal** vowels. These are present in German only in some loan words, mainly from French.

The normal pronunciation for all vowel sounds is voiced, and they are much less subject to devoicing than voiced consonants.

In sections 4.3 and 4.4 below we will be describing the individual German vowel sounds using the terminology just introduced and providing for each a vowel diagram to indicate the position of the tongue. It is worth emphasising, however, that it is not possible to learn the correct pronunciation of vowel sounds merely by following a verbal description, however accurate. The only way to learn new vowel sounds is to listen carefully to a model, to produce the sounds yourself and to compare your own pronunciation to that of the model. For vowel sounds the tactile feedback from the tongue and other organs of speech is much weaker than for consonants, and the auditory feedback therefore takes on an even greater importance. However, articulatory descriptions of the vowels can be a useful aid when taken in conjunction with auditory feedback, particularly in cases where repeated listening and saying on their own do not lead to satisfactory results.

4.2 The vowels of German

On the basis of minimal pairs we can distinguish nineteen vowel phonemes in German, sixteen monophthongs, or pure vowels, and three diphthongs. The monophthongs can be seen as forming seven pairs, the members of which differ from each other in both **quality** (G. *Qualität*, i.e. vowel sound, which is determined by the position of the organs of speech) and **quantity** (G. *Quantität*, i.e. vowel length). These pairs are:

/i:/ _ /ɪ/ as in	*Miete* ['mi:tə]	*Mitte* ['mɪtə]
/e:/ _ /ɛ/	*stehlen* ['ʃte:lən]	*stellen* ['ʃtɛlən]
/a:/ _ /a/	*lahm* [la:m]	*Lamm* [lam]
/u:/ _ /ʊ/	*Mus* [mu:s]	*muß* [mʊs]
/o:/ _ /ɔ/	*Ofen* ['o:fn̩]	*offen* ['ɔfn̩]
/y:/ _ /ʏ/	*fühlen* ['fy:lən]	*füllen* ['fʏlən]
/ø:/ _ /œ/	*Höhle* ['hø:lə]	*Hölle* ['hœlə]

There are also two unpaired monophthongs

/ɛ:/	as in	*Bären* ['bɛ:rən]
/ə/		*bitte* ['bɪtə]

and three diphthongs

/aɪ/	as in	*heiß* [haɪs]
/aʊ/		*Haus* [haʊs]
/ɔʏ/		*neu* [nɔʏ]

In addition to these nineteen vowel phonemes, we will also discuss a
twentieth vowel sound of German: the vocalic allophone of /r/, [ɐ] as in
besser ['bɛsɐ].

4.2.1 **Tenseness and laxness**

In the pairs of German monophthongs given above, the first-mentioned
members are **tense** (G. *gespannt*) and the others are **lax** (G. *ungespannt*).
Tense vowels are those produced on the edges of the vowel area. They
require greater muscular energy or tension than the lax vowels, i.e. those
pronounced more towards the centre of the vowel area, which is the
natural, relaxed position for the tongue. You can observe this distinction
for yourself in two ways when pronouncing tense vowels sounds like [i:]
or [u:], for which the distinction is clearest. (1) Pronouce an extended [i:]-
sound as in German *Liebe*, as close and fronted as possible, but the vowel
of English *feel* will also do. Notice how much more tension there is in the
tongue than for the lax vowel in German *Lippe* or English *fill*. (2) If you
pronounce these same two vowels in front of a mirror, you will notice
how the muscles in the region of the lower jaw and the larynx contract for
the tense [i:], but are relaxed for [ɪ]. You can also feel this difference in
muscle tension with your fingertips under the lower jaw. The same distinction can be felt between other tense and lax pairs of vowels, e.g. [u:]
and [ʊ], Engl. *pool* and *pull*; [e:] and [ɛ], German *Kehle* and *Kelle*, etc.
It is weakest for the open vowels, e.g. [a:] and [a] in German *Kahn* and
kann, but there is evidence from acoustic phonetics that a slight difference in tension exists even here.[1]

4.2.2 **Vowel length**

In the pairs of German monophthongs, the first, tense, members are
pronounced longer than the lax members when they occur in stressed
syllables. This is indicated in transcription by the use of the length mark
(:). Vowel length is thus a second factor which helps to distinguish
between tense and lax vowels in stressed position. However, this distinction is lost when the tense vowels occur in unstressed syllables, especially
preceding the main stress. In this position the tense vowels are pronounced short, e.g. *wieviel* [vi'fi:l], *zurück* [tsu'rʏk], also very commonly
in words of foreign origin, e.g. *Kritik* [kri'ti:k], *human* [hu'ma:n],
Psychologie [psyçolo'gi:]. These vowels are still distinguished from the lax
vowels /ɪ/, /ʊ/, /ʏ/ and /ɔ/ on the basis of their tense quality, at least in
formal pronunciation.[2] The short tense vowels can be regarded as con-

---

[1] See Iivonen (1989: 10f., 21f.).

[2] In conversational pronunciation, the distinction between short tense and short lax vowels
tends to be lost; see section 6.3 below.

textual variants of the tense vowel phonemes, which thus have two allophones: /i:/ – [i:, i]; /e:/ – [e:, e], etc.

Vowel length is not the same as the actual duration of the vowel sounds, which can vary greatly depending (a) on the nature of the vowel (open vowels are intrinsically longer than close vowels, because the articulators have to cover a greater distance to form a following closure) and (b) on the context in which the vowel sound occurs. Vowel length is phonemic, i.e. it serves to distinguish phonemes of a language, whereas vowel duration is phonetic, i.e. it can be measured (in milliseconds) in different environments. There is sometimes a discrepancy between vowel length and vowel duration, as in English, where long vowels are of considerably shorter duration before fortis consonants than when they occur before lenis consonants or in final position, e.g. /i:/ in *beat* is only about half as long as in *bee* or *bead*, and is frequently of shorter duration than the /ɪ/ of *bid*. German long vowels are not shortened before fortis consonants in this way, so English-speaking learners will have to make a conscious effort to maintain the length of vowels in words like *Lied* [li:t], *Hupe* ['hu:pə] and *Schaf* [ʃa:f].

On the other hand, English-speakers tend to lengthen short vowels, especially /æ/, in stressed positions, e.g. *It's in your hand, I'll get you a can*. Short vowels cannot be lengthened in this way in German, for example German *Hand* and *kann* must always be pronounced with short vowel sounds.

4.2.3 Non-syllabic vowels

The vowels /i:/ and /u:/ are usually non-syllabic, that is they are pronounced very short and do not constitute a separate syllable, when they occur before vowels. This occurs in words of foreign origin and is especially common in the Latin suffix *-tion*. In phonetic transcription it is indicated by the use of the diacritic [̯] under the vowel symbol, e.g. *Produktion* [prodʊk'tsi̯o:n], *Ferien* ['fe:ri̯ən], *manuell* [ma'nu̯ɛl]. A non-syllabic pronunciation of other vowels is found very occasionally e.g. [o̯] in *loyal* [lo̯a'ja:l] and [ỹ] in *Libyen* ['li:bỹən].

4.3   The German monophthongs

4.3.1   /i:/

(a) Description

The German /i:/ is a tense, close, front vowel, pronounced with spread lips and only a very slight opening of the jaw. The tip of the tongue

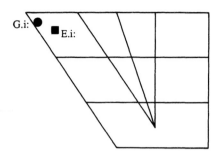

Fig. 27: German /i:/

touches the lower front teeth, and the sides of the front of the tongue
press against the inner sides of the upper molars. The German sound is
rather more close and fronted than the sound that most English speakers
have in their own language (a common tongue position for the English
sound has been included on the diagram using a square to distinguish it
from the German sound).

(b)   *Distribution and examples*
Spelling: ⟨i⟩, ⟨ih⟩, ⟨ie⟩, ⟨ieh⟩, ⟨y⟩ (rare)
In stressed syllables /i:/ occurs only as a long vowel. It occurs in the
following positions:
initial: *irisch* [ˈiːrɪʃ], *Igel* [ˈiːg̩l̩], *ihnen* [ˈiːnən]
medial: *Spiel* [ʃpiːl], *lies* [liːs], *Miete* [ˈmiːtə], *politisch* [poˈliːtɪʃ], *stiehlt*
[ʃtiːlt], *Schwyz* [ʃviːts]
final: *nie* [niː], *Vieh* [fiː], *Geographie* [geograˈfiː].
In unstressed position with reduced length: *Idee* [iˈdeː], *Kritik* [kriˈtiːk],
Philosophie [filozoˈfiː], *Militär* [miliˈtɛːɐ̯], *Mikroskop* [mikroˈskoːp],
Lineal [lineˈaːl].
Non-syllabic [i̯] before vowels: *Nation* [naˈtsi̯oːn], *finanziell* [finanˈtsi̯ɛl],
Sebastian [zeˈbasti̯an]

(c)   *Problems for English-speaking learners*
Some speakers of standard English have an /i:/ sound which is very
similar to the German sound and is thus a perfectly adequate substitute
for the German /i:/. For most speakers, however, the English /i:/ differs
quite considerably from the German /i:/: (a) the English /i:/ tends to be
slightly more open and more centralised than in German, and (b) there is
a strong tendency in many regional forms of English to diphthongise /i:/
so that it is pronounced [ɪi] or even [əi]. To overcome these habits of the
mother tongue, the learner should push the front of the tongue further
forward than for the English sound, try to feel the tension in the tongue

muscle, and make sure that the lips are widely spread. It is worthwhile exaggerating these features in exercises, as there is no danger of exaggerated features being carried over into everyday speech – the danger is rather that the features mentioned will be too weak. Contrast the following English and German pairs:

G. *lieb* [li:p]	closer and more fronted than E.	*leap*
Dieb [di:p]		*deep*
viel [fi:l]		*feel*
Miete ['mi:tə]		*meet*
lies [li:s]		*lease*

(d) *Regional variation*

Some southern speakers have a more open variety of /i:/, and there is a strong tendency to diphthongisation of this sound in the pronunciation of some southern dialect speakers (Bavaria, Switzerland).

4.3.2 /ɪ/

(a) *Description*

The tongue position for German /ɪ/ is more centralised than that of /i:/. It is pronounced with the front of the tongue raised above and retracted slightly from the half-close front position. The tongue is lax and the lips are spread, but less distinctly than for /i:/. /ɪ/ is always pronounced short.

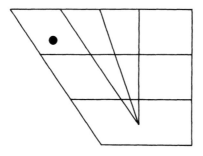

Fig. 28: German /ɪ/

(b) *Distribution and examples*
Spelling: ⟨i⟩
/ɪ/ occurs in the initial and medial positions, but not finally:

initial: *ich* [ɪç], *immer* ['ɪmɐ], *Interesse* [ɪntə'rɛsə], *Irrtum* ['ɪrtu:m]
medial: *bin* [bɪn], *Mitte* ['mɪtə], *König* ['kø:nɪç], *hinter* ['hɪntɐ], *Birne* ['bɪrnə]

(c) *Problems for English-speaking learners*
Most English-speakers have an /ɪ/ which is very similar indeed to the German vowel, so there are very few problems with this sound. Some English speakers may have a vowel which is slightly more open and more central than German /ɪ/, and for these speakers it may be desirable to make a small adjustment in the direction of [i:] (more close and more fronted than their English /ɪ/).

(d) *Regional variation*
In southern Germany (Bavaria, Swabia) and Austria the short open /ɪ/ is pronounced close and fronted, so that its quality is very similar to that of /i:/, from which it is distinguished mainly by length in these varieties.

4.3.3 /e:/

(a) *Description*
German /e:/ is a half-close, front, tense vowel pronounced with the lips in a loosely spread position, similar to that for /ɪ/. The tip of the tongue touches the lower front teeth and the sides of the front of the tongue are in contact with the inner sides of the upper molars, although not as strongly as for /i:/. There is a tendency towards a slightly more open pronunciation of /e:/ before /r/.

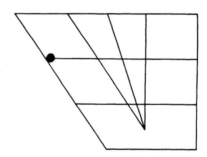

Fig. 29: German /e:/

(b) *Distribution and examples*
Spelling: ⟨e⟩, ⟨ee⟩, ⟨eh⟩
In stressed syllables /e:/ occurs only as a long vowel. It occurs in the following positions:
initial: *eben* [ˈeːbən], *Ehre* [ˈeːrə], *Elend* [ˈeːlɛnt]
medial: *Leber* [ˈleːbɐ], *Regel* [ˈreːgl̩], *Beere* [ˈbeːrə], *sehen* [ˈzeːən], *sehr* [zeːɐ], *Seele* [ˈzeːlə]
final: *Weh* [veː], *geh* [geː], *Schnee* [ʃneː].

In unstressed position with reduced length: *egal* [e'ga:l], *Reform* [re'fɔrm], *Realität* [reali'tɛ:t], *separat* [zepa'ra:t].

(c) *Problems for English-speaking learners*

This is one of the most difficult sounds of German for the English-speaking learner, as there is no corresponding long vowel in SBS. There are some regional varieties of English which have a long monophthong similar to the German sound, though some English monophthongs in words like *gate* are too open for German /e:/, e.g. Lancashire [gɛ:t]. Speakers of SBS tend to substitute the English diphthong /eɪ/ for German /e:/, but this tendency must be resisted. Contrast the following pairs:

English	German
Tay [teɪ]	*Tee* [te:]
gay [geɪ]	*geh* [ge:]
mail [meɪl]	*Mehl* [me:l]
lake [leɪk]	*leg* [le:k]
day [deɪ]	*D* (the letter D) [de:]

In the English words, there is a clear movement of the tongue during the vowel sound (from [e] to [ɪ]), whereas the tongue stays completely still during the pronunciation of the German long vowel. There are two things you have to get right in order to make this sound correctly:

(a) the tongue position, which is higher than for English (SBS) short /e/ as in [get], almost as high as many English speakers' /ɪ/, and as far forward as possible;

(b) you must make sure that the tongue is tense and remains in the same position until the end of the vowel sound.

It is a good idea to exaggerate the length of the vowel at first, starting with words containing /e:/ in the final position, and then going on to /e:/ in other positions. Try the following pairs of German words containing /i:/ and /e:/, remembering that the tongue position is different, but the length, tension in the tongue and lack of diphthongisation are the same:

/i:/	/e:/
I [i:]	*E* [e:]
sie [zi:]	*See* [ze:]
wie [vi:]	*weh* [ve:]
lieben ['li:bən]	*leben* ['le:bən]
liegen ['li:gən]	*legen* ['le:gən]
fielen ['fi:lən]	*fehlen* ['fe:lən]

(d) *Regional variation*

The tendency towards a more open variant of /e:/ before /r/ is present throughout Germany, but it is strongest in northern and western central parts.

In Swabia (south-west Germany) some words which elsewhere are pronounced with the close /e:/ (and are spelt with ⟨e⟩) have the more open vowel /ɛ:/, e.g. *Regen* ['rɛ:gn̩], *lesen* ['lɛ:zn̩]. This is one of the most noticeable features of the Swabian accent, jokingly referred to as *schwäbeln* ('to speak with a Swabian accent') by speakers of other varieties of German.

4.3.4 /ɛ/

(a) *Description*

German /ɛ/ is a short, lax vowel, pronounced with the tongue in the half-open position or slightly higher. The lips are slightly spread.

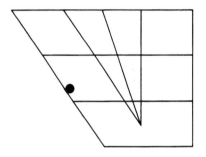

Fig. 30: German /ɛ/

(b) *Distribution and examples*

Spelling: ⟨e⟩, ⟨ä⟩

/ɛ/ occurs in the initial and medial positions, but not finally:

initial: *Ende* ['ɛndə], *etwas* ['ɛtvas], *Ernte* ['ɛrntə], *Ernst* [ɛrnst], *Änderung* ['ɛndərʊŋ]

medial: *Feld* [fɛlt], *Recht* [rɛçt], *kennen* ['kɛnən], *vergessen* [fɛɐ̯'gɛsn̩], *hätte* ['hɛtə], *läßt* [lɛst], *Hälfte* ['hɛlftə], *Gäste* ['gɛstə]

(c) *Problems for English-speaking learners*

Speakers of SBS have no problems with this German sound, since the English /e/ as in [get], although generally slightly more close than the German sound, is very similar.

(d) *Regional variation*

In parts of northern and western central Germany there is a more open variant of /ɛ/ before /r/ ([æ]).

In some southern and south-western varieties there are two different short e-sounds, a half-open one and one which is slightly more close, so that words like *Bett* and *fett* have different vowel sounds. These varieties have an extra vowel phoneme, but this pronunciation is restricted to a small geographical region and is not recommended to learners.

4.3.5 /ɛ:/

(a) *Description*

/ɛ:/ is a long vowel pronounced with the same tongue position as, or marginally more open than, the short vowel /ɛ/.

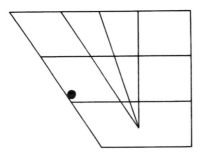

Fig. 31: German /ɛ:/

(b) *Distribution and examples*

Spelling: ⟨ä⟩, ⟨äh⟩

/ɛ:/ occurs in the initial, medial and final positions:

initial: *ähnlich* [ˈɛ:nlɪç], *ähneln* [ˈɛ:nəln], *Ähre* [ˈɛ:rə] ('ear of grain')
medial: *während* [ˈvɛ:rənt], *Jäger* [ˈjɛ:ɡɐ], *spät* [ʃpɛ:t], *Käse* [ˈkɛ:zə], *gefährlich* [ɡəˈfɛ:ɐlɪç], *fährt* [fɛ:ɐt],
final: *zäh* (tough) [tsɛ:], *jäh* (sudden) [jɛ:]

(c) *Problems for English-speaking learners*

Although there is no corresponding long vowel in English, this sound is not particularly difficult for learners. The best approach is to start with the short /ɛ/ in words like *trennen, Wellen,* and to lengthen the vowel sound. The tongue must, of course, be kept steady throughout the vowel sound, and there must be no diphthongisation: /eɪ/ is a common error for English-speaking learners attempting to produce /ɛ:/. Try the following minimal pairs:

/ɛ/	/ɛ:/
trennen [ˈtrɛnən]	*Tränen* [ˈtrɛ:nən]
Wellen [ˈvɛlən]	*Wählen* [ˈvɛ:lən]
Vetter [ˈfɛtɐ]	*Väter* [ˈfɛ:tɐ]
Teller [ˈtɛlɐ]	*Täler* [ˈtɛ:lɐ]
Welt [vɛlt]	*wählt* [vɛ:lt]

This phoneme is an exception to the German vowel system, as it is not a member of a tense/lax pair. The historical development and regional variety of this sound are extremely complex, but a very simple rule for its use in Modern Standard German can be given on the basis of spelling: /ɛ:/ is used wherever the vowel sound represented in writing by ⟨ä⟩ is to be pronounced long. Although all the pronouncing dictionaries of German regard only a pronunciation which includes /ɛ:/ as standard, the usage in Modern German actually varies greatly and the many millions of speakers in northern and eastern central areas of Germany do not have this sound at all, using the long half-close vowel /e:/ in its place (see (d) below). This means learners do not need to use /ɛ:/ at all if they do not wish to, particularly if their pronunciation model is a North German one. It should be pointed out, however, that /ɛ:/ is widely used, even in the north, in certain limited contexts: as the name of the letter ⟨Ä⟩ and to avoid misunderstanding where a distinction between /e:/ and /ɛ:/ is significant, e.g. *gebe* and *gäbe*.

Because of the more open pronunciation of /e:/ before /r/, the difference between /e:/ and /ɛ:/ tends to disappear in this position, e.g. *Beeren* = *Bären* [ˈbɛ:rən].

(d) *Regional variation*
Speakers in northern and eastern central areas tend to replace /ɛ:/ by /e:/, especially in colloquial speech, pronouncing pairs of words like *Dänen* and *denen*, *legen* and *lägen* identically. It is thus only in southern and western central parts of the German-speaking area that a regular distinction between these words is made.

4.3.6 /a:/

(a) *Description*
German /a:/ is a long, open, central vowel, pronounced with the tongue noticeably lower than for the other German vowels. The tip of the tongue touches the lower front teeth or gums and the lips are in a neutral position, neither spread nor rounded.

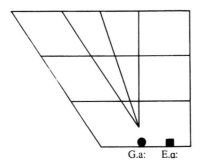

Fig. 32: German /a:/

(b) *Distribution and examples*
Spelling: ⟨a⟩, ⟨aa⟩, ⟨ah⟩
/a:/ occurs in the initial, medial and final positions:
initial: *Abend* ['a:bənt], *Adler* ['a:dlɐ], *Aachen* ['a:xn̩], *ahnen* ['a:nən], *atmen* ['a:tmən]
medial: *Tag* [ta:k], *habe* ['ha:bə], *Name* ['na:mə], *Paar* [pa:ɐ̯], *Staat* [ʃta:t], *wahr* [va:ɐ̯], *Zahl* [tsa:l]
final: *ja* [ja:], *da* [da:], *sah* [za:], *nah* [na:]

(c) *Problems for English-speaking learners*
Some English-speakers have a pronunciation which is rather similar to German /a:/ in words like *father* ['fɑ:ðə], but for many speakers of SBS this is a open **back** vowel (['fɑ:ðə]), as opposed to the German open **central** vowel. These English-speakers therefore have to get used to producing an a-sound which is further forward than their own long a, but not as far forward as the English short /æ/. Contrast the following pairs of English and German words:

English /ɑ:/	German /a:/
father ['fɑ:ðə]	*Vater* ['fa:tɐ]
Carmen ['kɑ:mən]	*kamen* ['ka:mən]
start [stɑ:t]	*Staat* [ʃta:t]
harbour ['hɑ:bə]	*habe* ['ha:bə]
tart [tɑ:t]	*Tat* [ta:t]
harder ['hɑ:də]	*Hader* ('dispute') ['ha:dɐ]

(d) *Regional variation*
In southern areas there is a tendency to pronounce /a:/ as a back open vowel with a certain amount of lip-rounding ([ɑ:] or [ɒ:]). This tendency is especially strong in Bavaria and Austria, but it can also be found in

other southern areas including Saxony and Thuringia. In some northern and central areas, on the other hand, there is a tendency towards a more fronted pronunciation of /a:/, rather similar in tongue position to the SBS /æ/ as in *can*, but pronounced long. Neither of these pronunciations should be imitated by the English-speaking learner, as the probable result will be the substitution of one of the English sounds for the German one.

4.3.7 /a/

(a) Description
The German /a/ is a short, open, central vowel pronounced by many speakers with exactly the same tongue position as for /a:/. The tense–lax distinction is not nearly so clear for the open vowels as it is for more close ones, but some speakers seem to have a marginally more lax (and thus more centralised) pronunciation of the short /a/. In the diagram it is depicted as being pronounced with the same tongue position as for /a:/.

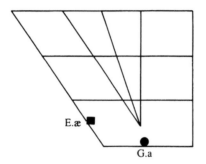

Fig. 33: German /a/

(b) Distribution and examples
Spelling: ⟨a⟩
/a/ occurs in the initial, medial and final positions:
initial: *alt* [alt], *alle* ['alə], *Apfel* ['apfl̩], *Alpen* ['alpən], *Armut* ['armu:t]
medial: *Hand* [hant], *Sache* ['zaxə], *lang* [laŋ], *Natur* [na'tu:ɐ̯], *warnen* ['varnən], *Karte* ['kartə]
final: *Afrika* ['a:frika], *Amerika* [a'me:rika], *rosa* ['ro:za], *lila* ['li:la]

(c) Problems for English-speaking learners
The SBS vowel /æ/ is more fronted and more close than the German /a/ and cannot be substituted for the German sound. German /a/ is an open central vowel, very similar to the a-sound in some northern and Midlands accents of English. For speakers of southern varieties of English, the closest sound to the German /a/ is /ʌ/ as in *but* and *hut*, which is also a

central vowel, but with a tongue position between half-open and open. However, this sound cannot be used in German for /a/, as it is very similar to another German vowel sound, the vocalic *r* [ɐ], and of course a distinction between these two must be maintained. For speakers of SBS it is probably best to start from the English sound /ʌ/ and to lower the tongue (and open the jaw) slightly.

Word pairs for practice are:

English	German
hut [hʌt]	*hat* [hat]
hunt [hʌnt]	*Hant* [hant]
luck [lʌk]	*Lack* [lak]
fund [fʌnd]	*fand* [fant]
lung [lʌŋ]	*lang* [laŋ]

(d)   *Regional variation*

As for /a:/, there is a more fronted variant of /a/ in some northern and central parts, whereas in the south-east (Bavaria, Austria) it tends to be pronounced as a back vowel with lip-rounding, as Standard German /ɔ/, e.g. *Ast* [ɔst], *Backe* ['bɔkə].

4.3.8   /u:/

(a)   *Description*

This is a tense, close, back vowel pronounced with the lips strongly rounded and protruding, considerably more so than for the corresponding English sound. The tongue is also higher and further back than for English /u:/, which is slightly fronted and a fraction below the close position. With the tongue in the higher position for the German vowel, contact is made between the sides of the tongue and the upper molars, a contact which is missing in the lower English tongue position.

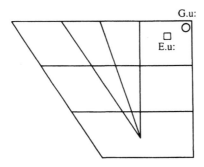

Fig. 34: German /u:/

(b) *Distribution and examples*
Spelling: ⟨u⟩, ⟨uh⟩
In stressed syllables /u:/ occurs only as a long vowel in the following positions:

🔈 **initial:** *Ufer* ['u:fɐ], *Uhr* [u:ɐ], *Urlaub* ['u:ɐlaʊp], *Ute* ['u:tə], *Udo* ['u:do], *Uwe* ['u:və]
medial: *Hut* [hu:t], *Juni* ['ju:ni], *Buch* [bu:x], *Zug* [tsu:k], *suchen* ['zu:xn̩], *nur* [nu:ɐ], *Natur* [na'tu:ɐ]
final: *du* [du:], *zu* [tsu:], *Schuh* [ʃu:], *Kuh* [ku:].
Unstressed with reduced length: *Union* [u'nio:n], *universal* [univɛr'za:l], *Universität* [univɛrzi'tɛ:t], *human* [hu'ma:n], *Humanität* [humani'tɛ:t], *zurecht* [tsu'rɛçt], *zurück* [tsu'rʏk]
Non-syllabic [u̯] before vowels: *Linguist* [lɪŋ'gu̯ɪst], *manuell* [ma'nu̯ɛl]

(c) *Problems for English-speaking learners*
German /u:/ causes problems for learners because it differs from the corresponding English sound in a number of ways. First, SBS /u:/ is usually diphthongised (a tendency which is even stronger in American pronunciation), [ʊu] and [əu] being two common British pronunciations. German /u:/ is a tense monophthong, in which the tongue position remains the same throughout.

Even for speakers of English who have a monophthongal pronunciation of /u:/, the German sound differs from their own in three ways: it is more close, it is further back and it has stronger lip-rounding. There may be a certain psychological barrier to the correct pronunciation of the German sound, as Gimson points out that in English 'a quality of /u:/ which is too near to a pure [back close vowel], with strong lip-rounding, is characterized as affected or over-cultivated' (1989: 121). The German sound does not have this connotation, of course, and learners should concentrate on producing a close back vowel, feeling the contact between the sides of the tongue and the back teeth, and rounding their lips tightly.

Some Scottish speakers have a more centralised tongue position for this vowel, which will not do in German because of its similarity to /y:/ and /ʏ/.

(d) *Regional variation*
There is very little regional variation associated with this sound in German. Some speakers in all regions have a slightly more open pronunciation, which is not recommended, since it is likely to encourage interference from English pronunciations of /u:/.

4.3.9 /ʊ/

(a) *Description*

/ʊ/ is a short, lax vowel pronounced with a tongue position slighly above half-close, and slightly fronted from the back position. There is either a very light contact between the sides of the tongue and the back teeth, or none at all.

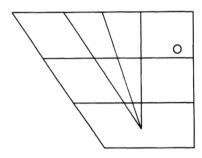

Fig. 35: German /ʊ/

(b) *Distribution and examples*

Spelling: ⟨u⟩

/ʊ/ occurs in the initial and medial positions, but not finally:

initial: *unser* [ˈʊnzɐ], *Unglück* [ˈʊnglʏk], *Urteil* [ˈʊrtaɪl], *Unschuld* [ˈʊnʃʊlt], *Ulrich* [ˈʊlrɪç]

medial: *Grund* [grʊnt], *Mutter* [ˈmʊtɐ], *Luft* [lʊft], *Nummer* [ˈnʊmɐ], *Stellung* [ˈʃtɛlʊŋ], *durch* [dʊrç], *Wurst* [vʊrst], *Furcht* [fʊrçt]

(c) *Problems for English-speaking learners*

The majority of English-speakers have no problems with this German vowel as it is very close to the corresponding sound in SBS. One slight difference is the greater lip-rounding that German-speakers give to their sound, which English-speaking learners should aim for. Many Scottish speakers use the same centralised sound for /ʊ/ in *pull* and /u:/ in *pool*. They must learn to distinguish long /u:/ from short /ʊ/ in German, and also to produce the sounds further back in the mouth.

(d) *Regional variation*

There is very little regional variation associated with this sound in German.

4.3.10 /o:/

(a) *Description*
/o:/ is a tense, half-close, back vowel, pronounced with the lips rounded and protruding quite noticeably, but not as strongly as for German /u:/. The sides of the front of the tongue are in contact with the inner sides of the upper molars, although not as strongly as for German /u:/. This vowel does not exist in SBS; it is pronounced with a tongue position about half-way between German /ɔ/ as in *Gold* and /u:/ as in *Fuß*.

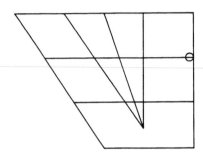

Fig. 36: German /o:/

(b) *Distribution and examples*
Spelling: ⟨o⟩, ⟨oh⟩, ⟨oo⟩, ⟨eau⟩ (there are some other rare spellings in words of foreign origin)

In stressed syllables /o:/ occurs only as a long vowel in the following positions:

initial: *ohne* ['o:nə], *oben* ['o:bən], *Oper* ['o:pɐ], *Ohr* [o:ɐ]
medial: *Sohn* [zo:n], *groß* [gro:s], *hoch* [ho:x], *Ton* [to:n], *wohl* [vo:l], *Montag* ['mo:nta:k]
final: *so* [zo:], *roh* [ro:], *Stroh* [ʃtro:], *Zoo* [tso:], *Niveau* [ni'vo:].
Unstressed with reduced length: *orange* [o'raŋʒə], *Olympiade* [olym'pi̯a:də], *Olive* [o'li:və], *Politik* [poli'ti:k], *Photograph* [foto'gra:f], *Phonologie* [fonolo'gi:], *Krododil* [kroko'di:l], *Radio* ['ra:di̯o], *Hugo* ['hu:go], *Otto* ['ɔto].
Non-syllabic [o̯] before vowels: *loyal* [lo̯a'ja:l], *Doyen* [do̯a'jɛ̃:] (in French loan words)

(c) *Problems for English-speaking learners*
There is a tendency on the part of English-speakers to replace this German monophthong with the English diphthong /əʊ/. Learners should try to overcome this, since it is one of the main characteristics of an

English accent in German. The correct tongue position is not difficult to find, about half-way between /ɔ/ and /u:/, and, as with the other long vowels, the tongue position should not change until the vowel sound has been completed. This is easier if the tongue is kept quite tense throughout the production of the vowel. Note the difference between the following pairs of words in English and German:

English	German
boat [bəʊt]	*Boot* [bo:t]
note [nəʊt]	*Not* [no:t]
loan [ləʊn]	*Lohn* [lo:n]
tone [təʊn]	*Ton* [to:n]
vole [vəʊl]	*wohl* [vo:l]

Some speakers of English, notably Scots and some northerners, have a very similar vowel sound in their pronunciation of English, which can be used quite well for German, too.

(d) *Regional variation*
In Saxony this sound is frequently realised as a diphthong, [ɔu] or [ʌu], a pronunciation which is not recommended to English-speaking learners, as it is reminiscent of many English pronunciations of /əʊ/ as in *boat*.

4.3.11 /ɔ/

(a) *Description*
German /ɔ/ is a lax, half-open, back vowel pronounced with loosely rounded lips. It is somewhat more close than the SBS vowel /ɒ/ in *got*, which is almost fully open.

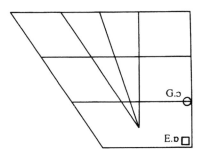

Fig. 37: German /ɔ/

(b)   *Distribution and examples*
Spelling: ⟨o⟩
/ɔ/ occurs in the initial and medial positions, but not finally:

🖵 **initial:** *oft* [ɔft], *offen* [ˈɔfn̩], *Ort* [ɔrt], *Ordnung* [ˈɔrdnʊŋ], *Onkel* [ˈɔŋkl̩], *Oktober* [ɔkˈtoːbɐ]
medial: *Gold* [gɔlt] *Sonne* [ˈzɔnə], *voll* [fɔl], *Form* [fɔrm], *Wort* [vɔrt]

(c)   *Problems for English-speaking learners*
The degree of lip-rounding is greater for German /ɔ/ than for SBS /ɒ/, but otherwise the sounds are very similar. Those speakers who have a very open /ɒ/ in English should try to achieve a half-open tongue position for German. This is the tongue position for English long /ɔː/ as in *born*, but the German sound must be pronounced short, of course: *Bonn*. Some speakers of English, e.g. most Irish and American speakers, have an open, unrounded vowel in words like *dock*, very similar to the vowel quality of SBS /ɑː/, but short. Some southern British speakers have a long /ɔː/ before fricatives in words like *off* and *cloth*. Neither of these sounds should be used in German, where /ɔ/ is always short and moderately rounded.

(d)   *Regional variation*
In southern varieties of German /ɔ/ is pronounced with a closer tongue position than in the north, e.g. *Gott* [got].

4.3.12   /yː/

(a)   *Description*
German /yː/ is a tense, close, front, rounded vowel, produced with strongly rounded and protruding lips (similar to the lip position for German /uː/). The tongue position is very similar to that of /iː/, but

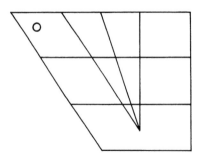

Fig. 38: German /yː/

slightly centralised. This means that the tip of the tongue touches the lower front teeth, and the sides of the middle and back parts of the tongue are in contact with the upper molars.

(b) *Distribution and examples*
Spelling: ⟨ü⟩, ⟨üh⟩, ⟨y⟩
In stressed syllables /y:/ occurs only as a long vowel. It occurs in the following positions:

🔊 **initial:** *Übung* ['y:bʊŋ], *über* ['y:bɐ], *übrig* ['y:brɪç], *Übel* ['y:bl̩], *überzeugt* [y:bɐ'tsɔʏkt], *üblich* ['y:blɪç]
medial: *Bühne* ['by:nə], *führen* ['fy:rən], *Tür* [ty:ɐ], *Bücher* ['by:çɐ], *Züge* ['tsy:gə], *Asyl* [a'zy:l], *Typ* [ty:p], *Zürich* ['tsy:rɪç]
final: *früh* [fry:], *Müh'* [my:] (= *Mühe*).
Unstressed with reduced length: *Dynamit* [dyna'mi:t], *Synonym* [zyno'ny:m], *Synagoge* [zyna'go:gə], *Psychologie* [psyçolo'gi:], *Psychiatrie* [psyçia'tri:], *Physiotherapie* [fyzi̯otera'pi:], *Zynismus* [tsy'nɪsmʊs]

(c) *Problems for English-speaking learners*
English speakers tend to find all the German front rounded vowels difficult, as English does not have any vowels which are both front and rounded. The difficulty is compounded in the case of /y:/ because (a) the tongue position is more extreme and (b) the degree of lip-rounding is greater than most English-speakers are used to. The best way to achieve this sound is to start with a German /i:/, making sure that the tongue is high, fronted and tense, and then, keeping the tongue perfectly still, to add the lip-rounding of the German /u:/. If you do this you will hear the vowel sound change: [i → y]. This sound is easiest to pronounce at the beginning of words, because then you have time to get your tongue and lips into the right positions, so start with these words and, once you have got used to producing the vowel, go on to words in which it occurs in later positions.

(d) *Regional variation*
In many central and southern varieties of German /y:/ tends to be unrounded and to sound like /i:/. This is regarded as substandard pronunciation in Germany and should not be imitated by the learner.

4.3.13 /ʏ/

(a) *Description*
German /ʏ/ is a short, lax, front, rounded vowel, which bears the same relation to /y:/ as the short /ɪ/ does to /i:/. The tongue position is more centralised than for /ɪ/, slightly above half-close. The front of the tongue

touches the bottom front teeth, and the sides of the tongue have contact with the upper molars. The degree of lip-rounding is weaker than for /y:/, about the same as for the short /ɪ/.

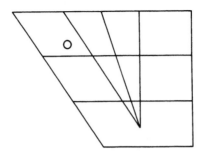

Fig. 39: German /ʏ/

(b) Distribution and examples
Spelling: ⟨ü⟩, ⟨y⟩
/ʏ/ occurs in the initial and medial positions, but not finally:
initial: *üppig* ['ʏpɪç], *Ypsilon* ['ʏpsilɔn] (rare in this position)
medial: *müssen* ['mʏsn̩], *Glück* [glʏk], *Künstler* ['kʏnstlɐ], *Gründe* ['grʏndə], *jünger* ['jʏŋɐ], *hübsch* [hʏpʃ], *fürchten* ['fʏrçtn̩], *würdig* ['vʏrdɪç], *Sylt* [zʏlt]

(c) Problems for English-speaking learners
The problems with this sound correspond to those for /y:/, and the procedure for learning it is the same: start with /ɪ/ and, while keeping the tongue completely still, add lip-rounding, although a smaller degree than for /y:/. Once you have learnt both these vowels, you will need to make sure that you can keep them apart; a good way of practising this is to say minimal pairs with /y:/ and /ʏ/, e.g.:

/y:/	/ʏ/
Hüte ['hy:tə]	*Hütte* ['hʏtə]
Wüste ['vy:stə]	*wüßte* ['vʏstə]
Düne ['dy:nə]	*dünne* ['dʏnə]
fühlen ['fy:lən]	*füllen* ['fʏlən]
Lüge ['ly:gə]	*Lücke* ['lʏkə]

(d) Regional variation
As with /y:/, /ʏ/ is also unrounded in some central and southern varieties of German, a pronunciation which again should be avoided by the learner.

4.3.14 /ø:/

(a) *Description*
German /ø:/ is a tense, front, rounded vowel pronounced with a tongue position slightly lower than half-close. For practical purposes, a tongue position the same as that for German /e:/ can be adopted. The tip of the tongue touches the lower front teeth, and the sides of the middle and back part of the tongue are in contact with the upper molars.

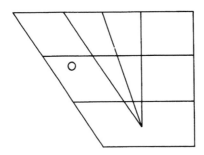

Fig. 40: German /ø:/

(b) *Distribution and examples*
Spelling: ⟨ö⟩, ⟨öh⟩, ⟨eu⟩ (in loan words from French)
In stressed syllables /ø:/ occurs only as a long vowel. It occurs in the following positions:
initial: *Öl* [ø:l], *öde* ['ø:də], *Österreich* ['ø:stəraɪç], *Öfen* ['ø:fn̩],
medial: *möglich* ['mø:klɪç], *schön* [ʃø:n], *Röhre* ['rø:rə], *Goethe* ['gø:tə], *Böhmen* ['bø:mən] ('Bohemia'), *Friseur* [fri'zø:ɐ]
final: *Bö* [bø:] ('gust'), *Milieu* [mi'ljø:], *Höh'* [hø:] (= *Höhe*).
Unstressed with reduced length: *Ökonom* [øko'no:m] ('economist'), *Ökologie* [økolo'gi:] ('ecology'), *ökumenisch* [øku'me:nɪʃ] ('ecumenical'), *Phönizier* [fø'ni:tsi̯ɐ] ('Phoenician')

(c) *Problems for English-speaking learners*
It is understandable that this German sound almost always causes problems for English speakers, for not only is it a front rounded vowel, but, whereas the tongue position for /y:/ and /ʏ/ were not too different from English /i:/ and /ɪ/, in the case of /ø:/ there is no English vowel sound at all made in this position. English speakers tend to substitute /ɜ:/ as in *bird* for this German vowel, pronouncing *Goethe* with the vowel sound of English *girder*, and *Töne* like *Turner*. Yet the differences between these vowels are clear: German /ø:/ is a half-close, front, rounded vowel,

while English /ɜ:/ is a central, unrounded vowel somewhere between half-close and half-open. There are two ways of tackling German /ø:/.

1 For learners who have mastered German /e:/, the same tongue position may be adopted, to which lip-rounding should be added for /ø:/. The following are word pairs containing /e:/ and /ø:/:

/e:/	/ø:/
Hefe [ˈheːfə]	*Höfe* [ˈhøːfə]
Schwere [ˈʃveːrə]	*schwöre* [ˈʃvøːrə]
Sehne [ˈzeːnə]	*Söhne* [ˈzøːnə]
Meere [ˈmeːrə]	*Möhre* [ˈmøːrə]
kehre [ˈkeːrə]	*Chöre* [ˈkøːrə]

2 Most learners, however, will probably find it easier to approach this vowel once they have mastered /ʏ/, which is the closest German sound to /ø:/ and can be used as a starting-point when learning it. The difference between the two vowel sounds lies not so much in the tongue position as in the lip-rounding, which is much more pronounced for /ø:/. For many German speakers the tongue position is almost indistinguishable from that of /ʏ/, for some it is slightly more open. As /ø:/ is a long vowel, the tongue is tense, compared to the lax /ʏ/. To pronounce /ø:/ then, first of all form [ʏ], make sure that the tongue is tense for the long vowel, and then increase the lip-rounding considerably. This should give a perfectly acceptable [ø:]-sound; you must, of course, make sure that the tongue position does not move towards /y:/, as otherwise there is a danger of confusing these two vowels. If you find this happening, you obviously need to lower the tongue position slightly for /ø:/. Try the following pairs of words to make sure you distinguish clearly between /y:/ and /ø:/:

/y:/	/ø:/
Güte [ˈgyːtə]	*Goethe* [ˈgøːtə]
Hühne [ˈhyːnə]	*höhne* [ˈhøːnə]
Sühne [ˈzyːnə]	*Söhne* [ˈzøːnə]
Grüße [ˈgryːsə]	*Größe* [ˈgrøːsə]
rühme [ˈryːmə]	*Römer* [ˈrøːmɐ]
kühne [ˈkyːnə]	*König* [ˈkøːnɪç]

(d) *Regional variation*

As with /y:/ and /ʏ/, /ø:/ is unrounded in many central and southern regions and is not distinguished from /e:/, resulting in pairs words like *Söhne* und *Sehne*, both pronounced [ˈzeːnə]. This pronunciation should be avoided by the learner.

4.3.15 /œ/

(a) *Description*

German /œ/ is considerably more open than /ø:/. It is a lax, front, rounded vowel, with the tongue in half-open or even slightly more open position and somewhat retracted from front. The tip of the tongue touches the bottom front teeth, and if there is any contact between the sides of the back of the tongue and the upper molars it is very slight.

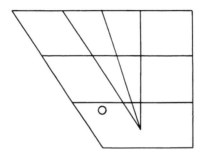

Fig. 41: German /œ/

(b) *Distribution and examples*

Spelling: ⟨ö⟩

/œ/ occurs in the initial and medial positions, but not finally:

initial: *östlich* ['œstlɪç], *Öffnung* ['œfnʊŋ], *öffentlich* ['œfn̩tlɪç], *öfters* ['œftɐs]

medial: *können* ['kœnən], *göttlich* ['gœtlɪç], *Köpfe* ['kœpfə], *Köchin* ['kœçɪn], *fördern* ['fœrdɐn], *Körper* ['kœrpɐ], *Köln* [kœln], *Böll* [bœl]

(c) *Problems for English-speaking learners*

As with /ø:/, the German vowel /œ/ causes problems for English-speakers because there is no vowel articulated in a similar place in the mouth in English. The best way to learn the pronunciation of this vowel is to start with the open German /ɛ/ or /ɛ:/ (which are between English /e/ in *bet* and /æ/ in *bat*), and to add lip-rounding. It is perhaps easiest to start with the long vowel. Take a word like *gähnen* and then add lip-rounding to the first vowel, keeping the original tongue position. The result should be a long vowel with the tongue position of /œ/; if the vowel is then pronounced short in the same context it will produce the word *gönnen* with an acceptable German /œ/ sound, even though the tongue position will probably be somewhat too far forward. This is not likely to be a problem, however, as a more centralised tongue position for the lax vowels is a natural tendency in English as well as German pronunciation. The same method can be applied to words with the short /ɛ/ like *helle*; if lip-rounding is added to the first vowel the result is the word *Hölle*.

For speakers of SBS it is often possible to start with English /æ/ as in *canon* and add lip-rounding to produce a perfectly adequate German *können*. This is course is not possible for northern speakers who have a more open variant ([a]) for SBS /æ/.

(d) *Regional variation*
As with the other front, rounded vowels there is a tendency towards unrounding in central and southern areas. This pronunciation is not recommended to the learner.

4.3.16 /ə/

(a) *Description*
/ə/ is a lax, central vowel with a tongue position between half-open and half-close and a neutral lip position. As in English, /ə/ is the most common vowel sound in German, and the pronunciation is for all practical purposes exactly the same in both languages in **non-final positions**. In final position, however, English /ə/ tends to be much more open than the German sound.

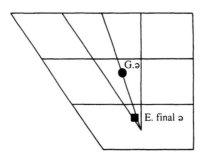

Fig. 42: German /ə/

(b) *Distribution and examples*
Spelling: ⟨e⟩
/ə/ occurs only in unstressed syllables in medial and final position; it does not occur initially in German:

🔲 **medial**, in prefixes: *berühmt* [bə'ry:mt], *bequem* [bə'kve:m], *Geschäft* [gə'ʃɛft], *geheilt* [gə'haɪlt]
medial, in unstressed final syllables: *Greuel* ['grɔʏəl], *Knäuel* ['knɔʏəl],

meinem ['maɪnəm], *neuem* ['nɔYəm], *Tränen* ['trɛ:nən], *dienen* ['di:nən],
gehen ['ge:ən], *Tieren* ['ti:rən]
final: *eine* ['aɪnə], *andere* ['andərə], *Seite* ['zaɪtə], *Liebe* ['li:bə], *ohne*
['o:nə], *sagte* ['za:ktə], *glaubte* ['glaʊptə], *Käthe* ['kɛ:tə], *Ute* ['u:tə]

(c) *Problems for English-speaking learners*

There are no problems for English-speakers with non-final German /ə/, as
the sound is pronounced just like in English. In final position, however,
English-speakers tend to have a much more open pronunciation of /ə/,
with about the same quality as the vowel in *but*. Thus, for many English
speakers, the two vowels in the words *mother, brother* are the same. This
more open final /ə/ must not be adopted in German, because it leads to
conflict with another German vowel, the vocalic allophone of /r/, ([ɐ]).
Both /ə/ and [ɐ] occur very frequently in final position in German and
they must be kept apart. For English-speakers this means that final /ə/ in
German should be more close than they are used to, approaching half-
close. In fact, it does not matter if the final German /ə/ sounds a bit like
/e/, or even /ɪ/, as this is a common pronunciation in southern parts of the
German-speaking area. For speakers of SBS (and some northern English
accents) it is useful to start with the pronunciation of some English words
ending in /ɪ/, which is quite close to the German pronunciation of final /ə/.
Compare:

English	German
bitty ['bɪtɪ]	*bitte* ['bitə]
oily ['ɔɪlɪ]	*Eule* ['ɔYlə]

The tongue position need only be centralised very slightly from English /ɪ/
to give a perfectly acceptable German /ə/, and a slight centralisation of
vowels is a natural tendency in unstressed syllables anyway.

Many southern English-speakers, of course, have a long vowel at the
end of these words (['bɪti:], ['ɔɪli:]), a pronunciation which is not helpful in
learning German final /ə/.

English has a tendency to reduce a great number of vowels to /ə/ in
unstressed syllables, for example:

Stressed syllable	Unstressed syllable
/ɒ/ *conflict* (n.) ['kɒnflɪkt]	/ə/ *conflict* (vb.) [kən'flɪkt]
/əʊ/ *protest* (n.) ['prəʊtest]	/ə/ *protest* (vb.) [prə'test]
/ɔ:/ *inform* [ɪn'fɔ:m]	/ə/ *information* [ɪnfə'meɪʃn̩]
/ʌ/ *industrial* [ɪn'dʌstrɪəl]	/ə/ *industry* ['ɪndəstrɪ]
/eɪ/ *major* ['meɪdʒə]	/ə/ *majority* [mə'dʒɒrɪtɪ]
/æ/ *adverse* ['ædvɜ:s]	/ə/ *adversity* [əd'vɜ:sɪtɪ]

This tendency should not be carried over into German, where /ə/ is only used for unstressed ⟨e⟩. The other vowels retain their quality even when unstressed (except in some weak forms; see section 6.3 below). Compare the following words in English and German:

English	German
conflict [kənˈflɪkt]	*Konflikt* [kɔnˈflɪkt]
protest [prəˈtest]	*Protest* [proˈtɛst]
information [ɪnfəˈmeɪʃn̩]	*Information* [ɪnfɔrmaˈtsi̯oːn]
industry [ˈɪndəstrɪ]	*Industrie* [ɪndʊsˈtriː]
majority [məˈdʒɔrɪtɪ]	*Majorität* [majoriˈtɛːt]
address [əˈdres]	*Adresse* [aˈdrɛsə]

(d) *Regional variation*
In southern accents /ə/ has a quality more like [e] both in unstressed prefixes (*be-*, *ge-*, etc.) and in final position.

4.3.17 [ɐ]

(a) *Description*
The final German monophthong differs from the others in that it is not a phoneme but an allophone of the consonant /r/. This vocalic allophone is a lax, central vowel with a tongue position somewhat below half-open and neutral lip position, very similar to the SBS vowel /ʌ/.

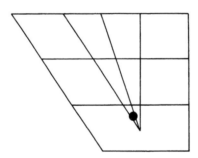

Fig. 43: German [ɐ]

(b) *Distribution and examples*
Spelling: ⟨er⟩, ⟨r⟩
[ɐ] occurs (1) as a monophthongal realisation of unstressed final /ər/, (even when followed by another consonant, e.g. *-ern*, *-ert*), and (2) as

a non-syllablic vowel [ɐ̯] for /r/ in the unstressed prefixes *er-*, *her-*, *ver-*, *zer-*, and after long vowels in final position and before consonants.

🖭 **-er:** *Lehrer* [ˈleːrɐ], *Mutter* [ˈmʊtɐ], *alter* [ˈaltɐ], *hinterlassen* [hɪntɐˈlasn̩], *interpretieren* [ɪntɐpreˈtiːrən], *Metern* [ˈmeːtɐn], *Ministers* [mɪˈnɪstɐs], *feiert* [ˈfaɪɐt]

er-: *ersetzen* [ɛɐ̯ˈzɛtsn̩], *erkennen* [ɛɐ̯ˈkɛnən], *Erfolg* [ɛɐ̯ˈfɔlk]

her-: *hervor* [hɛɐ̯ˈfoːɐ̯], *herbei* [hɛɐ̯ˈbaɪ]

ver-: *vergessen* [fɛɐ̯ˈgɛsn̩], *Versteck* [fɛɐ̯ˈʃtɛk]

zer-: *zerbrechlich* [tsɛɐ̯ˈbrɛçlɪç], *Zerstörung* [tsɛɐ̯ˈʃtøːrʊŋ]

after long vowels before consonants: *hört* [høːɐ̯t], *verliert* [fɛɐ̯ˈliːɐ̯t], *gewährte* [gəˈvɛːɐ̯tə], *bohrte* [ˈboːɐ̯tə]

after long vowels in final position: *hier* [hiːɐ̯], *nur* [nuːɐ̯], *hinterher* [hɪntɐˈheːɐ̯], *Friseur* [friˈzøːɐ̯]

(c) *Problems for English-speaking learners*

There should be no problems with this sound for speakers of SBS, as their own pronunciation of final /ə/ comes very close to German [ɐ]. In non-final positions they can substitute the SBS vowel /ʌ/ (as in *but*), although this vowel is not present in all varieties of English, of course; in many northern accents it is pronounced [ʊ], and some speakers (e.g. London) may have a pronunciation which is too close to [a], neither of which can be used for German [ɐ]. These speakers will have to use a little more care in acquiring the correct German pronunciation of [ɐ]. Some varieties of English, e.g. Scottish and Irish, have final /ər/ in words like *better* [ˈbetər]; speakers with this pronunciation will not be able to use it for German [ɐ].

The vowels /ə/ and [ɐ] occur very frequently in final position in German and must be kept distinct.

/ə/ occurs in:
nouns ending in *-e*: *Lehre*
many noun plurals: *Städte*
various adjective endings: *gute*

[ɐ] occurs in:
nouns ending in *-er*: *Lehrer*
some noun plurals: *Kinder*
various adjective endings: *guter*
comparative adjectives and adverbs: *besser*

Compare the following word pairs for making the distinction between /ə/ and [a]:

/ə/	[ɐ]
bitte ['bɪtə]	*bitter* ['bɪtɐ]
schöne ['ʃøːnə]	*schöner* ['ʃøːnɐ]
Wette ['vɛtə]	*Wetter* ['vɛtɐ]
meine ['maɪnə]	*meiner* ['maɪnɐ]
Fliege ['fliːgə]	*Flieger* ['fliːgɐ]
fette ['fɛtə]	*Vetter* ['fɛtɐ]
Größe ['grøːsə]	*größer* ['grøːsɐ]

(d)   *Regional variation*

There is great regional variation in the pronunciation of /r/ throughout the German-speaking area, and there are speakers, particularly in the south-west, who retain a consonantal pronunciation in all positions. However, the vocalic use described here is by far the most common and probably on the increase.

All varieties of German distinguish between the endings ⟨-e⟩ and ⟨-er⟩, but in southern and eastern central areas the distinction is different from that made in the north and in western central areas, as the following table shows:

	⟨-e⟩	⟨-er⟩
North	[-ə]	[-ɐ]
South	[-e]	[-ə]

For the learner, the main thing is that a distinction is made; it is of secondary importance whether the northern or the southern variety is adopted.

4.4   **The German diphthongs**

In addition to the seventeen monophthongs or pure vowels, German also has three diphthongs or vowel sounds during which there is a perceptible change in quality: /aɪ/, /aʊ/ and /ɔY/. Phonetically a diphthong consists of a relatively stable first element followed by a glide towards a second element, and it is usual to describe them by giving the starting-point and the point towards which the glide moves. The first element is clearly audible and readily recognisable, but the second is subject to great variation, and the actual duration or extent of the glide depends on the individual speaker and on the context: the glide may either go all the way to the point indicated (e.g. in careful speech), or it may stop considerably short (in fast speech, in unstressed syllables, etc.). All the German diphthongs are so-called **falling diphthongs** (G. *fallende Diphthonge*), i.e.

the first element carries most of the length and stress of the vowel sound, and there is a marked reduction in intensity during the transition to the second element.

4.4.1 /aɪ/

(a) *Description*

/aɪ/ is a glide from the position of German /a/, or sometimes a position slightly forward of this, in the direction of /ɪ/. It is only in careful speech that the glide reaches the half-close position of /ɪ/; in normal speech the tongue usually remains somewhat lower.

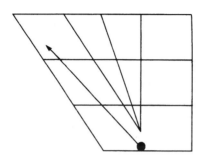

Fig. 44: German /aɪ/

(b) *Distribution and examples*

Spelling: ⟨ei⟩, ⟨ai⟩, ⟨ey⟩, ⟨ay⟩

/aɪ/ occurs in the initial, medial and final positions:

initial: *ein* [aɪn], *einzig* [ˈaɪntsɪç], *Eimer* [ˈaɪmɐ], *Eifer* [ˈaɪfɐ], *Eile* [ˈaɪlə], *Eisen* [ˈaɪzn̩]

medial: *sein* [zaɪn], *weit* [vaɪt], *klein* [klaɪn], *Reihe* [ˈraɪə], *Bayern* [ˈbaɪɐn], *Mainz* [ˈmaɪnts] *Rhein* [raɪn], *Meyer* [ˈmaɪɐ]

final: *Mai* [maɪ], *bei* [baɪ], *zwei* [tsvaɪ], *Blei* [blaɪ], *Hai* [haɪ], *Bäckerei* [bɛkəˈraɪ]

(c) *Problems for English-speaking learners*

Speaker of SBS have no great problems with German /aɪ/, as their own diphthong is rather similar to the German one described here, the main difference being that the tongue tends to be raised to a slightly closer level in German. However, there is a great deal of regional variation in the pronunciation of English /aɪ/, and those speakers whose own diphthong starts from a more central or back position ([ɜːɪ] or [ɑɪ]) should aim at an open and slightly fronted first element. The best starting-point is German /a/ (i.e. a more open vowel than SBS /ʌ/; see section 4.3.7 above). Speakers of northern varieties of English who have the pronunciation [a] for English /æ/ can quite satisfactorily use this as the starting point of German /aɪ/.

(d) Regional variation
Just as in English, there is a great deal of regional variation for this phoneme in the German-speaking countries, the most prominent deviation being south-western and Austrian varieties, which have a closer pronunciation of the whole diphthong, typical realisations being [eɪ] in the southwest and [ɛe] in Austria.

4.4.2 /aʊ/

(a) Description
/aʊ/ is a glide from the position of German /a/, or a position slightly backward of this, in the direction of /ʊ/. As with /aɪ/, the tongue frequently does not reach the half-close position of /ʊ/, but it can in careful speech. Loose lip-rounding, as is connected with the lax vowel /ʊ/, sets in during the glide.

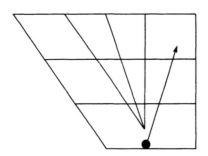

Fig. 45: German /aʊ/

(b) Distribution and examples
Spelling: ⟨au⟩
/aʊ/ occurs in the initial, medial and final positions:
initial: *auf* [aʊf], *auch* [aʊx], *Auge* [ˈaʊgə], *Aufgabe* [ˈaʊfgaːbə], *Ausdauer* [ˈaʊsdaʊɐ], *August* [aʊˈgʊst], *Augsburg* [ˈaʊksbʊrk]
medial: *Haus* [haʊs], *kaum* [kaʊm], *Glaube* [ˈglaʊbə], *Laut* [laʊt], *Dauer* [ˈdaʊɐ], *kaufen* [ˈkaʊfn̩]
final: *Bau* [baʊ], *Frau* [fraʊ], *genau* [gəˈnaʊ], *blau* [blaʊ], *grau* [graʊ], *rauh* [raʊ], *Donau* [ˈdoːnaʊ]

(c) *Problems for English-speaking learners*

Those speakers who have a very back first element in English /aʊ/, e.g. *now* [naʊ], can use this pronunciation for the German sound to too, as some German speakers also have quite a back starting-point. However, once again there are great regional differences in the pronunciation of English /aʊ/, and many speakers (e.g. in the south-east and particularly the London area) have a front vowel as a starting-point, resulting in [æʊ]. Others may have a more close front vowel as the first element and pronounce [ɛʊ] or even [eʊ]. Pronunciations with a front starting-point will not do in German, and these speakers must spend some time and effort on acquiring an acceptable German pronunciation. The best way to do this is to start with English /ɑː/ as in *father*, which for most English speakers is a back vowel, pronounce it short and then add a glide to the position of /ʊ/. If you are one of the speakers who has a front [a] even in words like *father*, you can try starting with a vowel sound which is as open and as far back as possible. When this is pronounced short, it should give a good starting-point for German /aʊ/.

(d) *Regional variation*

As with /aɪ/, speakers in south-western parts tend to have a closer pronunciation in both elements of /aʊ/. Speakers in some northern and central parts have a very open second element.

4.4.3 /ɔʏ/

(a) *Description*

The third and last of the German diphthongs, /ɔʏ/, starts from a half-close, back, loosely rounded vowel and moves in the direction of [ʏ] or [ɪ]. The lip-rounding of the first element is normally retained throughout the vowel in German, but there are also some German-speakers who

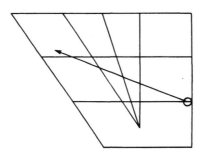

Fig. 46: German /ɔʏ/

have an unrounded second element in this diphthong, as is the case in the corresponding English diphthong /ɔɪ/ (e.g. *boy* [bɔɪ]).

(b) Distribution and examples
Spelling: ⟨eu⟩, ⟨äu⟩; also ⟨oi⟩ and ⟨oy⟩ in words of foreign origin.
/ɔʏ/ occurs in the initial, medial and final positions:
initial: *euch* [ɔʏç], *euer* [ˈɔʏɐ], *Eule* [ˈɔʏlə], *äußerst* [ˈɔʏsɐst], *Äußerung* [ˈɔʏsərʊŋ], *Europa* [ɔʏˈroːpa], *Eugen* [ˈɔʏgeːn]
medial: *deutsch* [dɔʏtʃ], *Freund* [frɔʏnt], *Leute* [ˈlɔʏtə], *Steuer* [ˈʃtɔʏɐ], *Häuser* [ˈhɔʏzɐ], *Häuschen* [ˈhɔʏsçən], *häufig* [ˈhɔʏfɪç], *läuft* [lɔʏft], *Boiler* [ˈbɔʏlɐ]
final: *neu* [nɔʏ], *treu* [trɔʏ], *Heu* [hɔʏ], *Scheu* [ʃɔʏ], *Gebräu* [gəˈbrɔʏ] ('brew'), *Allgäu* [ˈalgɔʏ], *Boy* [bɔʏ]

(c) *Problems for English-speaking learners*
The main differences between German /ɔʏ/ and the corresponding English sound are first that the German vowel normally has lip-rounding throughout and secondly that the second element is often closer and more fronted than in the English sound. These are not real problems, however, as both unrounded and slightly centralised second elements of /ɔʏ/ are to be found in German speech, too. If the English-speaking learner wishes to acquire a pronunciation with stronger lip-rounding, the sound should be practised retaining the same amount of lip-rounding as is normal for /ɔ/ in German, which as we have said is stronger than for the corresponding English sound, throughout the diphthong.

(d) *Regional variation*
Some southern and central speakers pronounce /ɔʏ/ more like /aɪ/, leading to homophones such as *Eule* and *Eile* [ˈaɪlə]. In some northern and central parts there is a tendency towards a much more open second element ([ɔø] or [ɔe]).

4.5 Nasal vowels

Nasal vowels occur in some French loan words in German, e.g. *Parfum* [parˈfœ̃], *Pension* [pãˈzi̯oːn], *Beton* [bɛˈtɔ̃], *Elan* [eˈlãː]. A nasal vowel is pronounced with the same tongue position as the corresponding oral vowel, but the soft palate is lowered, allowing air to escape through the nasal cavity as well as through the mouth.
    However, all common borrowings from French have been gradually assimilated into the German sound system and are now most commonly pronounced without nasal vowels, e.g. for our examples above: [parˈfyːm]

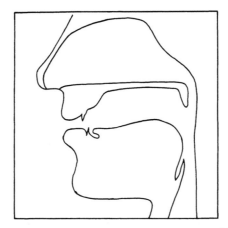

Fig. 47: Position of organs of speech for [ã]

(spellt *Parfüm*), [paŋ'zi̯oːn] or [pɛn'zi̯oːn], [be'tɔŋ] and [e'laːn], and nasal vowels are therefore restricted to foreign names of persons and places, and less common loan words.

Nasal vowels thus have a very marginal status in German, and as they do not belong to the native pronunciation they will not be treated in detail here.

4.6 Summary and comparison of German and English vowel articulations

We can summarise the similarities and differences between the German and English (SBS) vowels in the following diagrams, which depict separately the monophthongs and diphthongs of the two languages.

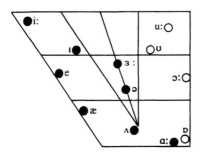

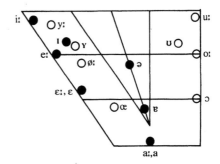

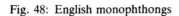

Fig. 48: English monophthongs   Fig. 49: German monophthongs

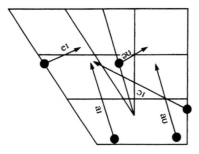

Fig. 50: English closing diphthongs

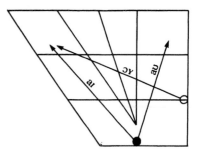

Fig. 51: German diphthongs

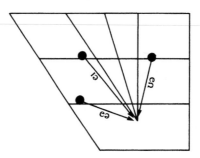

Fig. 52: English centring diphthongs

5

Stress and intonation

5.1 Word stress

In the pronunciation of German not all syllables are produced with the same force. Both in utterances and in individual words certain syllables are more prominent than others. These syllables are said to bear the **stress** (or **accent**, G. *der Akzent*). Phonetically stress is a complex phenomenon involving greater force in the production of the syllable, a longer duration of vowels and consonants, and a change in the pitch of the voice. The combined effect of these different factors is a greater acoustic prominence of the stressed syllable compared to unstressed ones in the same utterance. In phonetic notation a raised dash (') is used to indicate that the following syllable is stressed, e.g. 'Hamburg, Ber'lin, stressed on the first and second syllable respectively. This is known as the **primary stress** (G. *der Hauptakzent*), i.e. the most prominent syllable in the word. A weaker or **secondary stress** (G. *der Nebenakzent*) is marked with a lower dash ( ), e.g. 'Fußball‚mannschaft. **Unstressed syllables** (G. *unbetonte Silben*) are left unmarked in phonetic notation.

The stress pattern to be found in words is known as **word stress** or **lexical stress** (G. *der Wortakzent*). In German, as in English, this is **fixed for each individual word**. That means that it does not vary in different forms of words (as in Russian or Serbo-Croat), nor does it invariably occur on the same syllable in all words as it does e.g. in Finnish and Hungarian (on the first syllable) or Polish or Italian (on the penultimate syllable).

For English-speakers it is not the phenomenon of stress as such but the placement of stress in German words that causes problems, and we will now look at this in greater detail.

In words of one syllable (**monosyllabic words**, G. *einsilbige Wörter*), there is, of course, no doubt as to the placement of the stress. In words of two or more syllables (**polysyllabic words**, G. *mehrsilbige Wörter*), the place of the stress can be determined in German with the help of a fairly small number of rules. For a description of stress placement in German we will need to differentiate between native German words and foreign words, and also between simple and derived words on the one hand, and compound words on the other.

5.1.1 Native German words

(a) Simple words
Simple native German words (and many well-established loan words) are stressed on the first syllable of the root (G. *Stammsilbenbetonung*): *'Schwester, 'Wiese, 'Hügel, 'gestern, 'wenig, 'sieben, 'gegen.*

(b) Suffixes
The position of the primary stress is usually not affected by the addition of suffixes; in longer words a secondary stress may be added:

> *'fahren, 'Fahrer, 'Fahrerin*
> *'Arbeit, 'arbeiten, 'arbeitete*
> *'hoffen, 'Hoffnung, 'hoffnungs los, 'Hoffnungs losigkeit*

There are exceptions: the suffix *-ei* is always stressed, e.g. *Bäcke'rei, Träume'rei*, and there are some individual variations, e.g. *'Gegenwart – 'gegenwärtig* or *gegen'wärtig; Luther* ['lʊtɐ] – *'lutherisch* or *lu'therisch*.

(c) Unstressed prefixes
The prefixes *be-, ge-, ent-, er-, ver-*, and *zer-* are always unstressed: *be'deuten, ge'lacht, ent'halten, er'langen, ver'stehen, zer'stören*. This also applies in nouns derived from verbs containing these prefixes: *Be'deutung, Ver'stand, Zer'störung*.

(d) Stressed prefixes
Other prefixes, which also occur on their own as independent words (prepositions, particles or nouns), are stressed, e.g.: *ab-, an-, auf-, aus-, bei-, da-, dar-, ein-, her-, mit-, nach-, vor-, weg-, zu-*, e.g.: *'angeben, 'abfahren, 'ausgehen, 'mitmachen, 'nachgeben, 'weglaufen, 'zustimmen*. Forms such as these are sometimes regarded as compounds because both elements occur as independent words, and in fact they do have the typical compound stress (primary stress on the first element). However, in common with most descriptions of German, they will be regarded as prefixes here. Two other stressed prefixes are *ur-* and *erz-* as in *'Ursprung, 'Ursache, 'Erzengel, 'Erzbischof*.

(e) *Prefixes which can be stressed or unstressed*

A third group of prefixes are either stressed or unstressed: *durch-*, *um-*, *über-*, *unter-*, *wider-*. If the prefix is separable, it is stressed, otherwise it is unstressed, e.g. *ich setze über* from ˈ*übersetzen*, but *ich überˈsetze* from *überˈsetzen*. The different stress patterns are associated with different meanings of the words, e.g.:

ˈ*übersetzen*, 'to cross over'	*überˈsetzen*, 'to translate'
ˈ*durchsetzen*, 'to carry through'	*durchˈsetzen*, 'to intersperse with'
ˈ*umgehen*, 'to circulate''	*umˈgehen*, 'to go round'
ˈ*unterschlagen*, 'to cross (e.g. legs)'	*unterˈschlagen*, 'to embezzle'

Nouns created from these verbs by means of a suffix retain the stress pattern of the verb, e.g. ˈ*Durchsetzung*, *Umˈgehung*, but those without a suffix always have the stress on the prefix, e.g.: ˈ*Umzug*, ˈ*Unterschied*.

(f) *The prefixes miß- and un-*

The prefixes *miß-* and *un-* have variable stress patterns.

miß-: the verb root is stressed when *miß-* is added to a simple (underived) verb: *mißˈfallen*, *mißˈbrauchen*, *mißˈlingen*, etc. In nouns and adjectives and also in verbs containing another prefix, however, the stress is on *miß*: ˈ*Mißerfolg*, ˈ*Mißverständnis*, ˈ*mißmutig* ('sullen'), ˈ*mißverstehen*, etc.

un-: in nouns, verbs and most adjectives the prefix *un-* is stressed: ˈ*Unglück*, ˈ*Ungeheuer*, ˈ*Unsinn*; *beˈunruhigen*, *verˈunsichern*, *verˈunglücken*; ˈ*unbeliebt*, ˈ*unbegrenzt*, ˈ*uneben*, ˈ*ungenau*. However, there are some adjectives with *un-* in which the stress is on the root. These are cases in which the addition of *un-* to an adjective involves a clear change of meaning, e.g. *unerˈhört*, 'enormous' (compare ˈ*unerhört*, 'unanswered'), or adjectives which do not exist without the prefix *un-*: *unˈschätzbar* ('incalculable'), *unˈsagbar* ('unspeakable'), *unumˈstößlich* ('irrefutable'). Where the primary stress is on the root, the prefix *un-* may be given a secondary stress if there is a further prefix between *un-* and the root: ˌ*unverˈgeßlich*, ˌ*unerˈmüdlich*, ˌ*unbeˈschreiblich*.

5.1.2 **Foreign words**

In foreign words (i.e. words borrowed from other languages, principally Latin, Greek and French), the stress is usually on the final or penultimate syllable. Many foreign words are immediately recognisable on account of their endings (see, for example, the lists below), but this is not always the case, and the learner will sometimes have to consult a dictionary (either a pronouncing dictionary or a good general dictionary) in order to be absolutely sure of the stress pattern of a word.

(a) *Final stress*
There are a large number of endings which normally require stress on the final syllable:

-al	*for'mal, to'tal*
-ar/-är	*Bibliothe'kar, revolutio'när*
-ant/-ent	*Demon'strant, Assis'tent* (but note *'Leutnant* and *'Orient*)
-anz/-enz	*Rele'vanz, Assis'tenz*
-ell	*aktu'ell, for'mell*
-est	*Po'dest, Pro'test*
-ie	*Demokra'tie, Philoso'phie, Zeremo'nie* (but note *'Studie* ['ʃtu:di̯ə])
-ion	*Informa'tion, Produk'tion*
-ist	*Poli'zist, Rea'list*
-iv	*aggres'siv, impul'siv* (but note *'positiv, 'negativ, 'Nominativ* with initial stress)
-tät	*Universi'tät, Reali'tät*
-ukt	*Pro'dukt, Via'dukt*
-ur	*Architek'tur, Litera'tur, Na'tur*

Further examples with endings requiring final stress are: *Kon'takt, Me'tall, Fa'san* ('pheasant'), *Konsu'lat, Mati'nee, Biblio'thek, In'sekt, Pa'ket, Fri'seur, Konf'likt, Mono'pol, Symp'tom, grandi'os, skanda'lös, Insti'tut.*

Note the following words with final stress: *Trans'fer, oppor'tun, Ju'wel, Te'nor, Kame'rad,* and also some North German place-names, *Ber'lin, Schwe'rin* (both with a long vowel in the final syllable: [-i:n]).

(b) *Penultimate stress*
Other foreign suffixes, mainly those with *schwa* ([ə]) or short [ɪ] or [ʊ] in the final syllable, have the stress on the penultimate syllable. They include:

-abel/-ibel	*prakti'kabel, sen'sibel*
-ade	*Prome'nade, Marme'lade, Schoko'lade*
-age	*Bla'mage, Pas'sage*
-elle	*Frika'delle, Ta'belle*
-ieren	*spa'zieren, stu'dieren*
-ik	*Pho'netik, Gram'matik* (but note *Mu'sik, Katho'lik, Poli'tik,* etc., with a long final vowel)

-ismus	*Soziaˈlismus, Orgaˈnismus*
-itis	*Bronˈchitis, Hepaˈtitis*
-oge	*Sozioˈloge, Theoˈloge*
-or	*Diˈrektor, Ventiˈlator, ˈAutor*
-ose	*Narˈkose* ('anaesthetic'), *Hypˈnose*

Further examples with endings taking penultimate stress are: *Griˈmasse* ('grimace'), *Freˈgatte* ('frigate'), *Geˈnese* ('genesis'), *Delikaˈtesse, Paˈlette, Masˈseuse, Invaˈlide, Maˈschine, Anaˈlyse*.

Note the following words with penultimate stress: *Miˈnister, Minisˈterium, Triˈbüne* ('grandstand').

(c) Changes in stress patterns

Just as with native German words, the addition of inflectional endings does not usually affect the stress pattern of foreign words, nor does the formation of feminine nouns by means of the suffix *-in*, e.g. *Demonˈstranten, Informaˈtionen, Poliˈzistin*.

The exception to this rule is the suffix *-or*, which requires penultimate stress when inflectional endings or the suffix *-in* are added: *Diˈrektor/ Direkˈtoren/Direkˈtorin, ˈAutor/Auˈtoren/Auˈtorin, ˈTraktor/Trakˈtoren*. Note *ˈMotor* or *Moˈtor*, but always *Moˈtoren*.

However, changes of stress pattern occur regularly when derivational suffixes are added to foreign words. The native suffixes *-er* (often *-aner*) and *-isch*, which are frequently added to foreign words, usually require penultimate stress, and foreign suffixes take either penultimate or final stress, as was seen above. As the same root can appear with different suffixes, we find groups or families of words with the same root but different stress patterns, e.g.

> *ˈJapan – Jaˈpaner – jaˈpanisch*
> *ˈAfrika – Afriˈkaner – afriˈkanisch*
> *Sozioˈloge – sozioˈlogisch – Sozioloˈgie*
> *Demokˈrat – demokˈratisch – Demokraˈtie*
> *senˈsibel – Sensibiliˈtät – sensibiliˈsieren*
> *Muˈsik – musiˈkalisch – Musikaliˈtät – ˈMusiker* (this last word has adopted the native German stress pattern)
> *Maˈschine – maschiˈnell – Maschineˈrie*
> *Taˈbelle – tabelˈlarisch* ('tabular')

5.1.3 **Compounds**

Compounds are words that are made up of elements which themselves occur as independent words, e.g. *Bahnhof, Hochhaus* (*Bahn, Hof, hoch* and *Haus* are all words in their own right). The general rule for stress placement in German compounds is that the elements of the compound retain their original stress patterns, but that the first element has the primary stress and subsequent elements have a secondary stress. The secondary stress is normally suppressed in short compounds where it would be adjacent to the primary stress. Examples of the most common types (noun and adjective compounds) are:

ˈBahnhof, ˈHochhaus, ˈFrühstück, ˈHauptstraße, Geˈsichtspunkt, Beˈsuchszeit, ˈbarfuß, ˈviereckig, ˈherzkrank.

ˈAutoˌbahn, ˈBundesˌkanzler, Maˈschinenˌöl, Geˈmüseˌhändler, Fabˈrikbeˌsitzer, Faˈmilienˌname, ˈselbstbeˌwußt, ˈliebensˌwürdig, ˈwünschensˌwert, ˈgeistesˌkrank.

ˈFußballverˌein, ˈKrankenhausverˌwaltung ('hospital administration'), ˈLehrerˌausbildung ('teacher training'), ˈArbeitslosenverˌsicherung, ˈBundestagsˌabgeordnete, Verˈständnisˌschwierigkeiten, geˈsundheitsˌschädigend, tradiˈtionsbeˌwußt.

Verb compounds (comparatively few in number) also have the primary stress on the first element, e.g. ˈachtgeben, geˈwährleisten, ˈhaltmachen, ˈstattfinden, ˈteilnehmen.

There are a number of exceptions of this general rule, as follows.

(a) Multiple stress
Co-ordinating compounds, which consist of two parts of equal rank and are generally joined by a hyphen, have multiple stress, i.e. primary stress on each element: ˈBaden-ˈWürttemberg, ˈKlaus-ˈDieter, ˈdeutsch-franˈzösisch, ˈblau-ˈweiß, ˈschwarz-ˈrot-ˈgold, ˈhöflich-reserˈviert, ˈSchauspieler-Regisˈseur.

Multiple stress also occurs when the first element(s) serve to give emotional emphasis to the meaning of the final element: ˈblutˈjung ('extremely young'), ˈMordsˈkerl ('terrific fellow'), ˈTotenˈstille ('dead silence'), ˈtotˈsicher ('dead certain'), ˈkohlˈrabenˈschwarz ('jet black'), ˈjammerˈschade ('a great pity'), ˈmutterˈseelenalˈlein ('quite alone'). The same stress pattern is found with the prefixes *erz-*, *un-* and *ur-* when they are used with an intensifying meaning: ˈerzkaˈtholisch ('ultra-Catholic'), ˈunˈglaublich (note English ˈunbeˈlievable with similar stress pattern), ˈurˈalt ('ancient').

(b) Stress on second element
There are a relatively small number of compound nouns which have their primary stress on the second element: *Jahrˈzehnt* ('decade'), *Jahrˈhundert*,

Jahr'tausend, *Pfingst'sonntag* ('Whit Sunday'), *Oster'montag*, *Kar'freitag* ('Good Friday').

These include a small group which have an adjective, numeral or quantifier as their first element: *Grün'donnerstag* ('Maundy Thursday'), *Schwarz'weißfernsehen*, *Rot'kreuzfahne* ('Red Cross flag'), *Alt'weibersommer* (Indian summer'), *Drei'königsfest* ('Epiphany'), *Zwei'zimmerwohnung*, *Zwei'drittelmehrheit*, *Drei'groschenoper* ('Threepenny Opera'), *Elf'meter* ('penalty kick'), *Acht'stundentag*.

There are also some place-names with this stress pattern: *Bremer'haven*, *Trave'münde*, *Saar'brücken*.

Adverbial and prepositional compounds frequently have the stress on the second element, e.g.: *darauf'hin*, *dement'sprechend*, *hier'her*, *im'stande*, *so'fort*, *um'sonst*, *zu'nächst*, *zwischen'durch*, or they have variable stress, depending on their position in sentences, e.g. *nach'her* or *'nachher*, *dort'hin* or *'dorthin*.

5.2 Sentence stress and rhythm

(The numbered sentences which follow can all be found on the accompanying tape.)

Words are, of course, not usually used on their own, but in utterances. Not every word in an utterance is stressed: in general the words which are most important from the point of view of the meaning are stressed and the others are unstressed. The allocation of stress to certain syllables in utterances is known as **sentence stress** (G. *der Satzakzent*). If the sentence

(1)   Gestern hat er ein neues Fahrrad gekauft.

is pronounced with normal stress, the words *'gestern*, *'neues*, *'Fahrrad* and *ge'kauft* are likely to be stressed, while *hat*, *er* and *ein* will remain unstressed. The words which normally receive stress are those which contain most of the meaning, the **lexical** or **content words**: nouns, main verbs, adjectives and most adverbs. On the other hand, the words whose main function is to express the grammatical relationship between lexical words in a sentence, the **grammatical** or **function words**, are not usually stressed. Grammatical words include all articles, pronouns, prepositions, auxiliary verbs, conjunctions and some short adverbs.

In German, as in English, it is the stressed syllables which determine the rhythm of speech. Stressed syllables together with the following unstressed syllables form **stress groups** or **feet** (G. *der Takt*), each of which takes approximately the same time in an utterance, regardless of the number of unstressed syllables it contains. The sentence given above can be divided into stress groups as follows:

(1a) | 'Gestern hat er ein | 'neues | 'Fahrrad ge | 'kauft |

The number of unstressed syllables following the stress in these stress groups varies (4, 1, 2, 0), yet the interval between the stresses is aproximately the same in each case. This is achieved by shortening the syllables, particularly the unstressed syllables, in stress groups containing a large number of them. Another way of maintaining the rhythm is by making sure that the number of unstressed syllables in neighbouring stress groups does not vary too much. This can be achieved by adding stresses to normally unstressed grammatical words, or leaving the stress off lexical words if this is required by the rhythm.

Languages like English and German are said to be **stress-timed** languages (G. *akzentzählende Sprachen*), in contrast to others, like French and Spanish, in which each syllable has approximately the same duration, and which are thus referred to as **syllable-timed** (G. *silbenzählend*). The effect of fast speech in a syllable-timed language is sometimes compared to machine-gun fire by speakers of English and German, who are not used to each syllable being given the same weight. As the rhythm of German is based on the same principles as that of English, it should not cause any problems for the English-speaking learner.

Some problems do, however, arise for English-speakers because of a phenomenon closely related to rhythm. In stress-timed languages stressed syllables receive much greater articulatory effort than unstressed syllables, and as a consequence the latter show reductions in both consonant and vowel sounds, ranging from a slight weakening to a complete loss of sounds. It is this tendency which is responsible for the so-called 'weak forms' encountered in both English and German. Although this phenomenon is common to English and German, it is important to realise that there are differences in the actual reductions which occur in the two languages and also in the circumstances under which they occur. The question of reductions in unstressed syllables is treated in detail in chapter 6.

5.3 Intonation

The pitch of the voice is determined by the speed at which the vocal cords vibrate. When we speak, the pitch of our voice does not stay constant, but is continually changing, rising and falling. We are so used to these changes in pitch that we do not normally notice them; on the other hand we immediately notice when they are missing, that is when we hear a voice with constant pitch, e.g. a voice synthesised by a computer or a speaker with an artificial larynx. The variations of pitch over whole utterances in natural language are referred to as intonation.

The pitch of the voice rises and falls in singing as well, of course, but in a different way. In singing the pitch remains steady for the duration of a note and then moves up or down in steps to the following notes. In intonation, on the other hand, the movement in pitch does not take place in the form of steps between predetermined notes, but in the form of continuous glides. It is rare for the voice to be held at a constant level for an appreciable amount of time in speech.

The rules of intonation are much less strict than for other areas of language, e.g. grammar or stress patterns, and speakers have considerable freedom of choice as to the intonation they use with any utterance. But this does not mean that intonation is unsystematic, and, in spite of the possible variations, a number of basic intonation patterns, sometimes known as 'tunes', can be established. The aim of this short description of German intonation will be to establish what the intonation patterns of German are, how they are used, and how they differ from the English patterns.

Voice is not produced separately for individual sounds, but continuously throughout an utterance, interrupted only by voiceless sounds, which are in fact a minority of the sounds of speech. If we ignore these interruptions for voiceless sounds, we can represent the variations in the pitch of the voice as a continuous line between two parallel lines indicating the upper and lower limits of the speaker's range, as in the following example:

(2)

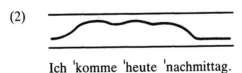

Ich 'komme 'heute 'nachmittag.

You can observe the changes in pitch more easily by saying an utterance like example 2 and then humming the same intonation pattern, which in fact is pronouncing all the syllables as [m]: [m'mm'mm'mmm]. You should be able to hear a noticeable downward change of pitch between the first and second syllables of *nachmittag*.

It is in fact more helpful if our diagram indicates not only the changes of pitch but also the syllables on which they occur, so we will represent intonation patterns by a series of dashes (for stressed syllables) and dots (for unstressed syllables), as in example 2a:

(2a)
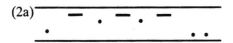

Ich 'komme 'heute `nachmittag.

In addition to these intonation diagrams, there is a second system of notation which can be seen in the text of example 2a above. This system makes use of **intonation** (or tonetic) **marks** (G. *Intonationszeichen*), ' indicating that the following syllable is stressed and ` indicating that there is a fall in pitch on the following syllable. Further intonation marks will be introduced at the appropriate places in this chapter, and they are summarised on p. xv. This notation system is considerably simpler than the full intonation diagrams and is particularly well suited to indicating the intonation of longer passages of speech.

5.3.1 Tone groups

In the above example, the intonation pattern fits together neatly with the grammatical unit of the sentence. This is frequently, but by no means always, the case, since intonation is quite separate from grammar. The unit within which intonation operates is a unit of meaning or communication which we shall call the **tone group**. Tone groups, sometimes also known as **intonation groups** or **sense groups** (G. *die Tongruppe* or *die Intonationseinheit*), are groups of words which belong closely together and which for the speaker form a single unit or piece of information. The speaker indicates that a group of words is being regarded as a single unit by saying them with a single intonation pattern. Pauses are not usual within a tone group, but they may occur between tone groups.

In spite of the fact that they are units of communication and not grammatical units, there are a number of ways in which tone groups correspond to grammatical units. In the following examples, a double bar ‖ is used to separate tone groups from each other.

(a) **Simple sentences** form separate tone groups: ‖ *Es ist spät.* ‖ *Laß uns nach Hause gehen.* ‖ *Wir müssen morgen früh aufstehen.* ‖
(b) **Co-ordinate clauses** (introduced by *und* or *aber*) usually form separate tone groups: ‖ *Wir wollten das Buch kaufen,* ‖ *aber wir hatten nicht genug Geld mit.* ‖
(c) **Non-restrictive (or non-defining) appositional phrases**: ‖ *Wir haben dein Lieblingsbild* ‖ *den Rembrandt gesehen.* ‖
(d) ***Ausrahmung*** (items placed outside of the syntactic 'frame' of the

sentence): ‖ *Wir wollen ihn besuchen* ‖ *am Sonntag.* ‖ Compare: ‖ *Wir wollen ihn am Sonntag besuchen.* ‖ with one tone group.

(e) **Ja** und **Nein** often have their own groups: ‖ *Ja,* ‖ *wir kommen mit.* ‖ ‖ *Nein,* ‖ *ich kann es nicht finden.* ‖

(f) **Tag questions** (which in German are not clauses but items like *nicht wahr, nicht,* or *oder*): ‖ *Ein phantastisches Gebäude,* ‖ *nicht wahr?* ‖

(g) **Subordinate clauses** usually form separate tone groups: ‖ *Wenn ihr kommt,* ‖ *fahren wir zusammen in die Stadt.* ‖ There are a number of exceptions to this last point, though, especially noun clauses, which are well integrated in their sentences and therefore do not usually form a separate tone group: ‖ *Ich hoffe, daß er kommt.* ‖ ‖ *Ich verstehe, was du meinst.* ‖

In the final analysis, however, it is not the grammatical units which determine the number of tone groups in an utterance, but rather the communicative intention of the speaker. The principles for determining the number of tone groups in an utterance are very much the same for English and German, so the English-speaking learner is unlikely to have any problems here.

5.3.2 The nucleus

A tone group contains one or more stress groups, which, as we have said, consists of a stressed syllable together with the following unstressed syllables. In every tone group, one stressed syllable will stand out as being more prominent than the rest: this is known as the **nucleus** or nuclear stress (G. *der Nukleus* or *die Tonsilbe*). The principal reason for the prominence of this syllable in the tone group is that the most notice-able change in pitch takes place on or immediately following the nucleus. As we have seen, a change in pitch is one of the factors (along with loudness and duration) which characterise stressed syllables, so non-nuclear stresses also involve a change in pitch, but this is smaller than that associated with the nucleus. In practice it is not difficult for the hearer to identify which syllable in a tone group is the most prominent and there-fore the nucleus.

We can distinguish different types of nucleus on the basis of the varia-tions in pitch which are associated with them. The most common types of nucleus in German have falling and rising pitch. An example of the **fall**, i.e. a jump down from a relatively high pitch to a considerably lower one, was given in (2a), which is repeated here:

(2a)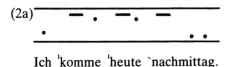

Ich 'komme 'heute `nachmittag.

The second type of nucleus is a **rise** (intonation mark ´), i.e. an upward movement from a relatively low pitch as in (3):

(3)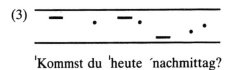

'Kommst du 'heute ´nachmittag?

In addition to these two most common types of nucleus, there are other patterns which involve level pitch or combinations of the fall and the rise. We will look at these in greater detail in the discussion of the individual intonation patterns in section 5.3.4 below.

5.3.3 The structure of the tone group

Every tone group contains a nucleus. It follows from this that, if there is only one syllable in the tone group, this syllable must contain the nucleus, as in the following examples:

(4)

`Nein.

(5)

´Ich?

Most tone groups are longer than just one syllable, however. They can contain further syllables both before and after the nucleus. Before the nucleus we have the **head** (G. *der Pränukleus*), which extends from the first stressed syllable to the syllable before the nucleus (italicised in the example):

(6)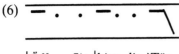

'Öffnen Sie 'bitte die `Tür.

(7)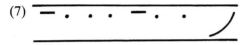

'Fahren Sie mit 'Rainer nach `Köln?

The most common type of head in German has a high-level pitch, as in the examples above. However, the pitch does not remain absolutely constant, as the diagram might suggest, but rises slightly on the stressed syllables and falls again on the unstressed syllables, so that there is a slight undulating movement of pitch on the head. Thus a more accurate representation of sentence 6 would be 6a:

(6a)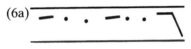

'Öffnen Sie 'bitte die `Tür.

The movement of pitch on the head is considerably smaller than that associated with the nucleus, so it can be disregarded in the following diagrams, as long as we remember that the high-level stresses do not mean absolutely constant pitch.

Any unstressed syllables before the head are referred to as the **prehead**, cf. examples 8 and 9:

(8)

Sie sind 'herzlich will`kommen.

(9)

Aber die Be'deutung ist `klar.

The prehead normally starts on a low to mid-level of pitch, so there is a jump up to the first syllable of the head.

Finally, we can also have syllables following the nucleus, which are known as the **tail** (G. *der Nachlauf*):

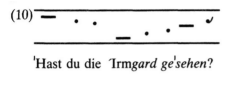

(10)

'Hast du die 'Irm*gard ge*'*sehen?*

(11)

Um `sieben ,*sollten wir an,kommen.*

The pitch level of the tail depends on the nucleus preceding it and is therefore best dealt with in section 5.3.4 together with the intonation patterns.

The following sentence illustrates the four parts of the tone group:

(12)	Wir	'haben 'heute das	`Schloß	be,sucht
	Prehead	Head	Nucleus	Tail

5.3.4 The intonation patterns of German

The nucleus is the most important and the most variable part of the tone group. There are variations in other parts of the tone group, but it is principally the variations in the nucleus which determine the different intonation patterns to be found in German. The three basic types of nucleus in German have falling, rising and level pitch respectively, in addition to which we have two intonation patterns in which the fall and the rise are combined. These five intonation patterns are described below in respect of their form and their function (or meaning).

While the description of the form (i.e. the actual changes in pitch which take place) is relatively straightforward, the functions are much more difficult to describe, partly because this is a more complex area, and partly because there are greater regional and indeed personal variations in the functions of intonation patterns than there are in the forms. A basic distinction is the one made by Fox (1984) between appeal and assertion. Rising intonation patterns make an **appeal** to the listener to respond in some way to what the speaker is saying. This is particularly obvious in their use in questions, but rising patterns can also be used with other types of utterance, e.g. statements or exclamations, indicating that a response from the listener is expected. Falling patterns do not function as appeals in this way, but are **assertions**, that is they indicate that the speaker regards the utterance as self-sufficient, not requiring completion by the listener.

Over and above this basic distinction, the intonation pattern gives the hearer information on the emotional attitude of the speaker, for instance friendliness, personal commitment or indifference. This attitudinal function of intonation is particularly subject to regional and personal variation, which means that it is very difficult to make statements which are universally applicable to all speakers of German. We will thus restrict ourselves to the most general and widely applicable features in the following description.

(a) *The fall*

The pitch of the voice falls sharply either within a syllable or between two syllables from a relatively high point to a lower one:

(13)

`Gut.

(14)

Ich 'komme so`fort.

(15)

Ich `komme.

(16)

`Schade!

(17)
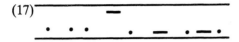

Wir haben `diesen ͵Film ge͵sehen.

In examples 13 and 14, in which the nucleus is on the last syllable, the fall has to take place within that syllable, but, if there is a tail following the nucleus, the fall usually takes the form of a jump down from the level of the nucleus to a much lower level for the tail, which continues at a low level of pitch until the end of the tone group (as in example 17). The German fall, whether within a syllable or from one syllable to the next, tends to be much steeper and more abrupt than the corresponding English pattern, which is more of a gentle glide than an energetic jump; compare the following examples:

German   **English**

(18)

`Gut.                                      `Good.

(19)

Ich `komme.                                I'm `coming.

The use of the German fall
The fall is assertive in character, i.e. it indicates that the speaker regards the utterance as complete and is not appealing for a reaction from the listener (see above). It is the most common nuclear pattern in the following types of utterance:

(a) statements (example 20);
(b) commands (example 21);
(c) questions introduced by a question word. These are sometimes referred to as 'W-Fragen' in German and 'wh-questions' in English, as most of the question words begin with these letters, e.g. *was, wer, wo, wie, wann* (example 22):

(20) Du 'hast jetzt ge`nug ge͵arbeitet.
(21) 'Gehen Sie 'bitte 'nicht `weg!
(22) Wann 'kommst du nach `Hause?

Problems for English-speaking learners
The use of the fall is very similar in German and English. The main difference between the two languages is in the realisation of the fall, which is much steeper in German than in English. English-speaking learners should concentrate on keeping the nucleus high before a tail in German, jumping down in pitch to the following syllable, and should aim for a steep fall within the syllable if the nucleus is at the end of the tone group.

(b) *The rise*
When the nucleus is on the final syllable of the tone group, the rise is simply the opposite of the fall: a sharp movement from a low point to a higher one:

(23)

´Hier?

(24)

´Wo?

However, when the tone group has a tail, the rise differs from the fall in one important respect: instead of a sudden movement between the nucleus and the first syllable of the tail, the rise takes place much more gently, starting on the nucleus and continuing throughout the whole of the tail.

(25)

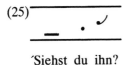

´Siehst du ihn?

(26)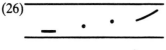

ˈKommt ihr denn ˈjetzt?

Where a rising nucleus is preceded by a head, there must be a sudden jump downwards before the nucleus, so that the pitch is low for the start of the rise:

(27)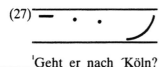

ˈGeht er nach ˈKöln?

(28)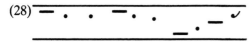

ˈWollen wir ˈheute ins ˈKino ˈgehen?

The use of the German rise
In contrast to the fall, the rise implies an appeal for a response from the listener. It is used in:

(a) Yes/No questions, i.e. questions not introduced by a question word, which can be answered by 'Yes' or 'No' (examples 29 and 30);
(b) questions introduced by a question word in order to make them sound more polite and friendly (example 31);
(c) questions introduced by a question word indicating that the speaker has not heard or does not believe what has just been said (example 32);
(d) sometimes also in non-final tone groups, indicating that the speaker has not finished, but wishes to continue speaking, although the level pattern is more common in German here (example 33).

Examples are:

(29) ˈKommst du ˈmit?
(30) ˈDieter war in Iˈtalien?
(Note that it is the rising intonation which makes this sentence into a question; with falling intonation it would be a statement.)
(31) Was ˈwillst du ˈmachen?

(With rising intonation this sentence expresses greater empathy and interest on the part of the speaker than the same sentence said with falling intonation.)

(32) ʾWievïel hat das ʾBuch geʾkostet?

(33) Wenn wir nach ʾHause ʾkommen, (essen wir was)

(This sentence is more likely to be said with level intonation; see below.)

Problems for English-speaking learners
As with the fall, the pitch also tends to rise more steeply in German than in English. However, differences between German and English are smaller for the rise than for the fall, and this intonation pattern does not generally cause problems for English-speaking learners.

(c) *Level pitch*
The third type of nucleus in German has **level** and mid to high pitch (intonation mark ˉ). Unlike the fall and the rise, there is no movement of pitch directly on or following the nucleus, so that this nucleus is distinguished from the other two types by the **absence of movement.** In tone groups which contain a head, though, there is also a step up from a lower level of pitch immediately preceding the nucleus, which helps to identify this pattern. In order to achieve this characteristic step up to a higher level of pitch, the head must drop down immediately before the nucleus, as in example 36.

(34) ‗

ˉJa (non-committal answer, used e.g. on the telephone to let the speaker know the hearer is still there)

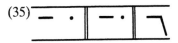

ˉAchtung, ˉFertig, ˎLos! (Ready, steady, go)

Wenn du ʾheute ʾnachmittag ˉkommst, (wirst du ihn treffen)

The use of the level pattern
The level pattern has two separate functions in German. First it is used
(more frequently than the rise) to indicate that the utterance is incomplete
(a–c), and secondly in (d):

(a)   non-final tone groups (example 37);
(b)   the first part of questions containing an alternative (example 38);
(c)   lists for all but the final element (example 39);
(d)   greetings and other short ritual expressions to express a non-
      committal attitude on the part of the speaker (examples 40 and 41).

Examples are:

(37)   Wenn wir nach ⁻Hause 'kommen, `essen wir was.
(38)   'Möchten Sie ⁻Tee oder `Kaffee?
(39)   Wir 'kaufen ⁻Butter, ⁻Milch, ⁻Eier und `Brot.
(40)   (guten) ⁻Morgen.
(41)   ⁻Danke.

Problems for English-speaking learners
A level intonation pattern is sometimes used for non-committal greetings
in English as well as German, so this use will not cause any problems
for English-speakers. However, it is much more common to use rising
intonation in non-final tone groups in English, so English-speakers must
practise the German use of level intonation in this context.

(d)   The rise–fall
The rise–fall (intonation mark ^) can be regarded as a variant of the fall
in which this is preceded by a rise. For the rise-fall the pitch starts at a
mid or low level and rises before it falls sharply to a low level. The fall is
either a jump down from one syllable to the next or a steep fall within the
syllable at the end of the tone group.

(42)

^wunderbar!

(43)

^danke!

(44)

ˆGerd!

(45)

Es hat geˆklappt!

The use of the German rise–fall
The rise–fall expresses a greater personal involvement, e.g. enthusiasm, on the part of the speaker than would be the case with the simple fall. It is used in:

(a)   statements (example 46);
(b)   commands (example 47);
(c)   questions introduced by a question word (example 48);
(d)   exclamations (example 49).

Examples are:

(46)   Ich 'hab' geˆwonnen!
(47)   'Komm doch heute ˆabend!
(48)   Wie 'hast du das geˆmacht?
(49)   phanˆtastisch!

Problems for English-speaking learners
As with the simple fall and rise, the changes of pitch in German tend to be more abrupt than in English. If the German intonation has been mastered for the simple rise and fall, there should be no problems with the rise–fall. The use of the rise–fall in German presents no problems for speakers of English as it is basically the same as in their own language.

(e)   *The fall–rise*
Just as the rise–fall can be regarded as a variant of the fall, so the fall–rise can be seen as a rise preceded by a fall. The pitch falls from a mid- or high position and rises again on the following syllable or syllables. If there is no tail, both the fall and the rise must take place within the single syllable of the nucleus, as in example (53). The intonation mark for the fall–rise is ˇ.

(50)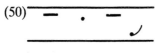

'Kommt er ˇwirklich?

(51)

Ist das ˇunser 'Wagen?

(52)

Hast ˇdu das ge'macht?

(53)

'Ist es ˇwahr?

The use of the German fall–rise
The fall–rise is used in the same sort of contexts as the rise to give special emphasis to the word on which the nucleus falls. It is therefore frequently used when a contrast is implied or stated in:

(a)   questions (example 54);
(b)   non-final tone groups (example 55);
(c)   it is also used in friendly warnings (example 56).

Examples are:

(54)   ˇLäufst du nach 'Hause? (fährst du nicht mit dem Bus?)
(55)   ˇÜbrigens, ‖ (wir können nicht mit dem Auto fahren.)
(56)   ˇVorsicht!

Problems for English-speaking learners
The German fall–rise has the same jump down from a high nucleus to a much lower following syllable as the simple fall or the rise–fall. Otherwise the fall–rise in German is similar to the corresponding English

pattern. The fall–rise is also used in English in contexts like those quoted for German in (a)–(c) above, but there is an additional pattern which is very frequent in English but not used at all in German: the rise–fall–rise (see section 5.3.7 below). English-speakers must learn to avoid using this pattern in German.

5.3.5 **The heads**

The nucleus is the most important and most variable part of the tone group, but there is also some variation to be found in the head, which we will now examine in greater detail.

The most common type of head, and the one we have used in our examples so far, is the **high head**, which has a high level of pitch from the beginning of the head to the syllable before the nucleus. Any unstressed syllables in the prehead are at low or mid-level pitch:

(57)
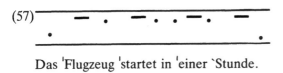

Das 'Flugzeug 'startet in 'einer `Stunde.

(58)

'Kannst du 'auch Ja´panisch?

The German high head is similar to the normal pattern in English, but there is a slight difference: whereas in English the pitch of the stressed syllables in the high head tends to drift downwards slightly, rising again on the unstressed syllables, in German there is the opposite tendency: a slight upward drift on the stressed syllables accompanied by a corresponding downward movement on the unstressed ones. Compare the following examples:

(59)

The 'men es'caped in a 'blue `car.

(60)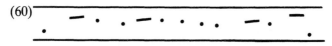

Die 'Männer ent'kamen in einem 'blauen `Auto.

As a result of this slight difference, German intonation sounds tenser, less relaxed than English-speakers are used to from their own language. It is important to listen out for the upward drift of the German high head and, once it has been recognised, to practise it, maintaining it even in emphatic utterances, which in English have a particularly strong tendency to a downward drift.

In addition to the high head, two further types of head are found in German. The first is the **low head**, in which the pitch of the whole head is at a low level. The low pitch reduces the prominence of the head and gives added weight to the nucleus, as there must be a step up to a high point for a following falling nucleus. The low head is used when the communicative content of the head is not particularly great; it carries the implication that the only important piece of information in the tone group is that marked by the nucleus:

(61)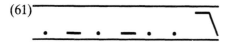

Wir ˌkommen ˌmorgen um `acht.

Finally we have the **rising head**, in which the stressed syllables in the head are at a low level, but there are slight rises on the unstressed syllables. This results in much greater pitch movements than are usual in the head and creates an emphatic effect.

(62)

ˌKannst du nicht ˌeinmal ´pünktlich 'sein?

The low and the rising heads do not cause any great problems for English-speaking learners, since English contains patterns which are phonetically similar and used in very much the same way as the German forms.

5.3.6 **The placement of the nucleus**

The nucleus is the most prominent syllable in a tone group, which as we have said is a unit of communication. It seems obvious, therefore, that the most prominent syllable will mark the most important word to be communicated in the tone group. The speaker can place the nucleus on whichever word is to be given the greatest importance, but there is also a 'neutral' or 'normal' position for the nucleus, in which no item in the tone group is particularly emphasised. The normal position for the nucleus in German is on the **last lexical word** of the tone group, except when the last lexical word is the verb:

(63) 'Gerd 'schreibt ein 'Buch über `Mozart.

but

(64) 'Gerd hat ein 'Buch über `Mozart ge͵schrieben.
(65) 'Gerd wird ein 'Buch über `Mozart ͵schreiben.

with the nucleus on *Mozart*.

If the nucleus is placed on any other item in the tone group, it has the effect of giving particular emphasis to that word. This is often referred to as **contrastive stress** (G. *kontrastive Akzentuierung*), as a contrast with another possible word is implied, if not mentioned:

(66) `Gerd schreibt ein Buch über Mozart (nicht Werner).
(67) Gerd schreibt ein `Buch über Mozart (nicht einen Artikel).
(68) Gerd hat ein Buch über Mozart ge`schrieben (nicht gelesen).

It is also possible to place the nucleus on grammatical words, which would normally be unstressed, or even to change the pattern of word stress if a contrast is intended:

(69) Gerd `hat ein Buch über Mozart geschrieben (er schreibt nicht mehr daran).
(70) Gerd hat `ein Buch über Mozart geschrieben (nicht zwei).
(71) Gerd hat das Buch über Mozart `gekauft (nicht `verkauft).

The placement of the nucleus in German follows rules very similar to those of English, so that English speakers do not have problems with this in German.

5.3.7 English intonation patterns to be avoided in German

It will be seen from the above that many of the basic features of German intonation are similar to English. There are some differences in the realisation of intonation patterns, in particular in the steepness of the German fall, and the use of level pitch, which are potential sources of difficulty for English-speaking learners. But there are no new intonation patterns for English-speakers to learn in German, since all the German intonation patterns also occur in English, with broadly similar functions. In fact, the main problem for those trying to master German intonation is that English has more intonation patterns than German, and the English-speaker is often tempted to use English patterns which do not occur in German. The intonation patterns in question are the low rise and the rise–fall–rise. Failure to avoid these patterns in German is a clear mark of an English accent.

(a) *The low rise*
The low rise is associated in English with reassuring, encouraging, pleading, etc. It is used to soften the effect of an utterance where a falling intonation would sound too peremptory. For example:

(72)

'What's the ˏmatter? (reassuring)

(73)

'Come aˏlong! (gentle command)

(74)

'Don't ˏworry! (encouraging)

With falling intonation these sentences sound much more aggressive, abrupt or impatient:

(75)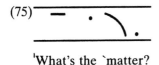

'What's the `matter?

(76)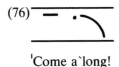

'Come a`long!

(77)

'Don't `worry!

German does not use intonation in this way to soften the effect of utterances. Instead, syntactic and lexical means can be employed. The use of syntactic means includes, for instance, formulating commands as questions, e.g. *Kommst du jetzt?* rather than *Komm jetzt!* This is also common in English, of course, e.g. *Are you coming?* in place of the abrupt example 76. The use of lexical means is a very typically German way of softening the effect of utterances, and there are a number of **modal particles** such as *mal, schon, wohl*, etc., which at least partly fulfil a similar role to that of the low rising intonation in English.

(78)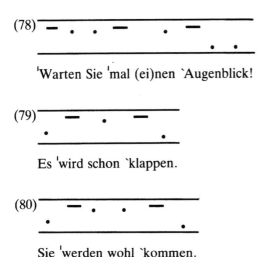

'Warten Sie 'mal (ei)nen `Augenblick!

(79)

Es 'wird schon `klappen.

(80)

Sie 'werden wohl `kommen.

Because they are used to softening the effect of utterances by the use of intonation, English-speakers tend to find that the lack of these patterns makes German sound abrupt and unfriendly. The correct use of German intonation involves the realisation that German uses syntactic and lexical means to soften the effect of utterances, and that intonation patterns which might sound abrupt and unfriendly in English do not necessarily have the same effect in German. The use of German intonation patterns (usually the fall) where English would use the low rise should then be practised.

(b)   *The rise–fall–rise*

In addition to the fall–rise, which occurs in both English and German, there is a very characteristic intonation pattern in English: the rise–fall-rise. This can be described as a rather shallow version of the fall–rise which is preceded by a rise. It is used very commonly in English to express hesitation, concession, reservation, or more generally politeness, warmth or encouragement:

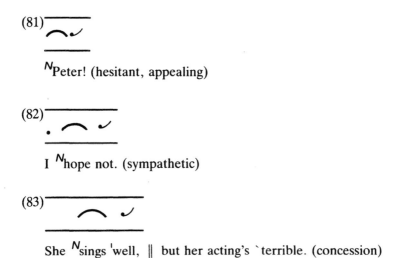

(81)

^{N}Peter! (hesitant, appealing)

(82)

I ^{N}hope not. (sympathetic)

(83)

She ^{N}sings 'well, ‖ but her acting's `terrible. (concession)

This pattern does not occur in German, which would use one of the five basic intonation patterns in these circumstances, for example:

(84)

'Du, `Peter!

(85)
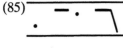

Ich 'hoffe `nicht.

Once again, German has different means of expressing the meaning contained in the English intonation patterns, such as word order (which is much freer than in English); cf. example 86, which is an approximate German rendering of example 83:

(86)
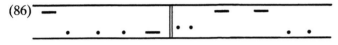

`Singen kann sie ‚gut, aber 'nicht `schauspielern.

Here too, there is a modal particle which can sometimes be regarded as the equivalent of the English intonation pattern: *zwar*, which expresses a concession, cf. examples 87 and 88:

(87)
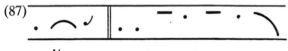

It's ^Ncheaper, but it 'doesn't 'look as `good.

(88)
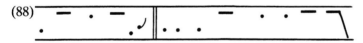

Es 'ist zwar `billiger, aber es 'sieht nicht so 'gut `aus.

The rise–fall–rise is an even more obvious mark of an English accent in German than the low rise, so every effort should be made to avoid it. Once again, the first step is to realise that the pattern is not used and to get to know which German patterns are used instead. Then German sentences should be practised in circumstances in which English would be likely to employ the rise–fall–rise.

6

Words in connected speech: formal and conversational pronunciation

When describing the consonant and vowel sounds of German in chapters 3 and 4, we tried to view them as far as possible in isolation and deliberately excluded any phenomena which go beyond the unit of the word. This enabled us to concentrate our attention on the individual sounds. However, human communication takes place in utterances, not in isolated sounds or words, and, even in the most careful speech, words are not pronounced individually, e.g.:

[viːɐ̯], [ˈhaːbən], [ɪn], [bɔn], [ˈʔaɪnən], [fɪlm], [gəˈzeːən]

but are joined together to form a single utterance: *Wir haben in Bonn einen Film gesehen*. When this happens, the words are not simply added together, each pronounced exactly as it would have been in isolation, but the pronunciation is affected by certain **reductions** or simplifications (G. *Verschleifungen*), which serve to minimise the muscular effort needed to produce utterances. An utterance containing the words given above can be pronounced in different ways, depending on the degree of the reductions, e.g. in careful speech we might hear example 1, in more relaxed speech example 2, and in fast casual conversation, finally, a typical pronunciation would be example 3:

(1) [viɐ̯ ˈhaːbm̩ ɪn ˈbɔn aɪnn̩ ˈfɪlm gəˈzeːən]
(2) [vɪɐ̯ ˈhaːbm̩ ɪm ˈbɔn aɪn ˈfɪlm gəˈzeːən]
                           ən
(3) [vɐ̯ ˈham ɪm ˈbɔn n̩ ˈfɪlm gəˈzeːn]

There are a number of processes at work here. The first is **assimilation** (G. *die Assimilation*), the process by which the articulation of a sound is modified to make it more similar to a neighbouring sound. Assimilation has to do with the way in which sounds are articulated in utterances. The speed of normal communication means that the organs of speech are in constant movement, forming several sounds every second. As each sound is being formed, the organs of speech are changing their position from that of the preceding sound, and also preparing to move on to make the following sound. The precise nature of each sound thus depends on its immediate environment and the **co-articulatory effects** of the preceding and the following sound. We encountered this phenomenon when describing the allophones of certain phonemes, e.g. the palatal and velar variants of /x/ in *dich* [dɪç] and *doch* [dɔx] (determined by the preceding sound), or the voiceless variants of /l/ and /r/ following strong plosives: *Platz* [pl̥ats], *Kreis* [kr̥aɪs]. In connected speech, assimilation works not only within words, as in these examples, but also at word and morpheme boundaries, and it involves alternations not just between allophones but also between different phonemes. In our examples 2 and 3, the preposition *in* is pronounced [ɪm]: [ɪm ˈbɔn]. The alveolar nasal /n/ of the preposition has been assimilated to the bilabial nasal /m/ under the influence of the following bilabial plosive /b/. Before a velar consonant, the /n/ can be assimilated to /ŋ/: [ɪŋ ˈkœln].

Two further processes operating in continuous speech are connected with the stress pattern of utterances. As we saw in the chapter on stress and intonation, not every word in an utterance is pronounced with equal strength or emphasis. The most important words from the point of view of the message are stressed, and less important ones are left unstressed. The unstressed parts of an utterance are subject to the **elision** or loss (G. *die Elision*) of sounds, e.g. the /ən/ of [ˈaɪnən] in example 2 or the second /ə/ of [gəˈzeːən] in the pronunciation [gəˈzeːn] in example 3. Elision sometimes creates the conditions for assimilation: in the form [ˈhaːbm̩], the /ə/ of [ˈhaːbən] has been elided, resulting in the combination [bn̩], which is assimilated to [bm̩].

Unstressed words are also subject to **vowel reduction** (G. *die Vokalreduktion*), which can be seen in the progressively reduced pronunciations of *wir* [viɐ̯, vɪɐ̯, vɐ] and *einen* [aɪnn̩, aɪn, ən, n̩] in examples 1–3. Vowel reduction is particularly striking in a group of common grammatical words such as pronouns and articles which are far more common in their reduced or 'weak' forms than in their full, unreduced forms.

All of these reduction processes apply in varying degrees depending on a number of factors: the *speed* of speech, the *tension* in the articulatory muscles and the *situation*. These factors are clearly interconnected: in formal situations (e.g. addressing a large audience) the muscular tension is typically greater and the speed of delivery less than in informal situations (e.g. chatting to a friend). This is the basis for distinguishing between formal pronunciation with its relatively low speed of delivery, high articulatory tension and fewer reduced forms, and conversational pronunciation, in which the articulatory tension is typically less, the delivery faster and the number of reduced forms greater. In distinguishing between various styles of pronunciation we must take into account that there are enormous personal differences in the use of spoken language. The speed of speech varies greatly between speakers, and judgements about which pronunciation style is suited to a given situation also differ. In this extremely complex area of language use we are thus clearly dealing with general tendencies and relative frequencies rather than with absolute values. For this reason the information given in this chapter on the use of reduced forms in the different pronunciation styles will have to be couched in very general terms.

One of the interpersonal differences in the use of language just mentioned is the speed of speech. The speed of delivery is not constant, however, even in the speech of one individual. The tendency of German towards isochrony (an equal amount of time between stresses in utterances) means that, when a large number of unstressed syllables occur together in a stress group, they tend to be pronounced at greater speed than when there are fewer. Forms that occur in such accelerated passages are referred to as **presto** (or **allegro**) **forms**, and those which occur at slower (i.e. normal) speed are known as **lento forms**. As we shall see, there are certain differences in the degree to which reduction processes operate in presto and lento forms.

In this chapter we will look in detail at the reductions which occur in connected speech in German. It is important to realise that all forms of spoken German (except the unnatural 'full pronunciation') involve some reductions. The difference between formal and conversational pronunciation is thus not an absolute one, but one of degree. For the learner this means that we cannot generally specify that the use of certain forms is definitely 'right' or 'wrong'; we can only say that certain forms are 'more suitable' or 'less suitable' in a given context. In contrast to the individual consonant and vowel sounds, which can be practised and perfected in the language laboratory, the natural use of reduced forms comes only with extensive practice of the conversational use of German. Learners are advised to observe the speech of German native speakers whenever they have the chance and to model their own use of reduced forms on what they hear. The description in the following sections is intended as an introduction and as a basis for this observation of native German usage.

6.1 Assimilation

Assimilation can take place in one of two directions: it can be **progressive** (or perseverative), i.e. a sound influences the following sound, or

regressive (or anticipatory), i.e. a sound influences the preceding sound. Assimilation can also be total or partial. **Total assimilation** is when a sound becomes exactly the same as a neighbouring sound, e.g. in *mitkommen* ['mɪkkɔmm̩] the /t/ has become a velar plosive under the influence of the following /k/ (total regressive assimilation) and the final /n/ has been totally assimilated to the preceding /m/ (total progressive assimilation). In **partial assimilation** the sound merely becomes more similar to the neighbouring sound, as in *haltbar* ['halpba:ɐ̯], where the /t/ has been replaced by the bilabial plosive /p/ under the influence of the following /b/, but has not become exactly the same (partial regressive assimilation).

Assimilation can affect the place of articulation, the manner of articulation or voicing, each of which will be dealt with separately in the following sections. In the examples, the dots (. . .) on either side indicate that the words are to be understood as occurring not in isolation, but in the context of larger utterances.

6.1.1 Assimilation of place

Assimilation of place involves a change in the place of articulation to make a sound more similar to a neighbouring sound. It is an extremely common phenomenon in both English and German, mainly affecting alveolar consonants.

(1) *Regressive assimilation*

Before word and morpheme boundaries, the alveolar plosive /t/ and the alveolar nasal /n/ may be assimilated to following labial and velar sounds:

/t/ → /p/

before /p/	. . . *Weltpremiere* . . .	['vɛlpprə͜mi̯e:rə]
	. . . *mit Problemen* . . .	[mɪp prob'le:mm̩]
before /b/	. . . *Stadtbücherei* . . .	['ʃtapby:çə͜raɪ]
	. . . *weit besser* . . .	['vaɪp 'bɛsɐ]
before /m/	. . . *Wandmalerei* . . .	['vampma:lə͜raɪ]
	. . . *geht mal* . . .	['ge:p ma:l]

/t/ → /k/

before /k/	. . . *hat kein* . . .	['hak kaɪn]
	. . . *Geld kassieren* . . .	['gɛlk ka'si:rən]
before /g/	. . . *Hartgummi* . . .	['haɐkgʊmi]
	. . . *geht gut* . . .	['ge:k 'gu:t]

/n/ → /m/

before /p/	. . . *anpassen* . . .	[ˈampasn̩]
	. . . *in Position* . . .	[ɪm poziˈtsi̯oːn]
before /b/	. . . *Einbahnstraße* . . .	[ˈaɪmbaːn͜ʃtraːsə]
	. . . *diesen Ball* . . .	[diːzəm ˈbal]
before /m/	. . . *einmal* . . .	[ˈaɪmmaːl]
	. . . *kann man* . . .	[kam man]

/n/ → /ŋ/

before /k/	. . . *Einkauf* . . .	[ˈaɪŋkaʊf]
	. . . *mein Kaffee* . . .	[maɪŋ ˈkafe]
before /g/	. . . *Unglück* . . .	[ˈʊŋglʏk]
	. . . *in Gefahr* . . .	[ɪŋ gəˈfaː ɐ̯]

Notice that assimilation can cause distinctions between cases to disappear, e.g. *diesen Ball* = *diesem Ball* [diːzəm bal]. This does not impede communication as long as the context supplies the necessary information.

Regressive assimilation of final /s/ to /ʃ/ before initial /ʃ/ or /ʒ/ is common, to simplify combinations which are difficult to pronounce:

/s/ → /ʃ/	. . . *schönes Spiel* . . .	[ˈʃøːnəʃ ˈʃpiːl]
	. . . *iß schon* . . .	[ˈɪʃ ʃoːn]
	. . . *das Genie* . . .	[daʃ ʒeˈniː]

The assimilation is total in the case of [ʃʃ] and partial in the case of [ʃʒ]. Similar assimilations take place in English too, cf. *this ship* [ʃʃ], *does she* [ʒʃ], but in English it goes further, as /s, z/ are assimilated to /ʃ, ʒ/ before /j/ too: *this year* [ðɪʃ jɪə], *those yachts* [ðəʊʒ jɒts]. This assimilation before /j/ does not take place in German, thus *dieses Jahr* [diː(zə)s jaːɐ̯].

Use: The regressive assimilations of place undergone by alveolars are almost universally used in conversational pronunciation, so much so that unassimilated forms sound unnatural. The assimilated forms are not impossible in moderate formal style, but they are less likely here.

(2) *Progressive assimilation*
Within words, the alveolar nasal /n/ can be assimilated to preceding labial and velar sounds when the intervening vowel /ə/ has been elided (see 6.2.1):

/n/ → /m/
    after /p/   . . . *Wappen* . . .   [ˈvapm̩]

after /b/ ... *leben* ...   ['le:bm̩]
          ... *schwebende* ...   ['ʃve:bm̩də]

/n/ → /ŋ/
    after /k/ ... *trinken* ...   ['trɪŋkŋ̍]
    after /g/ ... *Wagen* ...   ['va:gŋ̍]
               ... *liegend* ...   ['li:gŋ̍t]

Use: The progressive assimilation of place affecting /n/ is very common in conversational pronunciation.

6.1.2 Assimilation of manner

In assimilation of manner a sound is made more similar to a neighbouring sound by a change in the manner of articulation.

(1) *Regressive assimilation*
Before nasals, voiced plosives may be assimilated to the homorganic nasal (/b/ → /m/, /d/ → /n/, /g/ → /ŋ/) within the same word:

/bm/ → /mm/   ... *leben* ...   ['le:bm̩] → ['le:mm̩]
              ... *lebende* ...   ['le:mm̩də]
/dn̩/ → /nn/   ... *Händen* ...   ['hɛndn̩] → ['hɛnn̩]
              ... *fanden* ...   ['fandn̩] → ['fann̩]
/gn/ → /ŋn/   ... *resigniert* ... [rezɪŋ'ni:ɐt]
              ... *Magnet* ...   [maŋ'ne:t]

(2) *Progressive assimilation*
Voiced plosives following nasals may be assimilated to the homorganic nasal either within a word or across word boundaries:

/mb/ → /mm/   ... *zum Beispiel* ...   [tsʊm'maɪʃpi:l]
/nd/ → /nn/   ... *Bundesrepublik* ...   ['bʊnnəsrepu̩bli:k]
/ŋg/ → /ŋŋ/   ... *ungefähr* ...   ['ʊŋŋəfɛ:ɐ̯]

Use: The assimilated forms (both regressive and progressive) are usual in relaxed conversational style and as presto forms in careful conversational style, but they are unlikely to occur in formal pronunciation.

6.1.3 **Assimilation of voicing**

(1) *Devoicing*

In combinations of voiceless plosive or fricative + voiced plosive or /z/, the second element may be completely devoiced (progressive assimilation). This takes place at both word and morpheme boundaries:

/z/ → [z̥]	. . . *Fischsuppe* . . .	[ˈfɪʃz̥ʊpə]
	. . . *das Singen* . . .	[das ˈz̥ɪŋŋ̊]
	. . . *hat sein* . . .	[hat z̥aɪn]
/b/ → [b̥]	. . . *Regensburg* . . .	[ˈreːgn̥sb̥ʊɐk]
	. . . *geht baden* . . .	[geːp ˈb̥aːdn̥]
/d/ → [d̥]	. . . *aufdrücken* . . .	[ˈaʊfd̥ryˑkŋ̊]
	. . . *ab Donnerstag* . . .	[ap ˈd̥ɔn staːk]
/g/ → [g̊]	. . . *maßgeblich* . . .	[ˈmaːsg̊eːplɪç]
	. . . *hat gesungen* . . .	[hat g̊əˈzʊŋŋ̊]

After voiceless fricatives, /j/, /v/, /r/ and /l/ may be devoiced, although the devoicing is usually partial in these cases:

/j/ → [j̥]	. . . *Hans-Jakob* . . .	[hansˈj̥aːkɔp]
/v/ → [v̥]	. . . *das Wetter* . . .	[das ˈv̥ɛtɐ]
/r/ → [r̥]	. . . *mit Recht* . . .	[mɪt ˈr̥ɛçt]
/l/ → [l̥]	. . . *auflegen* . . .	[ˈaʊfl̥eːgŋ̊]

Use: The devoiced forms are not usual in formal pronunciation, but they are common in conversational pronunciation, with the degree of devoicing increasing in more relaxed forms.

(2) *Voicing*

In unstressed positions, voiceless fricatives and plosives may become voiced intervocalically:

/s/ → /z/	. . . *weiß er* . . .	[vaɪzɐ]
/t/ → /d/	. . . *hat er* . . .	[hadɐ]
/f/ → /v/	. . . *hoff' ich* . . .	[hɔvɪç]
/x/ → /ɣ/	. . . *mach' ich* . . .	[maɣɪç]

Use: These assimilated forms occur primarily in relaxed conversational style and are also common in some non-standard regional varieties of German.

6.2 **Elision**

A more extreme process than assimilation is the complete **elision** or loss of elements. In German this affects the vowel /ə/, the consonant /t/ and double consonants.

6.2.1 **Elision of /ə/**

(1) *Before nasals*
The vowel /ə/ occurs only in unstressed syllables in German as in English, and it can be further reduced (i.e. completely elided) before nasals in the particularly weakly stressed position following the main stress. The nasal becomes syllabic in the final position or before a consonant:

(a) In final position

/ən/ → /n/	. . . *treten* . . .	[ˈtreːtn̩]
	. . . *baden* . . .	[ˈbaːdn̩]
/ən/ → /m/	. . . *Lippen* . . .	[ˈlɪpm̩]
	. . . *Gaben* . . .	[ˈgaːbm̩]
/ən/ → /ŋ/	. . . *locken* . . .	[ˈlɔkŋ̍]
	. . . *wegen* . . .	[ˈveːgŋ̍]

(b) Before consonants

/ən/ → /n/	. . . *Vorsitzende* . . .	[ˈfoːɐ̯zɪtsn̩də]
	. . . *Reisende* . . .	[ˈraɪzndə]
	. . . *allenfalls* . . .	[ˈaln̩fals]
/ən/ → /m/	. . . *Lippenstift* . . .	[ˈlɪpm̩ʃtɪft]
/ən/ → /ŋ/	. . . *fliegende* . . .	[ˈfliːgŋ̍də]

Use: The forms with elision of /ə/ and assimilation of the final nasal are the usual realisation of the ending *-en* in conversational pronunciation and they are also common as presto forms in formal pronunciation.

(2) *Final /ə/*
The final /ə/ of the first person singular present tense of verbs can be elided, e.g.

ich hab' [ɪç ˈhap], *hab' ich* [ˈhab ɪç]

This is only possible as long as the result is not a syllabic nasal, thus:

zeichn' ich [ˈtsaɪçn ɪç], but only *ich zeichne* [ɪç ˈtsaɪçnə] (NOT **ich zeichn'* [ɪç ˈtsaɪçn̩])

In the past tense, the elision of final /ə/ can occur when the personal pronoun follows the verb directly, but only if the past tense ending /tə/ follows a consonant:

macht' ich [ˈmaxt ɪç], *konnt' ich* [ˈkɔnt ɪç], but only *redete ich* [ˈreːdətə ɪç] (NOT **redet ich* [ˈreːdət ɪç])

Use: The elision of final /ə/ described here is usual in conversational pronunciation, but not in formal pronunciation, where it only occurs as an occasional presto form.

6.2.2 Elision of /t/

/t/ may be elided if it is the middle member of a group of three consonants.

(1) *Before /s/ following /n/ and /l/*

/nts/ → /ns/	. . . *tanzen* . . .	[ˈtansn̩]
	. . . *ganz* . . .	[gans]
/lts/ → /ls/	. . . *hältst* . . .	[hɛlst]

(2) *Before /l/ following fricatives, especially /s/*

/stl/ → /sl/	. . . *festlich* . . .	[ˈfɛslɪç]
/ftl/ → /fl/	. . . *Häftling* . . .	[ˈhɛflɪŋ]
/çtl/ → /çl/	. . . *Frauenrechtlerin* . . .	[ˈfrauənˌrɛçlərɪn]

(3) *In complex series of sibilants (s-sounds) and plosives*

[sts] → [ss]	. . . *auszugehen* . . .	[ˈaussuɡeːn]
[stts] → [ss]	. . . *höchst zufrieden* . . .	[ˈhøːçs suˈfriːdn̩]
[tstts] → [tss]	. . . *jetzt zahlen* . . .	[jɛts ˈsaːln̩]

Use: The elision of /t/ in these contexts is a mark of conversational pronunciation. It is more common in relaxed conversational style than in careful conversational style.

6.2.3 **Reduction of double consonants**

Double consonants (G. *die Geminate*) may be reduced under various conditions.

(1) *In final position*

/nn̩/ → /n/	. . . *Tränen* . . .	['trɛ:nn̩] → [trɛ:n]
/mm̩/ → /m/	. . . *kommen* . . .	['kɔmm̩] → [kɔm]
/ŋŋ̩/ → /ŋ/	. . . *singen* . . .	['zɪŋŋ̩] → [zɪŋ]

As a result of such reductions the infinitive forms *kommen*, *singen*, etc., have the same pronunciation as the imperatives of the same verbs: *komm*, *sing*. This cannot lead to misunderstandings, as the context serves to disambiguate the form. If there were any danger of misunderstanding, the reductions would, of course, be avoided.

(2) *In other positions*

(a) Double consonants may be reduced if they are not the result of assimilation of place:

/tt/ → /t/	. . . *mitteilen* . . .	['mɪtaɪln̩]
/nn/ → /n/	. . . *annehmen* . . .	['ane:m(m̩)]
/kk/ → /k/	. . . *wegkommen* . . .	['vɛkɔm(m̩)]
/ʃʃ/ → /ʃ/	. . . *Eisschrank* . . .	['aɪʃraŋk]

(b) If they are the result of assimilation of place, they may be reduced as long as the double consonant does not immediately follow the stress:

/mm/ → /m/	. . . *den 'meisten* . . .	[də 'maɪstn̩]
/kk/ → /k/	. . . *hat 'keine* . . .	[ha 'kaɪn]
/mm/ → /m/	. . . *zum 'Beispiel* . . .	[tsʊ 'maɪʃpi:l]

Note that the following do not fulfil the conditions just specified and therefore retain the double consonant:

'*mitkommen* only ['mɪkkɔm(m̩)], NOT ['mɪkɔm(m̩)]
'*hat kein* only ['hak kaɪn], NOT ['hakaɪn]
'*Handpumpe* only ['hamppʊmpə], NOT ['hampʊmpə]

In these cases the double consonants are the result of assimilation of place AND are immediately preceded by the stress.

(c)   Double nasals may be simplified if they are followed by a large
number of unstressed syllables, especially before /ə/:

/nn/ → /n/   . . . *Bundesrepublik* . . .   ['bʊnəsrepublik]
/mm/ → /m/   . . . *Lebensversicherung* . . .['le:msfɛzɪçərʊŋ]
/ŋŋ/ → /ŋ/   . . . *ungefährliche* . . .   ['ʊŋəfɛ:ɐlɪçə]

Use: The reduction of double consonants is common in relaxed conversational style and it is also possible in presto forms in careful conversational
style.

6.3   Vowel reductions

In unstressed positions vowels are subject to a number of reduction
processes, which can be illustrated by means of the form of the definite
article *den*, pronounced [de:n] in isolation. The processes are:

1   Shortening of long vowels: [de:n] → [den]
2   Centralisation: replacement of tense vowels by the corresponding lax
    vowel: [den] → [dɛn]
3   Reduction to /ə/: [dɛn] → [dən]
4   Elision of vowel: [dən] → [dn̩]

The first of these processes applies to unstressed long vowels in all
pronunciation styles of German, including formal pronunciation, and can
be seen in words like *zurück* [tsu'rʏk], *Politik* [poli'ti:k], *Psychologie*
[psyçolo'gi:] and *Universität* [univɛrzi'tɛ:t], in which the unstressed tense
vowels are pronounced short. The other vowel reduction processes are
rare in formal pronuciation, but very common in the conversational
pronunciation of German, e.g. in the pronunciations [tsʊ'rʏk], [pɔlɪ'ti:k],
[psyçɔlɔ'gi:], [ʊnɪvɛɐzɪ'tɛ:t] for the words given above, in which the
unstressed tense vowels are replaced by the lax counterparts. The reduction processes can be seen most clearly, however, in the 'weak forms' of
certain high-frequency grammatical words.

6.3.1   Weak forms

In German, as in English, there is a group of frequently used grammatical
(or function) words, in the main consisting of one or two syllables, which
are especially affected by reductions in the spoken use of language. These
words carry very little information and are therefore generally unstressed.
In this unstressed position they have a special reduced or **weak form** (G.

schwache Form), as opposed to their full pronunciation (**strong** or **citation form**, G. *starke Form*), which is used when the words are pronounced in isolation or when they are stressed in sentences.

Some of the weak forms are indicated in the written form of both German and English, e.g.

German:	*im, zum, ins, durchs* . . .	(regularly used even in formal texts)
	hinters, unterm, raus . . .	(sometimes used in writing to indicate colloquial style)
English:	*we'll, won't, who's, we're, I'd, I'll, shan't* . . .	(mostly used in informal texts or to indicate colloquial spoken language)

However, the great majority of weak forms in both languages belong exclusively to spoken language and are not indicated in writing. Thus in normal connected speech the following sentences will contain several weak forms (the strong forms are given for comparison):

German:	*Hast du ihn gesehen?*	[hast] [duː] [iːn] [gəˈzeːən]
		[has dʊ ɪn gəˈzeːn]
	or	[has n̩ gəˈzeːn]
English:	*Have you seen him?*	[hæv] [juː] [siːn] [hɪm]
		[həv jʊ ˈsiːn ɪm]

A knowledge of the weak forms is essential for a natural pronunciation and rhythm in German. It is important to realise that, despite some similarities, the reductions encountered in German weak forms are not the same as those of English. English weak forms, for instance, frequently involve the elision of initial /h/ as in *have* [əv] or *him* [ɪm] in *The police have arrested him* [ðə pəˈliːs əv əˈrestɪd ɪm]; this is not a feature of German pronunciation at all. In the great majority of cases, English weak forms have the vowels /ə/ or /ɪ/, compared with greater variety in German, so the English-speaking learner will have to resist the temptation to reduce all vowels to one of these two in German weak forms. Most importantly, German has various stages of weak forms, with varying degrees of vowel reduction. In addition to vowel reduction, which is present in almost all the weak forms, many also contain elisions and some have assimilations, so that the three major reduction processes are all present in the phenomenon of weak forms.

6.3.2 List of weak forms

The following are the principal weak forms in German, divided into
various groups according to the part of speech they belong to. All of the
words given in the list are much more common in one of their weak forms
than in the strong form. Each word is illustrated by an example sentence
or phrase in phonetic transcription. The example is fully transcribed for
the first form, but thereafter only the words which change are given.

It should be pointed out that weak forms ending in /n/ are especially
prone to assimilation, to /m/ before bilabial consonants and to /ŋ/ before
velars, e.g.:

> *Ich sah ihn baden* [ç ˈza: (ɪ)m ˈba:dn̩]
> *Ich sah ihn kommen* [ç ˈza: (ɪ)ŋ ˈkɔmm̩]

The likelihood of assimilation increases with the degree of reduction, i.e.
it is much more likely with maximally reduced forms than with strong
forms or with forms showing only the first stage of reduction.

	Weak forms	*Example*	*Strong form*
(1) Pronouns			
ich	[ç][1]	ç ne:m(ə) ˈtsvaɪ	[ɪç]
mir[2]	[miɐ̯]	das ˈkan ɪç miɐ̯ ˈdɛŋkn̩	[mi:ɐ̯]
	[mɪɐ̯]	mɪɐ̯	
	[mɐ]	s mɐ	
du	[du]	ˈkanst du ˈkɔmm̩?	[du:]
	[dʊ]	dʊ	
	[də]	də	
er	[eɐ̯]	hat eɐ̯ ˈaŋgəru:fn̩?	[e:ɐ̯]
	[ɛɐ̯]	ɛɐ̯	
	[ɐ]	ɐ	
ihm	[im]	ɪç ˈhap s im gəˈge:bm̩	[i:m]
	[ɪm]	ɪm	
	[əm]	ç əm	
	[m]	m̩	
ihn	[in]	ˈru:f in ˈan	[i:n]
	[ɪn]	ɪn	
	[ən]	ən	
	[n]	n̩	

[1] Only in the initial position after a pause.
[2] Corresponding reductions take place in *dir*, *wir* and *ihr*.

sie	[zi]	'ha:bm̩ zi gə'ʃpi:lt	[zi:]
	[zɪ]	'habm̩ zɪ	
	[zə]	'ham zə	
ihrer	[irɐ]	'daŋk irɐ 'hɪlfə	['i:rɐ]
	[ɪrɐ]	ɪrɐ	
ihres	[irəs]	deɐ̯ 'frɔʏnt irəs 'bru:dəs	['i:rəs]
	[ɪrəs]	deɐ̯ ɪrəs	
ihrem	[iɐ̯m]	zi hat 'gɛlt fɔn iɐ̯m 'fa:tɐ	['i:rəm]
	[ɪɐ̯m]	zɪ fn̩ ɪɐ̯m	
ihren	[iɐ̯n]	zi hat 'gɛlt fɔn iɐ̯n 'ɛltɐn	['i:rən]
	[ɪɐ̯n]	zɪ fn̩ ɪɐ̯n	
es	[ɛs]	ɪç kan ɛs bə'haltn̩	[es]
	[s]	ç s	
ihnen	[inn̩]	ɛs gə'fɛlt inn̩ 'nɪçt	['i:nən]
	[in]	in	
	[ɪn]	s ɪn	

(2) Articles and relative pronouns

der	[deɐ̯]	'jɛtst kɔmt deɐ̯ 'tsu:k	[de:ɐ̯]
	[dɛɐ̯]	dɛɐ̯	
	[dɐ]	dɐ	
des	[dəs]	di 'zaɪtn̩ dəs 'bu:xəs	[dɛs]
dem	[dem]	'tsaɪk s dem 'hans	[de:m]
	[dɛm]	dɛm	
	[dəm]	dəm	
	[m̩]	m̩	
den	[den]	'le:ks aʊf den 'tɪʃ	[de:n]
	[dɛn]	dɛn	
	[dən]	dən	
	[dn̩]	dn̩	
	[n̩]	n̩	
die	[di]	viɐ̯ 'ge:ən aʊf di 'ʃtra:sə	[di:]
	[dɪ]	vɪɐ̯ dɪ	
	[də]	vɐ 'ge:n də	
das	[s]	'hi:ɐ̯ kɔmt s 'aʊto	[das]
ein	[ən]	'vɔln zi ən 'fo:to	[aɪn]
	[n̩]	zɪ n̩	
einem	[aɪmm̩]	'gi:p s aɪmm̩ ʃtu'dɛntn̩	['aɪnəm]
	[aɪm]	aɪm	
	[am]	am	
	[nəm]	nəm	
	[m̩]	m̩	

einen	[aɪnn̩]	ɪç ˈkaʊf aɪnn̩ ˈapfl̩	[ˈaɪnən]
	[aɪn]	aɪn	
	[ən]	ən	
	[n̩]	n̩	
eine	[nə]	ɛɐ̯ ˈblaɪpt nə ˈvɔxə	[ˈaɪnə]
dessen	[dəsn̩]	ˈhans, dəsn̩ ˈzoːn vɪɐ̯ ˈkɛnn̩	[ˈdɛsn̩]
deren	[deɐ̯n]	ˈuːtə, deɐ̯n ˈkɪndɐ vɪɐ̯ ˈkɛnn̩	[ˈdeːrən]
	[dɛɐ̯n]	dɛɐ̯n	
denen	[denn̩]	ˈlɔytə, denn̩ ɛs gəˈfɛlt	[ˈdeːnən]
	[den]	den	
	[dɛn]	dɛn s	
	[dən]	dən	

(3) *Auxiliary verbs*

bist	[bɪs]	du bɪs ˈnɪç ˈfɛrtɪç	[bɪst]
ist	[ɪs]	dɛɐ̯ ˈkafe ɪs ˈtɔyɐ	[ɪst]
	[s]	dɐ s	
sind	[zɪn]	di ˈɛpfl̩ zɪn ˈbɪlɪç	[zɪnt]
werden	[veɐ̯n]	di ˈʃtyːlə veɐ̯n gəˈliːfɐt	[ˈveːɐ̯d(ə)n]
	[vɛɐ̯n]	dɪ vɛɐ̯n	
wurden	[vʊɐ̯dn̩]	di ˈʃtyːlə vʊɐ̯dn̩ gəˈliːfɐt	[ˈvʊrd(ə)n]
	[vʊɐ̯n]	dɪ vʊɐ̯n	
würden	[vyɐ̯dn̩]	di ˈmylɐs vyɐ̯dn̩ ˈkɔmm̩	[ˈvʏrd(ə)n]
	[vyɐ̯n]	dɪ vyɐ̯n	
geworden	[gəvɔɐ̯dn̩]	ɛs ɪs ˈbɛsɐ gəvɔɐ̯dn̩	[gəˈvɔrd(ə)n]
	[gəvɔɐ̯n]	s gəvɔɐ̯n	
haben	[haːbm̩]	zi haːbm̩ s gəˈʃaft	[ˈhaːbən]
	[haːm]	zɪ haːm	
	[ham]	zə ham	

(4) *Prepositions*

zu	[tsʊ]	vɪɐ̯ zɪn tsʊ ˈhaʊzə	[tsuː]
	[tsə]	vɐ ˙ tsə	
von	[fn̩]	das ˈbɛstə fn̩ ˈaln̩	[fɔn]
für	[fyɐ̯]	das ˈraɪçt fyɐ̯ ˈhɔytə	[fyːɐ̯]
	[fʏɐ̯]	fʏɐ̯	
	[fɐ]	s fɐ	
vor	[foɐ̯]	ˈfynf foɐ̯ ˈdraɪ	[foːɐ̯]
	[fɔɐ̯]	fɔɐ̯	
	[fɐ]	fɐ	
nach	[nax]	ˈfynf nax ˈdraɪ	[naːx]
in	[ən]	zi ˈvoːnt ən ˈhambʊɐ̯k	[ɪn]
	[n̩]	zɪ n̩ dɐ ˈʃtat	

(5) Conjunctions

und	[ʊn]	maɪnə ˈda:mən ʊn ˈhɛrən	[ʊnt]
	[ən]	ən	
	[n̩]	n̩	
aber	[abɐ]	ˈklaɪn abɐ ˈfaɪn	[ˈa:bɐ]
	[aβɐ]	aβɐ	
oder	[odɐ]	ˈkalt odɐ ˈvaɐ̯m	[ˈo:dɐ]
	[ɔdɐ]	ɔdɐ	
wie	[vi]	zo ˈgu:t vi ˈni:	[vi:]
	[vɪ]	zɔ vɪ	
da	[da]	ˈɪst da ˈvas	[da:]

(6) Adverbs

nicht	[nɪç]	zɪ ˈkœn(n̩) nɪç ˈkɔmm̩	[nɪçt]
jetzt	[jɛts]	ˈkɔm jɛts ˈmɪt	[jɛtst]
	[jəts]	jəts	
sonst	[zɔns]	ɛs ˈklapt zɔns ˈnɪçt	[zɔnst]
	[zəns]	s zəns	
denn	[dən]	van ˈfɛŋt ɛs dən ˈan	[dɛn]
	[dn̩]	s dn̩	
	[n̩]	n̩	
so	[zo]	zo ˈbalt vi ˈmø:klɪç	[zo:]
	[z]	zɔ vɪ	
	[zə]	zə	
schon	[ʃon]	ˈzɪnt viɐ̯ ʃon ˈda:	[ʃo:n]
	[ʃɔn]	vɪɐ ʃɔn	
	[ʃən]	ʃən	
	[ʃn̩]	vɐ ʃn̩	
nun	[nun]	ɛs ˈɪst nun mal ˈzo:	[nu:n]
	[nʊn]	nʊn	
	[nən]	s nən ma	
nur	[nuɐ̯]	das ˈgi:pt ɛs nuɐ̯ ˈhɔʏtə	[nu:ɐ̯]
	[nʊɐ̯]	s s nʊɐ̯	
mal	[mal]	ˈkɔm mal ˈmɪt	[ma:l]
	[ma]	ma	
mehr	[meɐ̯]	ɛɐ̯ vɪl ˈnɪçt meɐ̯ ˈkɔmm̩	[me:ɐ̯]
	[mɛɐ̯]	ˈnɪç mɛɐ̯ ˈkɔm	

(7) Numerals

-zehn	[tsen]	ɛs ˈkɔstət ˈaxtsen ˈmark	[tse:n]
	[tsɛn]	ˈaxtsɛn	
	[tsən]	s ˈaxtsən	
	[tsn̩]	ˈaxtsn̩	

In longer numerals, the elements *-und-* (as above) and *-hundert-* are usually reduced:

| *-hundert-* | [hʊnɐt] | [draɪhʊnɐtfʏmftsɪç] | ['hʊndɐt] |
| | [nə] | [draɪnəfʏmftsɪç] | |

6.3.3 The use of weak forms and strong forms

Although the principle of weak forms, i.e. the existence of certain grammatical words which have a reduced form of pronunciation when unstressed in normal connected speech, is the same in English and German, there is an important difference in their use in the two languages.

English weak forms are dictated entirely by the stress and rhythm of the sentence and are completely unconnected with differences in style, in other words, weak forms in English are used even in very formal speech. There are no conditions under which strong forms would be used in unstressed position in natural speech.[3]

The use of **German** weak forms, on the other hand, depends decisively on the pronunciation style: the frequency of weak forms and the degree of reductions varies greatly between recitation style and relaxed conversational pronunciation. The general rule is that in formal pronunciation weak forms are less frequent and generally have only the first stage of vowel reduction (shortening), although the second stage (centralisation) is possible in presto forms. Weak forms with centralisation and reduction of vowel to /ə/ are typical of conversational pronunciation. The maximally reduced forms (with elision of vowel) are usually restricted to presto forms in relaxed conversational style.

The reality of linguistic usage is much more complex than this simple statement, however, and it should be pointed out that a large number of qualifications could be made. We will restrict ourselves to four rather general points here:

(1)   Strong forms are used if the word is stressed:

Wir haben 'den *Mann ge'sehen.*   [deːn]
Hast 'du *das ge'macht?*   [duː]
Wir 'konnten nur 'einen 'wählen.*   [ʔaɪnən]
Ich hab's weder 'ihm *noch* 'ihr *er'zählt.*   [ʔiːm], [ʔiːɐ̯]

---

[3] They might be used, for instance, in a dictation, but this, of course, is not natural speech.

Exceptions to this rule are the forms with an elided final /t/: *bist, ist, und, nicht, jetzt, sonst*. In these cases, both the strong and the elided forms can be used in stressed position:

Sie waren in 'Bonn 'und 'Köln. [ʊn(t)]
Wir haben's 'nicht ge'schafft. [nɪç(t)]
Sie 'müssen sich 'jetzt ent'scheiden. [jɛts(t)]

The weak form of *haben* [ham] can be used in stressed position as an auxiliary or even as a main verb:

Aber sie 'haben's ge'lesen. ['ha:bm̩], [ha:m] or [ham]
Wir 'haben die 'Bücher.

(2) Relative pronouns have a smaller degree of vowel reduction than the corresponding forms of the articles (*der, den, die*, etc.); in particular the maximally reduced forms of the article are not used for the relative pronouns:

Der 'Platz, den man uns 'anbot . . . [den, dɛn, dən], NOT [dn̩, n̩]
In der 'Stadt, die wir be 'sucht haben . . . [di, dɪ], NOT [də]
Der 'Mann, der uns ge'holfen hat . . . [deɐ̯, dɛɐ̯], NOT [dɐ]

(3) In their use as demonstratives, *der, den, die*, etc., have strong forms or forms with only the first stage of reduction even in unstressed position:

Wir wollen den 'Sessel da 'kaufen. [de(:)n]

(4) Strongly reduced forms are much less likely to occur in utterance-final position than in other positions:

Es ge'fällt ihnen. [in(n̩)], NOT [ɪn]
Wir be'suchen sie. [zi], NOT [zɪ, zə]
Gib 'mir einen! [aɪn(n̩)], NOT [ən, n̩]
'Kommt sie denn? [dɛn], NOT [dən, dn̩, n̩]

6.4 Other features of conversational pronunciation

Two further reductions typical of conversational pronunciation apply to /r/ and [ʔ].

6.4.1 /r/

The full pronunciation of the uvular variety of /r/, the uvular roll [ʀ], is unusual in conversational pronunciation. It is normally reduced at least to the uvular fricative [ʁ], and very frequently further to the frictionless continuant [ɤ]. This latter reduction is somewhat less likely in initial position in an utterance, but even here it is possible:

	Formal pronunciation	*Conversational pronunciation*
... *klare* ...	['klaːʁə]	['klaːɤə]
... *am Rhein* ...	[am ʁaɪn]	[am ɤaɪn]
Reinhold ist ...	['ʁaɪnhɔlt ɪst]	['ɤaɪnhɔlt ɪs]

The use of the vocalic allophone [ɐ] is more common among speakers of German who have a uvular type of /r/ than among those with an apical pronunciation. For speakers with a uvular variety ([ʀ, ʁ, ɤ]), vocalic [ɐ] is the most common realisation of /r/ even in formal pronunciation following long vowels (a) in final position and (b) before consonants. In conversational pronunciation it is also widely used in these positions following short vowels, e.g.:

	Formal pronunciation	*Conversational pronunciation*
... *wird* ...	[vɪʁt]	[vɪɐ̯t]
... *fern* ...	[fɛʁn]	[fɛɐ̯n]
... *Herr* ...	[hɛʁ]	[hɛɐ̯]

Following /aː/, [ɐ̯] is usually elided in conversational pronunciation (= total assimilation to the preceding vowel): *Haar* [haː], *Fahrt* [faːt], etc.

6.4.2 **The glottal stop**

In formal pronunciation the glottal stop is used before stressed initial vowels, and is also possible (though not obligatory) before unstressed initial vowels. In conversational pronunciation it is not used before unstressed vowels and can even be omitted before some stressed vowels, though not before an initial vowel which carries the nuclear stress in a tone group. In the following examples F = formal and C = conversational pronunciation.

> *Er hat ein ˋeigenes ˌAuto.*
> F: [(ʔ)eɐ̯ hat (ʔ)aɪn ˋʔaɪɡənəs ˌʔauto]
> C: [ɐ hat n̩ ˋʔaɪɡənəs ˌ(ʔ)auto]

Er ist im 'Augenblick *in* `Innsbruck.
F: [(ʔ)eɐ̯ (ʔ)ɪst (ʔ)ɪm 'ʔaʊɡənblɪk (ʔ)ɪn `ʔɪnsbrʊk]
C: [ɐ ɪs ɪm '(ʔ)aʊɡŋ̍blɪk ɪn `ʔɪnsbrʊk]

6.5 Reductions in common expressions

Common expressions such as greetings and other ritual phrases are subject to more severe reductions than is possible in normal utterances
because of their low semantic content: they do not contain any new
information, and merely need to be recognised as the appropriate greeting for the communication to be successful. Meinhold (1973: 53) gives
the pronunciation of the following greetings in five different styles
(Meinhold's transcription has been adapted slightly here to conform
with the one used in this book):

1 full pronunciation (hypercorrect, not used in normal communication);
2 formal style, used for greeting a large audience;
3 formal style, usual pronunciation;
4 conversational style;
5 relaxed conversational style (possibly accompanied by a quick
  gesture).

	Guten Morgen	*Guten Tag*	*Guten Abend*	*Auf Wiedersehen*
1	'guːtən 'mɔʁɡən	'guːtən 'taːk	'guːtən 'ʔaːbənt	aʊf 'viːdɐze:ən
2	guːtn̩ 'mɔʁɡŋ̍	guːtn̩ 'taːk	guːtn̩ 'ʔaːbm̩t	aʊf 'viːdɐze:n
3	gutn̩ 'mɔɐ̯ŋ̍	gutn̩ 'ta(k)	gutn̩ 'aːmt	f 'viːdɐze:n
	gʊtn̩	gʊtn̩	gʊtn̩	f 'viːdɐzen
	gʊn	gʊn	gʊn	
4	n̩ mɔ̃	n ta(ɣ)	n aːmt	'viː(d)ɐzen
5	mɔ̃	ta(ɣ)	n amt	

These greetings may serve as examples of the full range of different
pronunciations possible in modern German (excluding dialect forms, of
course). They illustrate the reduction processes discussed in this chapter:
assimilation (e.g. ['ʔaːbmt] in 2), elision (e.g. [gʊn, aːmt] in 3), and
vowel reduction (e.g. ['gutn̩], ['gʊtn̩], [f] in 3). They also contain reductions which would not be possible in other utterances because of the
necessity of making sure that the message is understood, e.g. the replacement of the sequence vowel + nasal consonant by a nasal vowel ([mɔ̃] for
[mɔɐ̯ŋ̍]) and the loss of the final consonant of the word *Tag* and of the
complete word *auf* in examples 4 and 5.

7

Exercises

The nineteen units in this chapter contain exercises on the German sounds which most frequently cause problems for English-speaking learners. The exercises are arranged in segments of increasing length: first single words containing the sound to be practised, then phrases, then sentences and, finally, for the sounds which need most practice, a dialogue. This scheme has not been followed slavishly, and there are variations where it seemed appropriate, but there is a progression from shorter and simpler exercises to longer and more demanding ones in each unit. This order should be adhered to when working with the exercises, although it is an individual question how much time a learner needs to spend on each unit. Some people find that they can learn new sounds very quickly and will be able to go on to the next set of exercises after working through a unit only once or twice; others will need to work through a unit several times before they are satisfied with their pronunciation. You should not hesitate to skip exercises, or even whole units, if you have a sound in your variety of English which will do in German too, for instance Irish speakers will mostly not need to practise the clear German /l/.

The accompanying tape contains a complete recording of the exercises and is suitable for use either in a language laboratory or on a cassette recorder at home. A language laboratory is ideal, of course, because it enables you to record your own voice and to listen to it alongside that of the native speakers on the tape. But if you do not have access to a language laboratory, a similar effect can be had using two cassette recorders at home, one for playing the accompanying cassette and the other for recording your own voice. If you are using a cassette recorder, you will find that the sound quality is greatly improved by listening through earphones.

The exercises have been recorded with gaps to allow you to repeat the word or sentence after the speaker. The gaps have been deliberately kept quite short in order to encourage you to speak at normal speed right from the start, but, if you find that you would like to practise some exercises more slowly and deliberately, it is possible to make a copy of the tape with longer gaps.

When practising a sound, first read through the section of the text in which it is described, then follow this up with the exercises, ideally straight away. A typical session in the language laboratory or with a cassette recorder at home will consist of several different phases:

1 Listen to the words (phrases, sentences, etc.). In this first phase you should not say anything yourself, but you should concentrate on recognising the German pronunciation of the sound or sounds in question.
2 Listen to the tape again, this time repeating after the native speaker on the tape and recording your voice (if possible).
3 Listen to your own voice and compare your pronunciation with that of the native speaker.

Phases 2 and 3 can be repeated as often as necessary. All three phases are important, but it is perhaps worth stressing the importance of listening, which is often overlooked, although you will certainly not be able to repeat a sound properly unless you have listened to it carefully first.

You should aim to make steady progress through the units. Do not allow yourself to get stuck at a sound you find particularly difficult. If you feel you have not mastered a sound, you can return to it later, but this should not stop you going on to other sounds in the meantime. Improvements in pronunciation do not occur overnight, but gradually as a result of repeated practice of problem areas. A point that should be remembered is that, although each unit concentrates on one aspect of German pronunciation, it also contains examples of many other German sounds, so you are constantly revising sounds you have already dealt with. Features of German intonation and connected speech are likewise contained in every unit. Finally: you should not be afraid to exaggerate certain features of German pronunciation in the language laboratory, e.g. lip-rounding for /o:/ and /u:/, or a vigorous pronunciation of [x] and [ç], especially when you are practising a sound for the first time. By exaggerating the sounds you will focus your attention on the ways in which these sounds differ from sounds of English, and you will learn more rapidly because the tactile feedback is greater. When speaking the language outside the language laboratory, for instance in conversation with Germans, there is no danger of retaining these exaggerated features.

UNIT 1: **Plosives**

1.1 **Words with /t/**

Tafel, Tomate, Tinte, teuer, tauschen, tätig, Thomas
Wetter, Butter, weiter, betrachten, leiten, Beutel
rund, Wind, kund, gesund, geschwind, Gerd, Held, Bord

1.2 **Contrasts with final and non-final ⟨b, d, g⟩**

(a) *[b] – [p]*		(b) *[d] – [t]*	
Diebe	: Dieb	Runde	: rund
Körbe	: Korb	Wunde	: wund
graben	: Grab	Kinder	: Kind
sieben	: Sieb	Rinder	: Rind
Stäbe	: Stab	Mörder	: Mord
Kälber	: Kalb	Bäder	: Bad

(c) *[g] – [k]*	
Tage	: Tag
Frage	: frag
Lage	: lag
sogen	: sog
trugen	: trug
zogen	: zog

1.3 **Words with ⟨b, d, g⟩ in syllable-final position**

abhalten, ablegen, abschalten, Abstand, abscheulich
endlos, handlich, Handarbeit, Sandhaufen, Geldsorgen
arglos, kärglich, Waagschale, Bergsteiger, Burgruine

1.4 **Words with ⟨b, d, g⟩ followed by a strong consonant in the same syllable**

du gibst, er hebt, ihr strebt, Herbst
du lädst, Landsmann, das blödste
du fragst, er sagt, sie erwägt, tagsüber

1.5 **Initial consonant clusters involving plosives**

[ps] Psalm, Psychologe, Psychologie, Psyche, Psychopath,
Pseudonym

[pn] pneumatisch, Pneumonie
[ks] Xenophobie, Xanten (Stadt), Xaver (Name)
[kn] Knabe, Knie, Knall, Knoblauch, Knoten, knicken
[gn] Gnade, gnädig, Gneis

1.6 Dialogue: *Beim Teetrinken*

Irmgard: Gerd, trinkst du lieber Tee oder Kaffee?
Gerd: Tee bitte, Tante Irmgard. Starker Kaffee ist doch schlecht
             für die Gesundheit.
Irmgard: Das stimmt aber nicht! Wer hat dir denn das erzählt?
Gerd: Dieter sagt das immer.
Irmgard: Dein Freund Dieter spinnt doch! Kaffee schadet der
             Gesundheit?! Dabei raucht er wie ein Schlot!
Gerd: Er raucht nicht mehr. Er hat letzte Woche aufgehört, als
             der Tabak wieder teurer geworden ist.
Irmgard: Na gut. Trinkst du den Tee mit Milch oder Zitrone?
Gerd: Zitrone bitte, Tante Irmgard. Und etwas Zucker.

UNIT 2:   /s/ and /z/

2.1 Words with initial /z/

so, Sonne, sozial, Sau, süß, Silber, Sorte, Sabine
Sackgasse, Sozialismus, Sicherheitsnadel, selbstlos

2.2 Words with final /s/

Fuß, Los, Hals, Fels, Krebs, rechts, Buches, Peters,
anfangs, schönes, Autos, Fotos, Marxismus, Realismus

2.3 Phrases with final /s/

etwas anderes   was ist es?
es ist Hans   dies und jenes
das Los des Mannes   iß etwas Warmes
das Haus des Professors   laß uns zu Fuß gehen

2.4 Words contrasting /s/ and /z/

reißen : reisen
heißer : heiser

weiße : weise
Muße   : Muse
Bußen : Busen
ließe : Liese (Name)

2.5 Sentences with /s/ and /z/

Seine Füße sind so groß.
Gestern sahen wir Susanne im Fernsehen.
Diese Skizzen sind besser als die im Museum.
Hans, weißt du, ob es was Besseres gibt?

UNIT 3: [x] and [ç]

3.1 Words with [ç]

Eiche, Bücher, Löcher, lächeln, Dichtung, Pärchen,
Brötchen, Häuschen, riecht, gleicht, vierzig,
Heinrich, Pech, hungrig, deutlich, Storch, Mönch

3.2 Phrases with [ç]

deutlich sprechen   hoffentlich pünktlich
richtig rechnen   nicht in der Küche
sechzig Pfennig   wirklich nicht schwierig
ein bißchen lustig   technisch nicht möglich

3.3 Words with [x]

Wache, Woche, fluchen, nachsuchen, Hochzeit, Macht,
kocht, gebraucht, versucht, Bauch, Geruch, haushoch

3.4 Phrases with [x]

in acht Wochen   unter Dach und Fach
ein Fachbuch brauchen   eine abgemachte Sache
einen Besuch machen   die Hochschule besuchen
nach den Ursachen suchen   in einfacher Sprache

3.5 Words contrasting [x] and [ç]

Buch   : Bücher   Frucht : Früchte
Sprache : sprechen   Nacht   : Nächte

lachen	:	Gelächter	Kuchen	:	Küche
auch	:	ich	kochen	:	Köche

3.6 Phrases containing [x] and [ç]

nicht lachen	Milch kochen
nichts machen	acht Nächte
dich besuchen	die Bücher suchen
ein bißchen Kuchen	das Mädchen besuchen

3.7 Sentences containing [x] and [ç]

Wir machen nächste Woche noch mehr chemische Versuche.
Die Sache ist noch nicht sicher.
Ach, ich kann es noch nicht versuchen!
Richards Tochter studiert an der Technischen Hochschule.

3.8 Dialogue: *Joachim studiert Chinesisch*

Ulrich: Michaela, ich hab' gehört, daß Joachim Chinesisch studiert. Ist das wirklich wahr? Ich dachte, er wollte Geschichte machen.

Michaela: Nein, er interessiert sich mehr für Sprachen als für andere Fächer.

Ulrich: Aber warum gleich Chinesisch? Das ist ein unheimlich schwieriges Fach.

Michaela: Du weißt doch, daß Joachim recht tüchtig ist. Und er will nächstes Jahr nach China.

Ulrich: Ach so, er will nach China. Deshalb kocht er immer diese chinesischen Sachen.

Michaela: Ich finde, daß er wirklich mutig ist. Ich könnte nicht diese ganzen Zeichen auswendig lernen. Aber was machst du denn selber, Ulrich? Möchtest du immer noch nach München?

Ulrich: Ich möchte schon, aber es hat nicht geklappt. Ich hab' einen Studienplatz in Architektur an der Technischen Hochschule in Aachen.

Michaela: Ich gratuliere! Aachen ist zwar nicht München, aber es ist auch nicht schlecht.

UNIT 4: /ŋ/

4.1 **Words with** /ŋ/

Wange, Menge, singen, fangen, Lunge, Hunger, jünger
schwankt, klingt, jüngst, Angst, eng, Gesang, gering

4.2 **Phrases with** /ŋ/

langsam anfangen	eine langweilige Sendung
geringe Mängel	die Zeitung bringen
ängstliche Jungen	auf die lange Bank schieben
Angst und Bange	mit Sang und Klang

4.3 **Sentences with** /ŋ/

Sie gingen die enge Straße entlang.
Lange trug sie den Ring am Finger.
Im Frühling fangen wir mit Gesangsübungen an.
Diese Zeitungen sind allerdings schrecklich langweilig.

UNIT 5: /l/

5.1 **Words with** /l/

kalt, Feld, wild, Volk, falsch, Erfolg, Schuld, Völker
handeln, sammeln, Mitteln, schnell, Kohl, Teil, Stil

5.2 **Words containing** /l/ **in prevocalic, final and preconsonantal position:**

viele	:	viel	:	vielmals
Wille	:	will	:	willst
Fehler	:	fehl	:	fehlt
Felle	:	Fell	:	Feld
volle	:	voll	:	Folter
faule	:	faul	:	Faulheit
Wahlen	:	Wahl	:	Wahltag

5.3 **Phrases with final** /l/

hell und dunkel	ein Teil der Insel
Löffel und Gabel	Beifall im Saal

Tal und Hügel

Fußballspiel

fall nicht vom Stuhl

gib mal ein Beispiel

5.4 Phrases with preconsonantal /l/

Wald und Feld

Gold und Silber

ein Bild gemalt

schnell handeln

gesellschaftliche Erfolge

er fällt bald

das Geld fehlt

du zählst falsch

5.5 Sentences with final and preconsonantal /l/

Der Zeltplatz soll voll sein.

Paul sammelt Pilze im Wald.

Der Abschlußball war ein voller Erfolg.

April, April, er weiß nicht was er will.

5.6 Dialogue: *Ein Bild von Emil Nolde*

Helmut: Hildegard, guck mal, Karl hat mir ein Bild geschenkt. Was hältst du davon?

Hildegard: Das ist mein Lieblingsbild! Von Emil Nolde. Gefällt es dir auch?

Helmut: Es ist mir zu dunkel. Ich mag lieber Bilder, die hell und freundlich sind.

Hildegard: Ich finde es toll! Ich habe das Original in Köln gesehen.

Helmut: Aber der Himmel ist zu dunkel. Und Hildegard, ehrlich, was sollen diese hellblauen Hügel – und die dunkelgelbe Kugel da?

Hildegard: Das ist die Sonne, du Esel! Welche Kunst gefällt dir denn, wenn du den Nolde nicht magst?

Helmut: Ich mag die alten Meister – Hals, Holbein, Breugel und so weiter.

Hildegard: Helmut, du bist halt hoffnungslos altmodisch!

UNIT 6: /r/

6.1 Words with /r/

Recht, Rose, reich, Rahmen, Presse, Bruder, tragen

hören, fahren, irren, führen, bohren, Beruf, Büro

Mark, wird, starb, scharf, Kurs, Wurst, Herr, starr

6.2 Words contrasting /x/ and /r/

Schacht	:	scharrt
wachte	:	Warte
Docht	:	dort
Sucht	:	surrt
Zucht	:	zurrt

6.3 Words with and without /r/

Arme	:	Amme
Darm	:	Damm
Schwarm	:	Schwamm
warfen	:	Waffen
Carmen	:	kamen
Charme	:	Scham

6.4 Phrases with /r/

drei Freunde	frische Brötchen
rot und schwarz	Reis und Makkaroni
ins Gebirge fahren	Zigaretten rauchen
Sport treiben	im Kraftwerk arbeiten

6.5 Sentences with /r/

Ihre Großeltern haben die Fabrik in Remscheid gegründet.
Rudi spricht außer Russisch noch drei andere Sprachen.
Unsere Sekretärin trägt eine rote Brille.
Rosis Bruder liest drei Werke von Bertold Brecht.

6.6 Dialogue: *Heinrichs neuer Roman*

Rolf: Grüß dich, Rosemarie. Das ist ja ein schreckliches Regenwetter!

Rosemarie: Grüß dich, Rolf. Hör mal, hat dein Freund Heinrich Rau wirklich einen Roman geschrieben?

Rolf: Warum fragst du? Hast du den Bericht im Radio gehört?

Rosemarie: Nein, ich habe gerade in der *Frankfurter Rundschau* darüber gelesen. Die Kritikerin hat den Roman sehr gelobt.

Rolf: Ach, Heinrich wird trotzdem nie reich. Er schreibt

so traurige Sachen. Seine Freunde raten ihm immer,
etwas Lustigeres zu schreiben.

Rosemarie: Warum traurig? Das ist ein historischer Roman über
Seeräuber vor der nordafrikanischen Küste.

Rolf: Heinrich schreibt über Seeräuber? Welche Ironie!
Er wird doch auf der Autofähre immer sofort seekrank!

Rosemarie: Aber trotzdem. Er scheint wirklich auf euren Rat zu
hören.

UNIT 7: [ts]

7.1 Words with [ts]

Zug, Zeile, zahlen, ziehen, Zauber, zwölf, Zweck
herzlich, überzeugt, einzig, Patient, Portion, trotz

7.2 Phrases with [ts]

zur Zeit	die Zuschauer zählen
zweiundzwanzig	das Zeugnis zeigen
zehn Zentimeter	ganz reizend
zwischenzeitlich	auf Zehenspitzen

7.3 Sentences with [ts]

Zwei Tassen Tee mit Zucker und Zitrone, bitte!
Die zwei Ärzte sind zusammen mit dem Zug gefahren.
Zürich ist das finanzielle Zentrum der Schweiz.
Herr Schulz hat die Zeitungen jetzt bezahlt.

7.4 Dialogue: *Heinz hat Zahnschmerzen*

Heinz: Tag Franziska, wie geht's? Wo bist du in letzter Zeit
gewesen? Du warst plötzlich verschwunden.

Franziska: Ich war zu Hause in der Schweiz. Mein Onkel Fritz hat
ein Haus in Zermatt. Ich fahre jedes Jahr zu dieser Zeit
dahin. Und wie geht's dir, Heinz?

Heinz: Nicht gut. Ich habe seit Tagen schreckliche
Zahnschmerzen. Ich glaube, ich muß mir einen
Weisheitszahn ziehen lassen. Kannst du mir einen guten
Zahnarzt empfehlen?

Franziska: Hast du nicht erzählt, daß du letztes Mal beim alten

Doktor Zottmann warst? Warum gehst du nicht zu ihm
zurück?
Heinz: Ach, es war ganz schrecklich, bei ihm im
Behandlungszimmer zu sitzen. Während er mir am
Zahn bohrte, hat er die ganze Zeit Witze erzählt!
Franziska: Entsetzlich! Aber ich kann dir eine ausgezeichnete
Zahnärztin empfehlen, eine reizende Frau, die bestimmt
keine Witze erzählt.
Heinz: Bist du ganz sicher, daß sie gut ist? Du weißt, daß ich
immer so eine Angst vor dem Zahnarzt habe.
Franziska: Sie ist ganz ausgezeichnet. Du kannst ruhig hingehen –
und wenn du nicht zufrieden bist, lade ich dich zum
Essen im neuen französischen Restaurant am
Friedensplatz ein.

UNIT 8:   [ʔ]

8.1   Words with initial [ʔ]

Eis, alles, oben, Unglück, Igel, Ente, üblich, Ärger
beachten, beeinflussen, vereinen, gearbeitet, geordnet

8.2   Phrases containing words with initial [ʔ]

ehrliche Arbeit   im In- und Ausland
unter Umständen   in Oberammergau
unheimlich aufregend   unnötige Arbeit
achthundert Autos   ungeduldige Autofahrer

8.3   Sentences with [ʔ]

Er beobachtet die Ereignisse am anderen Ufer.
Ihr ärgert Euch über eine unmögliche Übung.
Der Inhalt der Oper war unerwartet aktuell.
Heute abend um acht Uhr will er unsere Anfrage beantworten.

UNIT 9: /e:/

9.1 Words with /e:/

Eva, Erich, Esel, Ehe, ewig, Erdbeere, ekelhaft
Mehl, Weg, Krebs, Regen, lesen, wenig, gegen, kehren
Tee, See, Idee, Reh, je, Allee, Café, Gelee

9.2 Words contrasting /e:/ and /i:/

wegen	:	wiegen	Segel	:	Siegel
legen	:	liegen	weder	:	wieder
Wesen	:	Wiesen	denen	:	dienen
mehr	:	mir	Teer	:	Tier

9.3 Unstressed [e] with reduced length

General, Melodie, Republik, Resultat, Element, Demokratie,
demonstrativ, Kaffee ['kafe]

9.4 Phrases with /e:/

zehn Meter	der Weg zum See
vom Meer her	zum Steg gehen
wesentlich mehr	Schneeverwehungen
wesentlich weniger	Erdbeergelee

9.5 Sentences with /e:/

Peter hat den Weg mit dem Besen gekehrt.
Wir haben eben ihren Lehrer gesehen.
Zehn Meter vor dem Ziel hat Eva aufgegeben.
Ewald und Petra machen Ferien am Meer.

9.6 Dialogue: *Ein Café am Meer*

Angelika: Ehrlich, Peter, es sind nur noch wenige Meter bis zum Café.
Peter: Ich kann nicht mehr gehen. Mein großer Zeh tut weh!
Angelika: Aber guck, wir sind schon in der Beethoven Allee, ich kann das Café Dresden schon sehen.
Peter: Auf dem Heimweg nehmen wir aber ein Taxi. Zehn Kilometer laufe ich nicht mehr zurück.

Angelika:	Peter, es sind doch keine zehn Kilometer! Aber jetzt können wir einen Tee trinken und in Ruhe reden.
Peter:	Gut, daß das Café leer ist. Ich muß sehen, was mit meinem Zeh los ist.
Angelika:	Ich nehme einen Tisch in der ersten Etage. Von da aus kann man das Meer sehen.
Peter:	Angelika, das ist doch jetzt egal. Bei diesem Dezembernebel kann man eh nicht sehr weit sehen.

UNIT 10: /ɛ:/

All descriptions of Standard German pronunciation make a distinction between close /e:/ and open /ɛ:/, but this distinction is missing in the pronunciation of most northern German-speakers. This unit can therefore be omitted by those aiming for a northern type of German pronunciation, although it is useful to be able to pronounce an open /ɛ:/ as the name of the letter Ä and in some common verb forms (e.g. *gäbe*, *nähme*), in order to distinguish them from the forms containing /e:/.

10.1 Words with /ɛ:/

Ä, Ära, Nähe, Mädchen, Märchen, tätig, wäre, gäbe, käme, nähme, wählen, zählen, Gespräch, ungefähr, Städte

10.2 Phrases with /ɛ:/

ähnliche Märchen	rumänische Läden
den Plänen gemäß	gefährliche Bären
dänische Geräte	Märchen erzählen
die tägliche Fähre	während des Gesprächs

10.3 Sentences with /ɛ:/

Frau Jäger erzählte von ihren Plänen.
Die Dänen haben Käse gewählt.
Die Mädchen ähneln ihren Vätern.
In der Nähe waren nämlich zwei Läden.

10.4 Words contrasting /ɛ:/ and /e:/

Dänen	:	denen	Väter	:	Fete
wägen	:	wegen	zähe	:	Zehe

Säle   : Seele   säen   : sehen
Sägen : Segen   gäbe   : gebe

10.5 Phrases with /ɛ:/ and /e:/

in der Nähe des Sees   zwei Gläser Tee
sehr spät   die fehlenden Geräte
ungefähr zehn   wegen der Sekretärin
die Pläne sehen   die Fehler zählen

10.6 Sentences with /ɛ:/ and /e:/

Ich habe ungefähr zehn Bären gesehen.
Die dänischen Kollegen lesen täglich sehr viel.
Die Schweden nehmen mehr für ein ähnliches Gemälde.
Später hat Eva ungefähr zehn Gläser getrunken.

UNIT 11:   /a:/ und /a/

11.1 Words with /a:/

aber, aßen, Adam, Amen, Abenteuer, Asien, Adel
Bad, Vater, Waage, zahlen, Fahne, Gabel, Straßenbahn
warten, Parlament, Marmelade, Park, Bart, Quark

11.2 Phrases with /a:/

Er war schon da   mit der Bahn fahren
ja sagen   im Wagen schlafen
einen Namen haben   aus Erfahrung sagen
eine Fahrt planen   nach dem Fahrplan fragen

11.3 Words with /a/

anders, Antwort, Arbeit, halten, danken, Hammer, Last
lachen, Schachtel, Kanzler, Bart, warten, hart, Narr
Oma, Opa, Liga, Europa, Fulda, Helga

11.4 Phrases with /a/

Platz machen   Band acht
die Klappe halten   an der Wand

die Altstadt   am Stadtrand
alles ist kalt   die andere Hand

11.5 Words contrasting /a:/ and /a/

Bahn	:	Bann	Schlaf	:	schlaff
fahl	:	Fall	Stahl	:	Stall
lag	:	Lack	Wahl	:	Wall
Schal	:	Schall	Aal	:	All

11.6 Phrases with /a:/ and /a/

die Badewanne   an den Strand fahren
die Landstraße   dem Stadtrat danken
eine Glaskanne   mit dem Kaplan verwandt
eine Fahrkarte   lange Haare tragen

11.7 Sentences with /a:/ and /a/

Acht Tage lang haben wir nachts nicht schlafen können.
Für die lange Fahrt haben wir Platzkarten erhalten.
Herr Haarmann kauft seine Schallplatten in der Bahnhofstraße.
Der Mann mit dem schwarzen Haar war sehr begabt.

UNIT 12: /u:/

12.1 Words with /u:/

U-Bahn, U-Boot, Ursprung, Urenkel, Uhrmacher
gut, Schule, Mut, Kuchen, Puder, Tube, Blume, duzen

12.2 Unstressed [u] with reduced length

Student, studieren, Musik, musikalisch, Ural, kurios, lukrativ

12.3 Phrases with /u:/

ein gutes Buch   Hut und Schuhe
die Ruhe der Natur   Blumen für Uta
die Bluse suchen   genug zu tun
im Juni und Juli   die Schule besuchen

12.4 Sentences with /u:/

Rudi studiert Naturwissenschaften an der Universität.
Uta ist mit dem Zug in Urlaub gefahren.
Ihr Bruder hat nicht genug Geld für Hut und Schuhe.
Im Juli haben wir einen Flug nach Tunis gebucht.

12.5 Dialogue: *Rudis Geburtstag*

Uwe: Guten Abend, Ute. Was haben wir hier: ein Buch, einen
        Kuchen, Blumen – hast du etwa Geburtstag?
Ute: Du, der Rudi feiert heute seinen Geburtstag. Wir sollen ihn
        um 8 Uhr besuchen.
Uwe: Ich dachte, Rudi hätte erst im Juni oder Juli Geburtstag.
Ute: Eigentlich hat er Anfang Juni Geburtstag, aber er fährt dann
        mit seinem Bruder in Urlaub. Er hat den Flug schon gebucht.
Uwe: Und was ist das für ein Buch? 'Das blutige Tuch.
        Gruselgeschichten aus Husum'!!
Ute: Der Rudi findet das Buch bestimmt gut. Er studiert Literatur
        und liest gerne Gruselgeschichten.
Uwe: Wieviel Uhr haben wir übrigens? Ich suche ständig meine
        Uhr. Ich habe sie wohl auf dem Weg zur Uni in der U-Bahn
        verloren.
Ute: Du, such mal im Flur. Die Uhr liegt auf dem Stuhl, unter
        deinem Hut.

UNIT 13: /o:/

13.1 Words with /o:/

Ostern, Ofen, Ohren, Obst, Ober, Ohnmacht, Ozean
Boot, Lohn, Tod, Vogel, Botschaft, wohnen, Rotkohl
wo, Floh, froh, Büro, hallo

13.2 Unstressed [o] with reduced length

sozial, Kino, solidarisch, Produktion, Opposition, Moment, Hotel,
Notar, Polizei, Schokolade

13.3 Phrases with /o:/

Kohle holen	das verlorene Boot
frohe Ostern	eine modische Hose

rote Rosen   pro Person
das große Tor   ein hoher Ton

13.4 Sentences with /o:/

Ihr Sohn kommt am Montag vor Ostern zu Besuch.
Rosi ist mit dem Chor nach Polen geflogen.
Oder wir machen ein Foto vor der Oper.
Wir froren so sehr, daß unsere Ohren rot wurden.

13.5 Words contrasting /u:/ and /o:/

Mus	:	Moos		Gruß	:	groß
tun	:	Ton		Kur	:	Chor
Uhr	:	Ohr		gute	:	Gote
Ruhr	:	Rohr		Buden	:	Boden

13.6 Sentences with /u:/ and /o:/

Uwe hat ein rotes Tuch geholt.
Der Ober holte Brot, Butter, Obst und Kuchen.
Der Flug nach Polen am Montag ist ausgebucht.
Roland sucht ein Boot, das groß genug ist.

13.7 Dialogue: *Die Wohnung in der Mozartstraße*

Udo: Hallo Rosa, seid ihr schon umgezogen? Wo wohnt ihr denn
        jetzt?

Rosa: Hallo Udo. Seit Montag haben wir eine neue große
         Wohnung in der Mozartstraße. Komm doch zum Abendbrot.
         Der Bodo ist bestimmt schon zu Hause . . .

Udo: Die Wohnung ist großartig, Rosa. Aber was ist mit diesem
        großen Ofen hier?

Rosa: Das ist unser Kohleofen. Wir müssen leider immer Kohlen
         aus dem Keller holen. Was trinkst du denn, Udo? Wir haben
         Bier oder Rotwein.

Udo: Ich nehme gern ein Glas Rotwein. Du, was sind denn das für
        Fotos hier? Ist das Bodo als Kind?

Rosa: Ja, mit seinen Großeltern. Der Opa ist schon lange tot. Aber
         die Oma wohnt noch hier in Bochum. Und das hier ist unser
         Motorboot.

Udo: Wie, habt ihr so ein großes Motorboot?

Rosa: Das ist nur unser Traum. Der Bodo sagt immer, wenn wir im

Lotto gewinnen, kaufen wir uns so ein großes rotes Motorboot.

UNIT 14: /yː/ **and** /ʏ/

14.1 **Words with** /yː/

übrigens, Überfall, Überfahrt, übermütig, überflüssig
kühl, grün, prüfen, spülen, Brüder, Güte, für, Mühe
Gemüse, Gefühl, Vergnügen, Schülerin, Güterzug

14.2 **Phrases with** /yː/

berühmte Bücher	die grüne Tür
über die Stühle	hüben und drüben
müde Schüler	ein kühler Frühlingstag
Grüße aus Zürich	die Bettücher bügeln

14.3 **Sentences with** /yː/

Die Schüler spürten ihre müden Füße.
Herr Krüger soll die Stühle auf der Bühne prüfen.
Seine berühmten Brüder schickten Grüße aus Zürich.
Früher hatten wir überhaupt keine Bücher.

14.4 **Words with** /ʏ/

Bürste, Würstchen, Küche, Stück, tüchtig, würdig,
künftig, Bürger, Würde, Symbol, fünfzehn, verrückt,
entzückt, geschützt, Gerücht, Gewürz, zurück

14.6 **Phrases with** /ʏ/

fünf Stück	Glück im Unglück
Glückwünsche	Günter Müller
eine hübsche Brücke	die Bürger Münchens
die türkische Küche	einen Gürtel wünschen

14.7 **Sentences with** /ʏ/

Wir müssen Günter einen Füller kaufen.
Die Lücken müssen gefüllt werden.

Die Mütter der fünf Künstler waren glücklich.
Die Würstchen müssen zurück in die Küche!

14.8 Words contrasting /y:/ and /ʏ/

fühlen	:	füllen	Lüge	:	Lücke
Hüte	:	Hütte	Füßen	:	Füssen (Stadt)
müder	:	Mütter	gütig	:	gültig
Wüste	:	wüßte	Düne	:	dünne

14.9 Phrases with /y:/ and /ʏ/

Frühstück   die Gründe prüfen
die Südküste   fünfzig Bücher
süße Früchte   über die Brücke
das Stück üben   ein berühmter Künstler

14.10 Sentences with /y:/ and /ʏ/

Die Straße an die Küste führt über fünf Brücken.
Günters Brüder sind müde aber überglücklich.
Sie führte uns zurück zu den berühmten fünf Türmen.
Natürlich dürfen sie in der Küche frühstücken.

14.11 Words contrasting /u:/, /ʊ/, /y:/ and /ʏ/

Bruder	:	Brüder	Luft	:	Lüfte
Tuch	:	Tücher	Duft	:	Düfte
Flug	:	Flüge	Fluß	:	Flüsse
Wut	:	wütend	wußte	:	wüßte

14.12 Phrases with /u:/, /ʊ/, /y:/ and /ʏ/

in der Schule üben   die Stunde des Unglücks
Husten und Schüttelfrost   mit dem Hund im Büro
gute Bücher suchen   ein Stück Wurst
eine Prüfung im Juli   lustige Hüte

14.13 Sentences with /u:/, /ʊ/, /y:/ and /ʏ/

Unsere Überstunden wurden geprüft.
Die Übungen der russischen Musiker waren kürzer.
Meine Mutter müßte heute ins Büro gehen.
Die Tulpen blühen früher als unsere anderen Blumen.

14.14 **Words contrasting /iː/, /ɪ/, /yː/ and /ʏ/**

liegen	:	lügen	Kiste	:	Küste
Biene	:	Bühne	Mist	:	müßt
fielen	:	fühlen	sticken	:	Stücken
Kiel	:	kühl	Dingen	:	düngen

14.15 **Phrases with /iː/, /ɪ/, /yː/ and /ʏ/**

viele Hügel	sie liest Bücher
schüchterne Kinder	es ist typisch für sie
grüne Wiesen	wir spielen in München
ein Stück Fisch	sie üben die Lieder

14.16 **Sentences with /iː/, /ɪ/, /yː/ and /ʏ/**

Das Stück beginnt im Flugzeug über Island.
Sie ist im Film und auf der Bühne berühmt geworden.
Sie machen sich über ihn lustig.
Auf diesem Bild sieht man eine typisch griechische Wind mühle.

14.17 **Dialogue: *Beim Reisebüro Krüger in Lübeck***

Frau Bülow: Reisebüro Krüger in Lübeck, Bülow. Guten Tag.
Herr Müller: Guten Tag, Frau Bülow. Mein Name ist Müller. Ich würde mich gerne über billige Flüge informieren.
Frau Bülow: Ja, wo würden Sie denn gerne hinfliegen? Wir haben Flüge in die Türkei, nach Südfrankreich, Syrien, Ägypten, order sogar nach Südamerika und Südostasien.
Herr Müller: Nein, nicht so weit. Wie wär's mit Süddeutschland – München, Nürnberg, Tübingen. Haben Sie Wochenendflüge mit Hotel?
Frau Bülow: Ja wir haben viele Wochenendflüge. Von Hamburg Fuhlsbüttel nach München, Nürnberg, Zürich, usw. Freitag hin, Sonntag zurück.
Herr Müller: Und was ist so ein typischer Preis für eine Übernachtung mit Frühstück?
Frau Bülow: Ja, zum Beispiel im Hotel Südhof in München kostet die Übernachtung mit Frühstück hundertfünfzig Mark.
Herr Müller: Meine Güte, das ist viel zu teuer! Wie wäre es mit

einer gemütlichen kleinen Pension in Nürnberg? Die Übernachtung darf aber nicht über fünfzig Mark kosten.

UNIT 15: /ø:/ **and** /œ/

15.1 **Words with** /ø:/

mögen, böse, hören, Vögel, Römer, König, stören, zögern
Möbel, Möwe, verwöhnen, gewöhnlich, hör, stör

15.2 **Phrases with** /ø/

schöne Möbel	wir mögen die Löwen
fröhliche Töne	persönliche Größe
verwöhnte Söhne	weder möglich noch nötig
rötliche Vögel	Französisch ist schöner

15.3 **Sentences with** /ø:/

Wir mögen diese schönen Öfen.
Sie hören die höheren Töne nicht.
Es gehörte dem französischen König.
Ist es möglich, den Österreichischen Rundfunk zu hören?

15.4 **Words with** /œ/

öfter, örtlich, Öffner
möchte, könnte, Löffel, zwölf, plötzlich, wörtlich,
Köchin, Hölle, Hölzer, Göttin, Löcher, Pförtner, Völker

15.5 **Phrases with** /œ/

zwölf Mönche	die nördlichen Dörfer
nördlich von Köln	die östlichen Völker
den Oberkörper röntgen	ein Zwölftel der Bevölkerung
die Börse eröffnen	sie möchten zur Eröffnung

15.6 **Sentences with** /œ/

Diese zwölf Mönche möchten nach Köln.
Wir könnten die östlichen Dörfer besuchen.

Sie verstanden die Wörter plötzlich nicht mehr.
Wir könnten die Körbe jetzt öffnen.

15.7 Words contrasting /ø:/ and /œ/

Höhle	:	Hölle	Löwe	:	Löffel
Goethe	:	Götter	Öfen	:	öffnen
mögen	:	möchten	lösen	:	löschen
stören	:	störrisch	nötig	:	nördlich

15.8 Phrases with /ø:/ and /œ/

die Wörter hören
zwölf Löwen
Körpergröße
plötzliches Stöhnen

das schöne Köln
öffentliche Anhörung
die Töchter der Königin
ein größerer Löffel

15.9 Sentences with /ø:/ and /œ/

Die Öffnungszeiten sind völlig unmöglich.
Wir können die Vögel öfter hören
Seine Söhne und Töchter sind sehr verwöhnt.
Ich möchte die größeren Brötchen.

15.10 Phrases with /y:/, /ʏ/, /ø:/ and /œ/

wir mögen den Schnee
Brötchen zum Frühstück
schöne Blüten
die rötlichen Tücher

die schönsten Hüte
wir öffnen die Tür
die Güte des Königs
die göttlichen Wünsche

15.11 Sentences with /y:/, /ʏ/, /ø:/ and /œ/

Er überhört seine Schüler.
Wir können die Schüssel mit Öl füllen.
Die Königin hat fünf fröhliche Brüder.
Frau Köhler möchte französische Bücher lesen.

15.12 Dialogue: *Ein schönes Schlößchen in Österreich*

Frau Höfer: Darf ich Sie mal stören, Herr König? Ich habe da
eine persönliche Frage. Sie waren doch gerade in
Österreich. Wir möchten nämlich dort Urlaub
machen.

Herr König:	Nein, Frau Höfer, wir waren jetzt in den französischen Alpen. Ich könnte Ihnen aber ein Hotel in Österreich empfehlen, wenn Sie möchten.
Frau Höfer:	Ach so, Sie waren in den französischen Alpen. Ich hätte schwören können, Sie wären in Österreich gewesen.
Herr König:	Wir mögen Österreich sehr gern. Wir waren letztes Jahr dort, in einem sehr schönen Hotel. Ein kleines Schlößchen östlich von Innsbruck.
Frau Höfer:	Wir möchten irgendwo ganz ungestört sein. Möglichst keine größeren Städte in der Nähe, höchstens ein paar kleine Dörfer.
Herr König:	Ungestört waren wir aber nicht. Nebenan wohnte eine Familie mit zwei Söhnen und zwei Töchtern. Die Söhne spielten beide Flöte . . .
Frau Höfer:	Das hätte mich nicht gestört, ich höre gern Flöte. Haben Sie sich übrigens schnell an die Höhenluft gewöhnt?
Herr König:	Kein Problem. Und das Essen dort ist köstlich. Sie haben eine ungewöhnlich gute Köchin, die österreichische und französische Gerichte kocht.

UNIT 16:   /ə/ and [ɐ]

16.1 Words with /ə/

Besuch, Geburt, Gerücht, Beweis, Gebirge, Gebäude
gelangen, bekommen, gesungen, berichtigen, bezahlen
hätte, wollte, bitte, heute, Eule, Schule, Ehe

16.2 Words with [ɐ]

erzählen, Eroberung, versprechen, zerstreuen, Zerstörung
Bier, Tier, Schnur, Uhr, größer, schöner, meiner
Brettern, scheitern, Vätern, Vetters, Kölners, Schülers

16.3 Words contrasting final /ə/ and [ɐ]

bitte	:	bitter	Mitte	:	Mütter
schöne	:	schöner	Größe	:	größer
Wette	:	Wetter	fette	:	Vetter
meine	:	meiner	Hüte	:	Hüter

16.4 Words contrasting /ə/ and [ɐ] before final /n/

Betten	:	Brettern	meisten	:	meistern
wetten	:	wettern	hüten	:	Hütern
fetten	:	Vettern	fliegen	:	Fliegern
verlieren	:	Verlierern	siegen	:	Siegern

16.5 Words contrasting /ə/ and [ɐ] before final /s/

kühles	:	Kühlers	Dampfes	:	Dampfers
leeres	:	Lehrers	Fisches	:	Fischers
fettes	:	Vetters	Schweißes	:	Schweißers
Rittes	:	Ritters	Sieges	:	Siegers

16.6 Phrases with /ə/ and [ɐ]

viele Wörter	ein schlanker Ire
brave Kinder	ein schneller Bote
dicke Bücher	die Bonner Straße
deine Mutter	die Leipziger Messe

16.7 Sentences with /ə/ and [ɐ]

Meine Schwester möchte die neue Sommermode kaufen.
Die Berliner haben gute Bücher und Magazine.
Peter meinte, daß alle Väter ihre Kinder lieben.
Eine Gruppe amerikanischer Lehrer blieb vier Tage in Bayern.

16.8 Dialogue: *Zu müde fürs Theater*

Beate: Du Rainer, ich wollte heute abend ins Theater gehen, aber ich bin zu müde. Willst du meine Karte haben?

Rainer: Ich war schon lange nicht mehr im Theater. Was gibt's denn heute abend?

Beate: *Die Räuber* von Schiller. Es soll eine sehr gute Aufführung sein.

Rainer: Ja, einige Freunde von mir waren letzte Woche drin. Sie waren alle begeistert. Aber bist du sicher, daß du nicht selber hingehen willst?

Beater: Ich würde schon gerne, aber ich bin totmüde.

Rainer: So kenne ich dich aber gar nicht, Beate. Du hattest doch früher immer mehr Energie als alle anderen.

Beate: Du, ich habe nächste Woche meine letzte Prüfung in

Geschichte. Ich habe jetzt vier Nächte hintereinander
durchgearbeitet.

Rainer: Kein Wunder, daß du müde bist! Aber sag mal, wie teuer
ist die Karte eigentlich? Ich gebe dir das Geld später, am
Wochenende vielleicht.

UNIT 17:   Revision unit: /r/ in combinations

17.1   Words with consonant + /r/

Prima, Prosa, Preis, Tracht, trug, Kragen, Krawatte
brav, Brite, Drachen, schreiben, Schritt, Schrank

Dachrinne, Fachrichtung, nachreichen, wachrütteln
Nichtraucher, Nachtruhe, Fischrestaurant, Milchreis

17.2   Phrases with consonant + /r/

ich reise   Briefe schreiben
ich ruhe   eine Grube graben
mich reizt es   Krach ertragen
sich revanchieren   frisch gestrichen

17.3   Words with /r/ + consonant

Furcht, durch, Mord, Ort, warten, arg, Narbe
Zwirn, Irland, Bürger, Hürde, Mord, Mörder, Ordner

17.4   Phrases with /r/ + consonant

durch Irland   furchtbar hart
der vierte Irrtum   Hermann und Karl
herzlich gern   furchtbare Sorgen
hartes Herz   im Warteraum schnarchen

17.5   Words with combinations of /r/ sounds

traurig, Traurigkeit, rare, Rarität, Reiberei
Fahrerin, Lehrerin, Professorin, Krankenpflegerin
'rumrennen, 'rumrasen, Reproduktion, Rekrut, Rohre

17.6 **Phrases with combinations of /r/ sounds:**

mehrere	mehrere Ruderer
klare Regeln	klarere Rechte
schwere Ringer	schwerere Rinder
teure Ringe	teurere Reisen

17.7 **Sentences with /r/**

Rosemarie rettete ihren Bruder vor dem Ertrinken.
Brigitte riet mir, eine rote Brille zu tragen.
Raimund und sein Freund Ralf reisten durch Rußland.
Die Frankfurter Rundschau berichtet über die Radfahrerin.

17.8 **Words with /r/ + /y:/, /ʏ/, /ø/ and /œ/**

Rüdiger, Rüssel, Römer, rühren, Röhre, Rübe, Brötchen
schöpferisch, erröten, hören, berühmt, führen, stören

17.9 **Phrases with /r/ + /y:/, /ʏ/, /ø/ and /œ/**

'rüber rennen	bedrückende Rede
'runter führen	rötliche Rüben
drüber reden	frische Möhren
'runterstürzen	grüne Kräuter

17.10 **Sentences with /r/ + /y:/, /ʏ/, /ø/ and /œ/**

Ihre Brüder möchten Rinderbrühe und frische Brötchen dazu.
Rüdiger erhielt bedrückende Nachrichten aus Lörrach.
Das Geburtshaus Albrecht Dürers ist in Nürnberg.
Die Künstlerin ist durch ihre Radierungen berühmt geworden.

Unit 18: **Word stress**

The purpose of this unit is to test your knowledge of German stress patterns. Read the words below and then listen to the pronunciation on the tape. In this unit, the pause is *before* each word to allow you to read it before you hear the answer. If you find that the pauses are not long enough, press the pause button on your tape recorder until you are ready to answer.

Assistent, Polizist, Protest, Demonstrant
Sensibilität, Demokratie, Invasion, Juwel, Labor

Sozialismus, Theologe, Invalide, studieren, Analyse
praktikabel, importieren, Blamage, Narkose

Psychologe, Psychologie, Fotograf, Fotographie
Maschine, maschinell, Musik, musikalisch, Musiker

Direktor, Direktoren, Afrika, Afrikaner
olympisch, Olympiade, Autor, Autorin

liebenswürdig, bekanntmachen, Tonbandgerät, Versuchskaninchen
Bundestagsabgeordnete, traditionsbewußt, Fußballverein

beunruhigen, verarbeiten, Verwaltung, Bestätigung
robust, Politik, Grammatik, Zeremonie, negativ

UNIT 19:   Intonation

19.1 **The fall**

Practise saying the following sentences with falling intonation. Remember
that the German fall is much steeper and more energetic than the usual
English fall.

Wir `gehen jetzt.                     Ich heiße `Karl.
Sie `kommen bald.                     Wir hatten `recht.
Ich kann es nicht `glauben.           Ich hatte es nicht ge`ahnt.
Ver`zeihen Sie bitte.                 Denk an das `Brot!
Es war phan`tastisch!                 Die Gäste sind schon `da.

Wann fährt der Bus nach `Stuttgart?
Wieviel hast du ge`schafft?
Wen `kennst du von diesen Leuten?
Wo ist die nächste `Tankstelle?
Was kostet hier das Ben`zin?

19.2 Level pitch

Level pitch is used in German in non-final tone groups and also in non-committal greetings. English tends to have rising intonation in these situations.

Ich muß jetzt ⁻gehen, sonst verpasse ich meinen ˋZug.
Als wir in ⁻Köln ankamen, fing es gerade an zu ˋregnen.
Wir sind da ge⁻wesen, als es pasˋsierte.
Ich wohne in ⁻Hamburg, und Michael wohnt in ˋFlensburg.

Meine Damen und ⁻Herren, jetzt können wir ˋanfangen.
Liebe ⁻Freunde, ich habe eine Überˋraschung für euch.
Sie ⁻schreiben, daß sie ˋkommen wollen.
Wir werden ge⁻beten, uns zu setzen.

Möchten Sir ⁻Tee oder ˋKaffee?
Wir waren in ⁻Frankfurt, ⁻München und ˋBerlin.
Unsere Studenten kommen aus Eu⁻ropa, A⁻merika und ˋAsien.
Guten ⁻Morgen.

19.3 Avoiding English intonation patterns

English has two intonation patterns which are missing in German. These are the low rise, frequently used to express for instance a reassuring, encouraging or pleading attitude, and the rise–fall–rise, commonly used to express hesitation, a reservation or a concession. This section contains sentences which express these attitudes and might commonly be said with one of these intonation patterns in English.

Was ist denn ˋlos? (sympathetic question)
Wo tut's denn ˋweh? (sympathetic question)
Sind Sie verˋletzt? (sympathetic question)
⁻Brauchst du noch was? (sympathetic question)
Mach dir keine ˋSorgen. (encouraging)
Es ˋmacht nichts. Wir werden's schon ˋfinden. (encouraging)
Warten Sie mal 'n ˋAugenblick! (polite command)
Komm mal! ˋmit! (polite command)
Ich ˋkomme ja schon. (appealing: 'Don't be impatient')

Ich bin nicht ganz ˋsicher. (hesitant)
ˋVorsicht! Du machst es kaˋputt! (friendly warning)
Paß ˋauf! Es kommt ein ˋAuto! (friendly warning)

Wir möchten `schon, aber wir haben keine `Zeit. (concession)
`Singen kann sie gut, aber nicht `schauspielern. (concession)
Es ist zwar `billiger, aber es sieht nicht so gut `aus. (concession)

Further practice in intonation patterns is provided in the sentences and dialogues of earlier units, which could be worked through again, concentrating on the intonation.

Sources and further reading

Chapter 1

For further information on the stylistic levels of German pronunciation, see chapter 6 of this book and the further reading listed there. Details of regional variations in German pronunciation are to be found in König (1985 and 1989).

There are a number of excellent recent publications in English on the question of variety in the German language, i.e. (in the order most general to most detailed): Clyne (1984), Barbour & Stevenson (1990), Russ (1990). This last-named work provides descriptions of the most important German accents and dialects, including a wealth of detail on regional German pronunciation.

For a discussion of the question of German as a pluricentric language, see Clyne (1984), ch. 1.

The most comprehensive treatment of regional variety in English pronunciation (world-wide) is Wells (1982). Gimson (1989) also gives some details of regional pronunciation within Britain.

Chapter 2

There are a number of good introductions to phonetics on the market, e.g. O'Connor (1973), Ladefoged (1975), Clark & Yallop (1990). Two very readable 'practical' introductions (with exercises) are Wells & Colson (1971) and Catford (1988).

The standard treatment of German phonetics is Kohler (1977). For English pronunciation, see Gimson (1989).

Chapter 3

Information on the pronunciation of the German consonants is given in the introductory sections of the three pronouncing dictionaries of German and in Kohler (1977). Phonological problems of German are discussed in detail in Werner (1972) and Meinhold & Stock (1982) in German, and Benware (1986) in English. A briefer discussion in English is contained in Fox (1990), ch. 2.

For a description of the consonants of English, see Gimson (1989).

Chapter 4

The works mentioned in the section on chapter 3 also provide further information on the German vowels. For acoustic studies of regional differences in vowel realisation, see Iivonen (1987 and 1989).

Chapter 5

The word stress of German is given in the word lists of all three major pronouncing dictionaries; short treatments of the principles of German word stress are given in Siebs (1969: 115–32), and *Großes Wörterbuch der deutschen Aussprache* (1982: 106–13).

The most recent and comprehensive treatment of German intonation in English is Fox (1984), on which the description given here draws heavily. There is a greater number of works in German, based on several different theoretical approaches; among the more recent are Pheby (1975 and 1981) and the sections in Kohler (1977: 196–207) and the *Duden-Grammatik* (1984: 730–55). A novel theoretical description is given in Isačenko and Schädlich (1970) and applied in the workbook by Stock & Zacharias (1973). Of the older descriptions, von Essen (1956) is a readable account and is still useful, not least because of its copious exercises.

Descriptions of English intonation are far more numerous than those of German. The most influential approach is that of Halliday, described for instance in Halliday (1967) and applied in the practical coursebook, Halliday (1970). This approach also underlies a number of descriptions of German intonation, for instance those of Kohler, Pheby and Fox. A very widely used coursebook in English intonation is O'Connor & Arnold (1973), and a good concise description is contained in Gimson (1989: 269–88).

The connection between English intonation and German modal particles is raised in Schubiger (1965 and 1980), but see also the critical discussion of this work in Fox (1984: 109–15).

Chapter 6

The pioneering study of pronunciation styles in German is Meinhold (1973), which contains a wealth of detailed observations and analysis. This, together with the briefer treatment in Kohler (1977), has provided the basis for the description in chapter 6. Further detailed studies of reductions in German speech are contained in Vater (1979). Very little has been written in English on this topic, the exception being a chapter in Benware (1986: 120–36), in which two German texts are transcribed in different pronunciation styles. For a treatment of the corresponding phenomena in English pronunciation, see Gimson (1989).

Glossary

Acoustic phonetics The study of the physical properties of speech (e.g. pitch, frequency and amplitude) as it is transmitted between the speaker and the hearer in the form of sound waves.

Affricate A plosive in which the closure is released slowly, resulting in friction as the air escapes, e.g. German [ts] and [pf] in *Netz* and *Apfel*.

Allophone See **phoneme**.

Alveolar A consonant which is pronounced with contact or proximity between the tip or blade of the tongue as the active articulator and the alveolar ridge as the passive articulator, e.g. English and German [d], [s], [n].

Alveolar ridge The part of the roof of the mouth immediately behind the front teeth.

Apex The tip of the tongue.

Apical An articulation which involves the tip of the tongue as the active articulator, e.g. German trilled [r].

Approximant (or frictionless continuant) A sound for which the organs of speech are brought together, but the narrowing thus formed is not close enough, or the force of articulation is not great enough, to cause audible friction, e.g. English [j] as in *yes*.

Articulation The modification of an airstream by means of movements in the organs of speech above the larynx in order to produce sounds.

Articulator Any of the organs in the vocal tract involved in the production of sounds. We can distinguish between **active articulators**, such as the tongue or the lower jaw, which are moved in the process of articulation, and **passive articulators**, such as the palate or the upper teeth, towards which the active articulators move.

Articulatory phonetics The study of the way in which speech sounds are produced or articulated by the organs of speech in the vocal tract.

Aspiration The strong release of a plosive with an audible puff of air, phonetic symbol [ʰ], e.g. *Tal* [tʰaːl].

Assimilation A process by which a sound becomes more similar, or identical, to a neighbouring sound, e.g. the conversational pronunciation of German *haben* as [ˈhaːbm̩], the final /n/ having changed to /m/ under the influence of the preceding bilabial sound.

Auditory phonetics The study of the processes in the ear, auditory nerve and brain which lead to the perception of sounds by the hearer.

Auslautverhärtung Process in German by which voiced, lenis plosives and fricatives are replaced by their voiceless, fortis counterparts when they occur in word-final position or in syllable-final position before a morpheme boundary, e.g. *Hände* [hɛndə] but *Hand* [hant], *Liebe* [liːbə] but *lieb* [liːp], *lieblich* [liːplɪç], etc.

Bilabial The articulation of a sound involving both lips, e.g. for [p], [b] and [m].

Blade (or **lamina**) The part of the tongue immediately behind the apex. The blade lies under the alveolar ridge when the tongue is in a normal, relaxed position in the mouth.

Coarticulation An articulation of a sound which is influenced by a neighbouring sound, e.g. the different h-sounds in German *hier* and *Hut*, caused by the tongue and lips taking up the position for the following sound during the pronunciation of [h]. Coarticulation leads to **assimilation**.

Consonant Along with **vowel**, one of the two major categories of sounds. Consonants are sounds which are formed by obstructing the airstream in the vocal tract by means of either a complete closure or a narrowing of the organs of speech. The usual position for consonants is at the edge of the syllable, whereas vowels occupy the central position.

Devoiced The pronunciation of a sound which is usually voiced without any vibrations of the vocal cords. The phonetic symbol for devoicing is [̥], e.g. *Platz* [pl̥ats].

Diphthong A vowel sound in which there is an audible change in quality caused by a change in tongue position, e.g. German [aɪ] in *mein* or [aʊ] in *Haus*.

Elision The complete loss or omission of a sound in certain types of pronunciation, e.g. the final /ə/ of *habe* in the pronunciation [hap] or the /t/ of *nicht* in the pronunciation [nɪç].

Flap A sound formed by a single rapid tap of one articulator against another as in the common American pronunciation of *writer* or in a very rapid pronunciation of German apical [r] in *unsere* [ˈʊnzərə].

Fortis (or **strong consonant**) A pronunciation of plosives and fricatives involving a high degree of muscular energy and breath, e.g. German and English [p] or [f], compared with weaker, or **lenis** pronunciation of [b] and [v].

Fricative A group of consonants formed by bringing the organs of speech very close together to form a narrow channel through which the airstream flows with increased speed, causing turbulence which is audible as a friction sound, e.g. [f], [s], [ç].

Glottal A sound produced in the larynx by a closing or narrowing of the vocal cords, e.g. [h].

Glottal stop A plosive articulated in the glottis. The airstream is cut off by a complete closure of the vocal cords. The release of the closure is accompanied by a characteristic sound, as in Cockney pronunciation of *bottle* [ˈbɒʔl̩] in English, and before words beginning with a vowel in German, e.g. *Ecke* [ˈʔɛkə].

Glottis The opening between the vocal cords.

Head The part of a tone group from the first stressed syllable until the syllable before the nucleus.

Homorganic Sounds formed with the same place of articulation, e.g. [t] and [s] as in German *Netz* [nɛts].

Labio-dental The articulation of a sound involving the upper front teeth and the lower lip, e.g. for [f] and [v].

Lamina The blade of the tongue.

Larynx The part of the windpipe which contains the vocal cords, visible in men as the 'Adams's apple'.

Lateral A sound articulated with a closure only in the centre of the mouth, thus allowing air to escape at the sides, e.g. [l].

Lateral plosion The release of a plosive before a homorganic lateral consonant by lowering the sides of the tongue and allowing the airstream to escape between the tongue and the sides of the palate, e.g. German *Beutel* ['bɔʏtl̩].

Lax See **tense**.

Lenis (or **weak consonant**) See **fortis**.

Lento form See **presto form**.

Manner of articulation The way in which a sound is formed, i.e. the type of closure or narrowing of the organs of speech which is involved in its articulation, e.g. plosive, fricative, etc.

Monophthong A vowel sound which retains the same quality (and therefore the same tongue position) throughout, e.g. German [u:] or [e:]. Compare **diphthong**.

Nasal A sound articulated with the soft palate lowered so that air can escape through the nasal cavity. For the nasal consonants [m], [n] and [ŋ] there is a complete oral closure so that the air escapes only through the nasal cavity, but for nasal vowels (which are common in some languages, e.g. French) the air escapes through both the nasal and the oral cavities. The IPA symbol for a nasal vowel is ˜ placed above the vowel symbol, e.g. French *bon* [bɔ̃].

Nasal plosion The release of a plosive before a homorganic nasal consonant by lowering the soft palate and allowing the air to escape through the nasal cavity, e.g. German *hatten* ['hatn̩].

Nucleus (or **nuclear stress**) The most prominent syllable in a tone group, usually associated with a significant change in pitch.

Palatal The articulation of a sound by means of contact or proximity between the front of the tongue and the hard palate, e.g. [j], German [ç], etc.

Palate The roof of the mouth from behind the alveolar ridge to the uvula. It is divided into the hard palate at the front and the soft palate or velum at the back.

Palato-alveolar The articulation of a sound in which the blade and front of the tongue approach the alveolar ridge and the hard palate, e.g. [ʃ] and [ʒ].

Pharynx The part of the vocal tract between the larynx and the oral cavity or mouth.

Phoneme An abstract unit consisting of a group of similar sounds which are perceived by the speakers of a language as being one sound. Variants of phonemes are known as **allophones**, e.g. the different realisations of the German phoneme /r/ as [r] (apical roll), [ʁ] (uvular fricative), etc. In transcription, phonemes are enclosed in slash brackets, e.g. /r/, and allophones in square brackets, e.g. [ʁ].

Place of articulation The place in the vocal tract at which a sound is formed, e.g. bilabial (upper and lower lips), velar (soft palate).

Plosive (or **stop consonant**) A consonant articulated with a complete closure of the vocal tract, i.e. with a complete oral closure and with the soft palate raised so that air cannot escape through the nasal cavity. Air pressure builds up behind this closure and escapes with a slight puff or explosion when the closure is released. Examples of plosives are [p], [t] and [k].

Prehead All the unstressed syllables which precede the first stressed syllable in a tone group.

Presto (or **allegro**) **form** A form which occurs in rapid or accelerated passages of speech. Forms which occur at a slower rate of speech are known as **lento forms**.

Roll (or **trill**) A consonant articulated by rapid tapping of one articulator against another, e.g. the tip of the tongue against the alveolar ridge in the German apico-alveolar (front) rolled [r], or the uvula against the back of the tongue in the German uvular roll [ʀ].

Rounded A position of the lips used for the pronunciation of certain sounds, e.g. English [w] and German [u] and [o]. The degree of lip-rounding varies, e.g. it is less for German [ʊ] than for [u]. The opposite of rounded is **spread**.

Spread A position of the lips in which they are fairly close together or extended sideways as in a smile, the opposite of **rounded**. The spread-lip position is used for [i:] in English *meet* and German *Miete*. The degree of lip-spreading varies, e.g. it is less for German *Mitte* than for *Miete*.

Stress group (or **foot**) A unit of rhythm consisting of a stressed syllable and the following unstressed syllables. In stress-timed languages, the stress groups in an utterance are isochronous, i.e. they take approximately the same amount of time to say.

Stress-timed In stress-timed languages the rhythm of speech is determined by the stressed syllables, which occur at regular intervals of time, e.g. English and German.

Syllabic consonant A consonant (nasal or lateral) which forms a syllable on its own, e.g. German *Beutel* [ˈbɔʏtl̩], *hatten* [ˈhatn̩] (indicated by [̩] under the consonant in question).

Syllable-timed In syllable-timed languages the rhythm of speech is determined by the syllable, each of which tends to take approximately the same length of time, e.g. French.

Tail The part of a tone group following the nucleus.

Tense Vowel sounds which are articulated towards the edge of the vowel area are pronounced with greater muscular effort and tension in the organs of speech (particularly the tongue) than those pronounced nearer the centre of the vowel area, which are referred to as **lax**. Examples of tense vowels in German are /i:/ and /u:/, whereas /ɪ/ and /ʊ/ are lax.

Tone group (or **intonation group, sense group**) A unit of intonation consisting of a number of words which the speaker regards as forming a single unit or piece of information and which are pronounced with a single intonation pattern.

Trachea Windpipe.

Velar The articulation of a sound by means of contact or proximity between the back of the tongue and the velum, e.g. [k], [g], [x], etc.

Velum The soft, moveable back part of the palate which can be lowered to allow air from the lungs to escape through the nasal cavity or raised to block off the passage through the nasal cavity.

Vocal cords (or **vocal folds**) Bands of tissue in the larynx which vibrate in the airstream coming from the lungs to produce voice.

Vocal tract The air passages above the larynx in which articulation takes place. It consists of the pharynx, the oral cavity and the nasal cavity.

Voiced Sounds pronounced with vibrations of the vocal cords.

Voiceless Sounds pronounced without vibrations of the vocal cords.

Vowel Along with **consonant**, one of the two major categories of sounds. Vowels are articulated without a closure or narrowing of the organs of speech sufficient to cause audible friction as the airstream escapes from the mouth. The usual position for vowels is at the centre of the syllable, whereas consonants occur at the edge of syllables.

List of German phonetic terms

This list is intended to facilitate the use of German reference works on pronunciation by providing the English equivalents of some of the most common German phonetic terms. The list does not include terms which are exactly the same as English ones, or which differ only in spelling.

akzentzählend	stress-timed
Allophon (das)	allophone
Alveolen (pl.)	alveoli, alveolar ridge
Ansatzrohr (das)	vocal tract
Anschlag (der)	flap
Artikulationsart (die)	manner of articulation
Artikulationsbasis (die)	basis of articulation
Artikulationsorgane (pl.)	organs of speech
Artikulationsort (der)	place of articulation
Artikulationsspannung (die)	articulatory tension
artikulatorische Phonetik (die)	articulatory phonetics
auditive Phonetik (die)	auditory phonetics
behaucht	aspirated
betont	stressed
Dauerlaut (der)	continuant
einsilbig	monosyllabic
entstimmt	devoiced
Gaumen (der)	palate
Gaumensegel (das)	velum, soft palate
gerillt	grooved
gerollt	rolled, trilled
gerundet	rounded
geschlossen	close

gespannt	tense
gespreizt	spread
Glottisschlag (der)	glottal stop
Glottisverschluß (der)	glottal stop
halbgeschlossen	half-close
halboffen	half-open
harter Gaumen	hard palate
Hauptakzent (der)	main stress
Hinterzungenvokal (der)	back vowel
Kehlkopf (der)	larynx
Kehlkopfverschlußlaut (der)	glottal stop
Intonationseinheit (die)	tone group, intonation group
laterale Verschlußlösung (die)	lateral plosion
Lateralsprengung (die)	lateral plosion
Luftröhre (die)	windpipe
mehrsilbig	polysyllabic
Mittelzungenvokal (der)	central vowel
Mundhöhle (die)	oral cavity
nasale Verschlußlösung (die)	nasal plosion
Nasalsprengung (die)	nasal plosion
Nasenhöhle (die)	nasal cavity
Nasenlaut (der)	nasal
Nebenakzent (der)	secondary stress
offen	open
Phonem (das)	phoneme
Pränukleus (der)	head (of a tone group)
Rachen (der)	pharynx
Rachenhöhle (die)	pharynx
Reibelaut (der)	fricative
Satzakzent (der)	sentence stress
Schwinglaut (der)	roll, trill
Seitenlaut (der)	lateral
silbenzählend	syllable-timed
silbischer Konsonant	syllabic consonant
Sprechwerkzeuge (pl.)	organs of speech
Stimmbänder (pl.)	vocal cords
stimmhaft	voiced

Stimmlippen (pl.)	vocal cords
stimmlos	voiceless
Stimmritze (die)	glottis
Takt (der)	stress group, foot
Tongruppe (die)	tone group, intonation group
Tonsilbe (die)	nucleus
ungespannt	lax
Verschleifung (die)	reduction, simplification
Verschlußlaut (der)	plosive
Vibrant (der)	roll, trill
Vokal (der)	vowel
Vorderzungenvokal (der)	front vowel
weicher Gaumen	velum, soft palate
Wortakzent (der)	word stress, lexical stress
Zahndamm (der)	alveolar ridge
Zäpfchen (das)	uvula
Zungenblatt (das)	blade of the tongue, lamina
Zungenschlag (der)	flap
Zungenspitze (die)	tip of the tongue, apex

Bibliography

Pronouncing dictionaries of German

Duden-Aussprachewörterbuch (1990), ed. M. Mangold, 3rd edn. Mannheim (*Der Duden*, vol. 6).
Großes Wörterbuch der deutschen Aussprache (1982), ed. E.-M. Krech *et al.* Leipzig.
Siebs, T. (1969). *Deutsche Aussprache*, ed. H. de Boor, H. Moser and C. Winkler, 19th edn. Berlin.

Other works

Barbour, S. & Stevenson, P. (1990). *Variation in German: a critical approach to German sociolinguistics*. Cambridge.
Benware, W. A. (1986). *Phonetics and Phonology of Modern German: an introduction*, Washington, DC.
Catford, J. C. (1988). *A Practical Introduction to Phonetics*. Oxford.
Clark, J. & Yallop, C. (1990). *An Introduction to Phonetics and Phonology*. Oxford.
Clyne, M. (1984). *Language and Society in the German-speaking Countries*. Cambridge.
Crystal, D. (1987). *The Cambridge Encyclopaedia of Language*. Cambridge.
Duden-Grammatik der deutschen Sprache (1984), ed. G. Drosdowski *et al.*, 4th edn. Mannheim (*Der Duden*, vol. 4).
Essen, O. von (1956). *Grundzüge der hochdeutschen Satzintonation*. Ratingen.
Fox, A. (1984). *German Intonation: an outline*. Oxford.
Fox, A. (1990). *The Structure of German*. Oxford.
Gimson, A. C. (1989). *An Introduction to the Pronunciation of English*, 4th edn. revised by S. Ramsaran. London.
Halliday, M. A. K. (1967). *Intonation and Grammar in British English*. The Hague.
Halliday, M. A. K. (1970). *A Course in Spoken English: Intonation*. Oxford.

Iivonen, A. (1987). Monophthonge des gehobenen Wienerdeutsch. In: *Folia Linguistica*, **21**, 293–336.

Iivonen, A. (1989). *Regional German Vowel Studies*. Department of Phonetics, University of Helsinki.

Isačenko, A. V. & Schädlich, H. J. (1970). *A Model of Standard German Intonation*. The Hague.

Kohler, K. (1977). *Einführung in die Phonetik des Deutschen*. Berlin.

König, W. (1985). *dtv-Atlas zur deutschen Sprache*, 6th edn. Munich.

König, W. (1989). *Atlas zur Aussprache des Schriftdeutschen in der Bundesrepublik Deutschland*, 2 vols. Munich.

Ladefoged, P. (1975). *A Course in Phonetics*. New York.

MacCarthy, P. (1975). *The Pronunciation of German*. London.

Meinhold, G. (1973). *Deutsche Standardaussprache: Lautschwächungen und Formstufen*. Jena.

Meinhold, G. & Stock, E. (1982). *Phonologie der deutschen Gegenwartssprache*. Leipzig.

O'Connor, J. D. (1973). *Phonetics*. Harmondsworth.

O'Connor, J. D. & Arnold, G. F. (1973). *Intonation of Colloquial English*, 2nd edn. London. (1st edn 1961).

Pheby, J. (1975). *Intonation und Grammatik im Deutschen*. Berlin.

Pheby, J. (1981). Phonologie: Intonation. In: K. E. Heidolph *et al.*, *Grundzüge einer deutschen Grammatik*, ch. 6. Berlin.

Russ, C. V. J. (ed.) (1990). *The Dialects of Modern German: a linguistic survey*. London.

Schubiger, M. (1965). English intonation and German modal particles – a comparative study. In: *Phonetica*, **12**, 65–84.

Schubiger, M. (1980). English intonation and German modal particles II – a comparative study. In: *The Melody of Language*, ed. L. R. Waugh & C. H. van Schooneveld. Baltimore 279–98.

Stock, E. & Zacharias, C. (1973). *Deutsche Satzintonation*. Leipzig.

Vater, H. (ed.) (1979). *Phonologische Probleme des Deutschen*. Tübingen.

Weiher, E. (1982). *Praktische englische Phonetik*. Bonn.

Wells, J. C. (1982). *Accents of English*, 3 vols. Cambridge.

Wells, J. C. & Colson, G. (1971). *Practical Phonetics*. London.

Werner, O. (1972). *Phonemik des Deutschen*. Stuttgart (Sammlung Metzler).

Index